C000258936

The Colossus-Class Aircraft Carriers 1944 – 1972

Neil McCart

To all those who have served in the Colossus-class aircraft carriers
1944 - 1972

Front Cover: A splendid painting of HMS *Ocean* by artist Brian Conroy.

Cover Design by Louise McCart

ISBN: 1 901225 06 2

Typesetting By: Highlight Type Bureau Ltd,
Clifton House, 2 Clifton Villas, Bradford,
West Yorkshire BD8 7BY.

Printing By: The Amadeus Press,
Ezra House, West 26 Business Park,
Cleckheaton, West Yorkshire BD19 4TQ.

Published By FAN PUBLICATIONS
17 Wymans Lane, Cheltenham, GL51 9QA, England.
Fax & Tel: 01242 580290
Email: info@fan-publications.i12.com

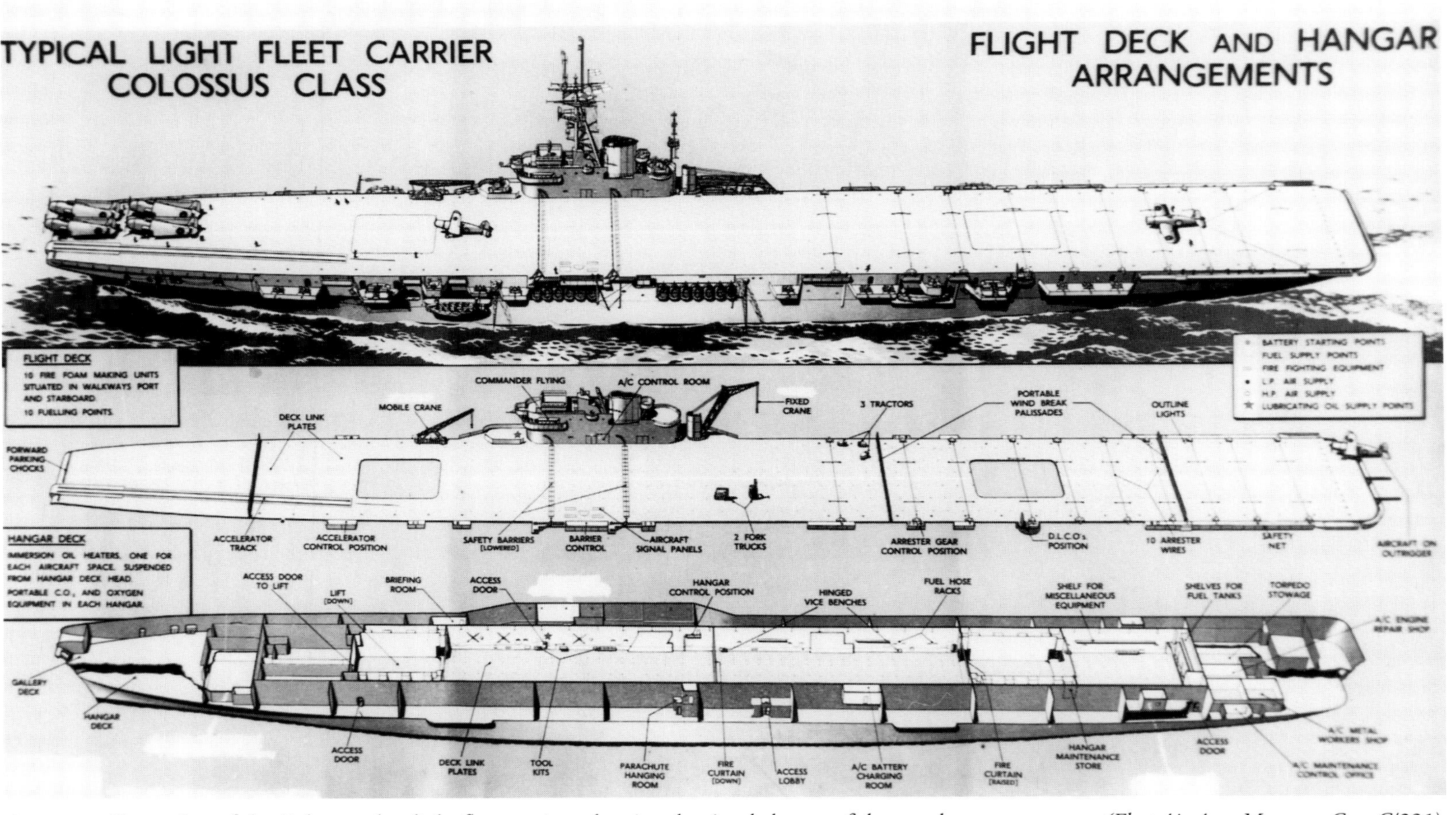

A cutaway illustration of the Colossus-class light fleet carriers, showing the simple layout of the vessels. *(Fleet Air Arm Museum, Cars C/221)*

Contents

Page No.

Introduction

When the Second World War broke out on 3 September 1939, the Royal Navy had only seven aircraft carriers and of those just one, HMS *Ark Royal*, could be said to be modern. Only she and the small, obsolete *Hermes* had been designed specifically as aircraft carriers, with *Argus* and *Eagle* having been converted from a merchant ship hull and from the hull of what was to have been a battleship for the Chilean Navy respectively. The other three, *Furious, Glorious* and *Courageous,* had all been converted from light battlecruisers in the 1920s. During the pre-war years the Fleet Air Arm was controlled by the Royal Air Force, and subsequently it had suffered a great deal of neglect as resources were used to build up the RAF's fighter and bomber forces. In 1937, when the Admiralty gained full control of the Fleet Air Arm, an expansion programme was initiated, but it could not be completed before war came in 1939. Only 14 days after the declaration of war the fleet carrier HMS *Courageous,* which was carrying out an anti-submarine patrol in the South West Approaches, a role for which she was totally unsuited, was sunk by a U-boat. Nine months later, in June 1940, her sister ship HMS *Glorious* was sunk by gunfire from the German battlecruisers *Scharnhorst* and *Gneisenau* during the Allied withdrawal from Norway. At this early stage of the war the battleship still reigned supreme as the Navy's capital ship.

Fortunately, it had been recognized that air power at sea was vital to the fleet, and in April 1937 the keel had been laid for the first of six large 23,000-ton fleet aircraft carriers. However, with their heavily armoured flight decks and hangars, and their 4-inch defensive armament, each ship would take over three years to build and it would be 1944 before the final two, *Implacable* and *Indefatigable,* were commissioned. As the Second World War progressed the vital importance of air power at sea became even more apparent. In November 1940, 20 Swordfish aircraft from HMS *Illustrious* attacked the Italian naval base at Taranto, and for the loss of only two of the outdated biplanes, three enemy battleships were crippled, keeping them out of action for most of the war. Six months later it was aircraft from *Victorious* and *Ark Royal* that disabled the German battleship *Bismarck,* allowing units of the Home Fleet to then catch and sink her. Without the Fleet Air Arm it is likely that this mighty battleship would have reached the safety of north-western France. Later that year, on 7 December 1941, carrier-borne aircraft of the Imperial Japanese Navy delivered a devastating blow to the US Navy's Pacific Fleet at Pearl Harbor, when they sank four battleships and seriously damaged four others. Just three days later, on a calm and sunny day in the South China Sea, one hundred torpedo bombers of the Japanese Navy's First Air Force, based at Saigon, settled the 'battleship v aircraft' argument once and for all when they sank the elderly battlecruiser *Repulse* and the modern battleship *Prince of Wales.* In 90 minutes the Japanese had delivered a stunning blow to British power and prestige in the Far East, and the action marked the first time in the history of naval warfare that capital ships under way were sunk by an attack carried out exclusively by aircraft. It convinced even the most sceptical, who had scoffed that the battleships sunk at Pearl Harbor had been 'sitting ducks' for aerial attack. Without doubt it signalled the end of the battleship as the Navy's capital ship, and aircraft carriers took over this role.

For the Royal Navy the answer came in early 1942 when it was decided to design a small, unprotected, class of aircraft carrier, which was capable of a speed of 25 knots and which could carry at least 35 to 40 fighter aircraft. The basic design work was entrusted to Vickers Armstrong Shipbuilders, who had experience of both merchant ship and warship construction, for it had been decided that the new carriers would be built largely to merchant ship standards. This would allow the vessels to be constructed quickly and it would enable more shipbuilding companies to tender for contracts. In the event, to expedite the completion of the ships it had been decided to limit the defensive armament to anti-aircraft weapons and, apart from splinter protection for exposed personnel, they were to have no conventional side armour. Instead there would be a complete sub-division of the main machinery compartments and the steering gear. It was also decided that the operational life of these new carriers would be limited to just three years, or until the end of the war which, at that time, could not be foreseen. With a displacement tonnage of just over 13,000, an overall length of 695 feet and a beam of 112 feet, the vessels would give the appearance of being smaller versions of the Illustrious-class fleet aircraft carriers. Altogether there were to be 16 light fleet carriers, but only the first eight, the Colossus class, would serve with the Royal Navy. The fact that two of these carriers served with foreign navies until the last decade of the 20th century, one of them opposing the Royal Navy in the South Atlantic in 1982, is a tribute to the fact that they were one of the most successful classes of warship ever built for the Royal Navy.

Chapter One

HMS *Colossus*
December 1944 – August 1946

The contract for the first of the light fleet aircraft carriers went to Vickers Armstrong Shipbuilders at their Wallsend-on-Tyne naval shipyard with the first keel plates being laid on 1 June 1942, just three days before the start of the decisive Battle of Midway, which saw a turning point in the Pacific War and during which US Navy aircraft carriers fought Japanese carriers and battleships without ever making contact. Just over 12 months later, in July 1943, the first key Royal Navy personnel, under the command of Commander (E) N. E. Bagshaw, travelled up to the Tyne to stand by the ship as preparations were made for her launch. The ceremony itself took place on Thursday 30 September 1943 when, after being named *Colossus,* the new carrier took to the waters of the River Tyne and was towed to her fitting-out berth. In June 1944, one member of the ship's company who was standing by *Colossus* was Torpedo Operator Peter Chamberlain who, despite early difficulties with the 'Geordie' dialect, enjoyed his time at the Vickers Armstrong shipyard, as he remembers: 'My work involved looking after the electrical circuit charts and stores and, as this was at the time of the Normandy landings, it was a pleasant "nine-to-five" job. With the living accommodation on board still being fitted out I lived ashore in lodgings, where I was treated like one of the family. A number of us who were standing by *Colossus* courted local girls, and I met my future wife during this time.'

On 26 July 1944, with the fitting-out work on *Colossus* nearing completion, the carrier's first commanding officer, Captain G. H. Stokes CB DSC RN, joined the ship. Captain Stokes had first gone to sea in 1919 as a midshipman in the old battleship *King George V,* and in the inter-war years he served in the submarine depot ship *Maidstone* and the submarine *L56.* He also served in the light cruiser *Danae* and the destroyers *Keppel, Tempest, Wakeful* and *Griffin.* In late 1939 he was appointed to command the destroyer *Mackay,* and following that he commanded the powerful Tribal-class destroyer *Sikh.* During operations against *Bismarck* on 25/26 May 1941 he was awarded the DSC, and in December 1941, after

HMS *Colossus* takes to the water on 30 September 1943.

(Author's collection)

leading a division of four destroyers in a night action which resulted in the destruction of two Italian cruisers at the Battle of Sirte, he was made a Companion of the Bath (CB). In 1943 and 1944, having been promoted to Captain, he commanded the Royal Naval Air Station, HMS *Jackdaw,* and it was from there that he was appointed to *Colossus.*

At 09.00 on Friday 1 December 1944 *Colossus* was commissioned into the Royal Navy, and the main body of the ship's company was embarked. With basin trials having been carried out on Monday 4 December, at 14.50 the next day, assisted by four tugs, the carrier slipped her moorings and moved ten miles downriver to secure alongside the Tyne Commissioners' Quay at North Shields, where she remained for nine days whilst the builders completed the final adjustments to her main propulsion machinery. Peter Chamberlain remembers this time, when it was much more difficult to get ashore, but at 09.15 on Thursday 14 December the carrier got under way again and by 10.00 she was clear of the River Tyne and steaming north for Rosyth, where she anchored eight hours later. Next day her initial trials began in earnest and, escorted by the destroyer *Verdun,* she put to sea to carry out steaming and gunnery exercises. On Saturday 16 December she carried out full-power trials, before returning to the safety of the Firth of Forth and anchoring off the naval base at Rosyth. She remained at Rosyth for nine days and Christmas was celebrated there, but at 09.00 on Boxing Day she sailed to carry out further machinery trials and at 22.15, escorted by the destroyers *Obedient* and *Orwell,* she commenced her passage of the Pentland Firth, bound for Greenock, where she arrived at 19.19 on Wednesday 27 December. It was from here that the carrier's work-up was to be carried out and between 28 December and 1 January 1945 she sailed at 09.00 each day to carry out various trials and evolutions, anchoring off Greenock each afternoon, when leave would be piped.

Finally, at 09.40 on Tuesday 2 January she embarked the official trials party and weighed anchor to carry out her first flying operations. As she rounded the Tail o' the Bank the trials were almost brought to a premature end when *Colossus* narrowly averted a collision with a boom defence vessel, but by 11.26 she was in the Firth of Clyde, just north of Lamlash where the first aircraft, a Seafire, landed on without a hitch. This was followed in quick succession by a Grumman Wildcat, a Fairey Barracuda, a Grumman Avenger and a Vought Corsair, all of which landed safely. Throughout the rest of the day, and during the following three days, the flying trials continued, with only one minor mishap on 5 January, when a Corsair was damaged on landing. On Sunday 7 January, with the winds too strong for flying operations, *Colossus* made a number of runs over the Skelmorlie measured mile, and during the forenoon of the next day she secured to a buoy off Greenock for a five-day break. The trials and work-up had been successful, with the ship performing well which was, in the words of Peter Chamberlain, 'a tribute to the shipyard workers of Walker-on-Tyne'.

At 08.30 on Saturday 13 January 1945 *Colossus* slipped her moorings and this time she steamed out of the Firth of Clyde into the Irish Sea where, at just after midday, she landed on 18 Barracudas of 827 Squadron. Later that day she anchored in Belfast Lough where the squadron personnel were embarked. At 19.20, with the last baggage lighter having been slipped, *Colossus* weighed anchor and set course for the Firth of Clyde again. En route she passed the outward bound Cunard liner *Queen Mary* which, having embarked German prisoners of war and wounded US servicemen, was sailing for New York from where she would return with thousands more troops of the US Expeditionary Force. Next day the Barracudas carried out deck landing practice and accelerated launchings in the Firth of Clyde and on 15 January *Colossus* rendezvoused with her sisters *Venerable* and *Vengeance,* while all three carriers were operating independently in the area. During the second half of January, *Colossus* carried out intensive flying practice each day and anchored off Greenock later in the afternoon when leave was usually granted. At 14.30 on Monday 22 January ten Corsairs of 1846 Squadron landed on and, with the Barracudas, they too carried out flying practice. Finally, during the afternoon of Saturday 27 January, 17 of the 21 embarked aircraft were launched to RNAS Eglinton near Londonderry, and *Colossus* secured to a buoy off Greenock for a two-week break, during which most of the ship's company were able to take some leave.

It was Tuesday 13 February 1945 when *Colossus* sailed from the Tail o' the Bank to carry out more machinery and gunnery exercises, and next day the flying operations were resumed. For the next two weeks the Barracudas of 827 Squadron and the Corsairs of 1846 Squadron continued their flying, and on Friday 23 February there was a more serious accident than in the previous month, when a Corsair crashed into the sea close to the ship. Fortunately, within 20 minutes the sea boat had rescued the pilot and returned him to the ship, and later that day there was a more unusual visitor when a Fairey Swordfish biplane landed on and, two hours later, took off again. On Monday 26 February the Flag Officer Flying Training spent the day aboard *Colossus* to watch the day's flying events, and next day the carrier secured to a buoy off Greenock for a seven-day break. This was the last opportunity for members of the ship's company to take leave before the carrier left home waters for the British Pacific Fleet, although for the Engineering Department most of the time was spent cleaning the main boilers. With the war in Europe coming to an end, but with no end in sight to the Pacific War, there was the gloomy prospect of a long commission east of Suez, with constant action against an increasingly desperate

A fine aerial view of *Colossus* at sea. *(Fleet Air Arm Museum, Cars C/73)*

Colossus at sea with aircraft on deck. *(Fleet Air Arm Museum, Cars C/83)*

A view along the flight deck as *Colossus* arrives in Sydney on 23 July 1945. *(Fleet Air Arm Museum, Cars C/20)*

The hangar cleared of aircraft and with camp beds set out for the repatriation of former POWs. Note the spare propeller blades still fixed to the bulkheads.
(Fleet Air Arm Museum, Cars C/88)

Japanese enemy as the US-led Allied forces closed in to invade Japan itself.

On Monday 5 March *Colossus* sailed to carry out more flying practice, this time with the converted merchant ship *Pretoria Castle.* This continued until the afternoon of 9 March when she anchored off Greenock, and next day she steamed upriver to secure alongside the west wall of Glasgow's King George V Dock, just off the Renfrew Road on the south bank of the River Clyde, close to RNAS Abbotsinch (now Glasgow's international airport). Once alongside squadron stores and aircraft were embarked, and Rear-Admiral C. H. J. Harcourt, Flag Officer 11th Aircraft Carrier Squadron, hoisted his flag in *Colossus.* At 10.00 on Monday 12 March, 48 hours after her arrival, *Colossus* left King George V Dock to make a slow passage downriver. Once into the Firth of Clyde she rendezvoused with *Venerable* and *Vengeance,* and the escorts *Assiniboine, Escort, Inman, Stockham, Tartar* and *Ulysses*, before the whole force set course for the Mediterranean. On Friday 16 March, as they approached Gibraltar, the destroyers *Malcolm, Verity* and *Wolverine* joined them. *Colossus* stopped for an hour in Gibraltar Bay to take on stores and mail, and by the forenoon of 20 March she had arrived off Malta. Once again there was a brief halt, when Admiral Harcourt transferred to *Venerable,* and at just after midday on 22 March, having left her sisters at Malta, *Colossus* flew off most of her aircraft and secured to a buoy in Alexandria Harbour where she was to undergo a refit.

For almost six weeks, including two days in the floating dry dock, *Colossus* remained at Alexandria, and it was on Wednesday 2 May that she sailed to land on her aircraft and to carry out further flying practice. Acting as planeguard during this period was an Italian destroyer and, for three weeks as the carrier operated from Alexandria, the Corsairs and Barracudas carried out intensive flying operations. During the afternoon of 22 May *Colossus* returned to harbour and two days later she was joined by *Venerable, Vengeance* and *Glory.* During the early evening of 27 May, together with *Venerable* and *Vengeance,* and escorted by the destroyers *Tuscan* and *Tyrion, Colossus* left Alexandria and set course for Port Said, where she arrived the following morning. That same afternoon all three carriers made their southbound transit of the Suez Canal before setting course for Aden, where they arrived on Friday 1 June. The 24 hours spent at the barren South Arabian port is best summed up by Peter Chamberlain who celebrated his 21st birthday that day: 'I didn't get the opportunity to go ashore, which was just as well because it looked pretty grim.' The three carriers and their escorts left Aden on 2 June and set course for Trincomalee where, after carrying out flying practice en route and detaching *Venerable* to Colombo, *Colossus* arrived during the forenoon of 9 June. Although *Vengeance* entered harbour, *Colossus* remained offshore just long enough to disembark two hospital cases, before she set course into the Bay of Bengal bound for Madras, where she anchored during the forenoon of 10 June. During her nine hours at anchor the personnel and spare aircraft of 1846 Squadron were landed, before the carrier made the passage to Colombo where, on 13 June, the personnel of 827 Squadron were disembarked.

There was just time for a run ashore before *Colossus* left for Trincomalee, where she arrived during the forenoon of 15 June to carry out a short maintenance period.

On Sunday 24 June *Colossus* sailed for Madras where she re-embarked the Corsairs and personnel of 1846 Squadron, before steaming round to Colombo where, on 27 June, she picked up the personnel of 827 Squadron. During the first week of June she exercised with the squadrons between Madras and Colombo, but finally on Saturday 7 July she rendezvoused with *Venerable* (Rear-Admiral Harcourt), *Vengeance, Tuscan* and *Tyrian* off Trincomalee, before setting course across the Indian Ocean for Fremantle. Having crossed the equator in the early hours of 8 July, King Neptune visited the ship next day for a full Crossing the Line ceremony. During the passage aircraft from all three carriers practised full-scale bombing attacks and the anti-aircraft gunners rehearsed for the expected suicide attacks on the fleet. On Monday 16 July there was a distant view of Fremantle as *Colossus* spent the day at anchor off the port, but then she made a fast passage to Sydney and on Sunday 22 July, whilst operating in Jervis Bay, the aircraft were flown off to RNAS Nowra. Next day, at 11.50, she steamed into Sydney Harbour to secure at No 6 berth Woolloomooloo Docks.

Having joined the British Pacific Fleet, the carriers of the 11th Aircraft Carrier Squadron had to train and prepare themselves for operations against the Japanese, and to relieve the fleet carriers which were engaged in bombing targets on the main Japanese islands. However, known only to a few senior politicians, for some time the Japanese Government had been trying to end the war on their own terms. On 16 July, the day that *Colossus* had spent at anchor off Fremantle, the first atomic bomb was exploded at the US test facility in the New Mexican desert and preparations were immediately made for the first two atomic weapons to be moved to the US base on Tinian Island, north of Guam in the Pacific Ocean. For *Colossus'* ship's company, however, the immediate future meant enjoying runs ashore in the bright lights of Sydney where, according to Peter Chamberlain, 'There was very little evidence of war and we enjoyed ourselves in the dance halls where "Story of a Starry Night" was the hit tune and was being played almost everywhere. It was taken from one of Tchaikovsky's pieces and I will always associate it with the end of the Pacific War.'

On Sunday 5 August *Colossus* was opened to visitors and next day the US Air Force's B29 bomber *Enola Gay* dropped the first atomic bomb, unleashing destructive power previously unimagined on the centre of the Japanese city of Hiroshima. Within seconds over 30,000 people had been killed. Four days later, on 9 August, the second atomic bomb was dropped on the city of Nagasaki and next day the Japanese Government declared its willingness to surrender. For *Colossus,* however, it was to be 'business as usual' and on Monday 13 August she left Sydney to embark her squadrons and to set course, in company with *Vengeance,* for Manus and the operational area. That evening she anchored in Jervis Bay and at 04.30 on 14 August she weighed anchor to set course for Manus. Within an hour of getting under way, however, she was ordered to return to Sydney and by 10.00 she had secured to dolphins in Sydney Harbour. At 09.00 on Wednesday 15 August, to everyone's relief, came the official announcement that hostilities were over, and the entry in the ship's official log sums up the mood on board, with the word 'PEACE' written in block capitals. That afternoon, at 14.30, *Colossus* left Sydney bound once again for Manus, but at least the war was over.

Five days after leaving Sydney, at 08.00 on Monday 20 August, *Colossus* anchored at Manus, which was the forward operating base for the British Pacific Fleet, and stores, ammunition and fuel were embarked. Later that day, at 17.50, she weighed anchor and, in company with Task Group 111.3, which included her sister *Venerable* and the fleet carrier *Indomitable,* as well as the cruisers *Argonaut, Belfast* and *Bermuda,* and the destroyers *Quiberon* and *Tumult,* she sailed for a position Lat 25° - 02'N/Long 122° - 20'E, off the island of Formosa (Taiwan). Once in position the Corsairs patrolled the skies over Japanese airfields to ensure that no flying operations took place, which would be in breach of the terms of surrender which had been signed two days earlier. On Tuesday 11 September, *Colossus* was ordered north to close a point off the Chinese port of Shanghai by dawn the next day and from there, at 07.00 on 14 September, nine Barracudas carrying prisoner of war liaison teams were flown off to the city. The teams were to organize the relief and repatriation of Allied POWs and civilian internees who had been held in camps in the region. For six days *Colossus* patrolled the Chinese coast, with her aircraft providing air cover for Allied forces at Shanghai, where the political situation was very delicate and where the threat of serious civil disorder was ever present. On 18 September she anchored some 14 miles from the coast, close to Gutzlapp Island (Chongming Dao), at the mouth of the Yangtse Kiang. Six days later, at 09.00 on Monday 24 September, having been ordered to Korea, she steamed north once again, this time into the Yellow Sea and to Chemulpo (Inchon) on the west coast of Korea, 25 miles south-west of Seoul. She arrived in harbour during the afternoon of 26 September, to find the port was packed with US Navy destroyers and auxiliaries, as well as two Japanese destroyers and patrol craft. Once at anchor she embarked 350 British and Australian ex-prisoners of war, all of whom had been taken at the fall of Singapore in February 1942. Next day she left for the Philippines and arrived in Manila Bay on 4 October, where the fleet carrier *Formidable,* which was preparing to leave for Sydney, and the escort carrier *Speaker* were already in harbour. With the final surrender of Japan there came the urgent task of repatriating the Allied prisoners and internees, all of whom had suffered almost four years of neglect and ill-treatment at the hands of their captors. However, with her squadrons still embarked, space was limited and after disembarking the army personnel she took on board a mixture of 174 POWs and civilian internees, including women and children, for passage to Hong Kong. *Colossus* then left Manila to make the 48-hour passage to Hong Kong, where she arrived on Sunday 7 October and disembarked her passengers. Whilst she was in Hong Kong the ship's company provided armed patrols to assist with security on Hong Kong Island and at Kowloon, and a number of ratings who were due for demobilization were discharged ashore to await a passage home. On Monday 15 October, whilst the ship was at anchor and using her main engines, she was turned into the wind and the Barracudas were launched to Kai Tak.

On Friday 19 October *Colossus* sailed from Hong Kong, and after landing on her aircraft she set course for Ceylon (Sri Lanka). Four days later she steamed round the south coast of Singapore where the cruisers *Jamaica* and *Sussex* were escorting a minesweeping flotilla which was clearing both British and Japanese minefields, the former dating back to the early months of the war. On 26 October all the aircraft were flown ashore and next morning *Colossus* secured to buoys in Colombo Harbour, where she officially became part of the East Indies Fleet. Five days later, with her hangars clear of aircraft and laid out with camp beds, she steamed north to Bombay (Mumbai) where, at 15.00 on 4 November, she secured alongside the Alexandra Dock. Once alongside stores, transport and 1,150 troops of the Indian Army were embarked, and at 13.00 on 8 November she sailed for Singapore where the troops were to reinforce the island's garrison. Six days later, after steaming south through the Strait of Malacca, she arrived off Singapore Island once again, and there then followed a slow seven-hour passage through the newly swept channels to secure alongside the naval base on the north shore of the island at 14.00. Over the following two days all the military personnel and vehicles were disembarked, before *Colossus* steamed round to Singapore Roads, where she anchored off the city` alongside the escort carriers *Smiter* and *Trumpeter,* as well as numerous destroyers which were moored nearby. As soon as her anchors were secured lighters came alongside and this time she embarked 50 naval officers and 400 ratings for passage to Trincomalee. That afternoon ten hours' shore leave until 23.00 was granted to the ship's company, and after another short stay in harbour, on 17 November she sailed for Trincomalee, where her passengers were disembarked. The carrier then proceeded to Bombay where she took on more troops of the Indian Army, together with their transport, heavy guns and stores, before sailing for Singapore once again. On 8 December she anchored in Singapore Roads where some military personnel and equipment were disembarked, but later that day she left for the Dutch East Indies.

In August 1945, just a few days before they surrendered, the Japanese authorities in the former Dutch colony had deliberately fanned the flames of nationalism in South-East Asia by declaring the independence of the country, with Dr K. S. Sukarno as the President of the Republic of Indonesia. On 29 September, however, Mountbatten's South-East Asia Command, into whose sphere of war the former Dutch possessions came, landed the first British troops at Batavia (Jakarta), ostensibly to repatriate the Allied POWs and internees. They immediately met fierce resistance from the nationalist forces, who had been armed by the Japanese, and they quickly became embroiled in a vicious war to pacify the nationalists until Dutch troops could reoccupy the country, which they did in March and April 1946. It soon became apparent that reinforcements were needed and the troops embarked in *Colossus* were earmarked for the task. At 07.30 on Monday 10 December the carrier secured alongside No 3 Quay at Tanjong Priok, the port for Batavia, where all the troops and their equipment were disembarked. As soon as this had been completed the ship's company set about cleaning up the ship and preparing the makeshift accommodation for the repatriation of Dutch civilian internees. At 09.00 on the following day the next batch of passengers was embarked, and by the end of the afternoon 200 women, 150 children, 25 elderly men and 12 seriously ill hospital patients had been taken on board. At 15.10 *Colossus* weighed anchor to steam east along the coast of Java to the port of Semarang which, despite having been designated a 'safe haven', had been the scene of a massacre of Dutch internees by nationalists. The carrier anchored off the port at 07.40 on 12 December, and over the next six hours she embarked a further 211 women, 143 children, 36 elderly men and 21 sick patients. At 14.00 she weighed anchor and set course for Colombo. Peter Chamberlain remembers that during the six-day passage the women and children proved to be quite a problem for the ship's company, and one young lady passenger became quite 'attached' to one of the officers who had to be confined to his cabin. On 18 December *Colossus* secured to buoys in Colombo Harbour to disembark all the passengers and next day she steamed round to Trincomalee where she remained for the Christmas celebrations.

After a nine-day break at the naval base, *Colossus* left harbour to land on her squadrons once again, before re-embarking the squadron personnel at Colombo and sailing for East Africa. The New Year was seen in en route to Mombasa and six days later she anchored in Kilindini Harbour for just 24 hours. After leaving the East African port on 8 January 1946 she made a 24-hour stop at Durban where she was greeted by the 'Lady in White',

A starboard side view of *Colossus* at sea with aircraft on deck. *(Peter Chamberlain)*

Below: A mess deck decorated for Christmas 1945. *Colossus* was in Trincomalee for Christmas and the New Year. *(Peter Chamberlain)*

Perla Gibson, and where, on the quayside, long queues of cars were waiting to whisk members of the ship's company ashore for some wonderful hospitality. Peter Chamberlain recalls, however, that 'just beneath the surface' lurked the evil of Apartheid which was brought home to him when he saw a warning that it was a criminal offence to 'mix with the coloured population'. After leaving Durban *Colossus* set course for the naval base at Simonstown, where she anchored at just after midnight on 17 January. Later that forenoon she weighed anchor and flew the aircraft off to RNAS Wingsfield, north of Cape Town, before securing alongside the city's Duncan Dock, where both squadrons' personnel were disembarked. Her stay in Cape Town was limited to just three days and by Monday 21 January she had secured alongside the wall in Simonstown Dockyard, to begin an 11-week refit.

During this period *Colossus* spent just over seven weeks in dry dock, she received an informal visit from Field Marshal Smuts, the South African Prime Minister, and the air group operating from their shore base made an 'attack' on the battleship *King George V* whilst she was approaching Cape Town. The ship's company enjoyed seven days' station leave, which Peter Chamberlain remembers spending at a guest house in the relaxing atmosphere of Kalk Bay. On 26 March *Colossus* was shifted out of the dry dock to be secured alongside the wall once again, and 13 days later she sailed to land on her aircraft. During the landing operations one Corsair was lost overboard, but fortunately the pilot was rescued safely and once the operation was completed the carrier went back to Cape Town's Duncan Dock to embark the squadron personnel and surplus aircraft for ditching. With the war over there were hundreds of ex-US Lend-Lease aircraft which were no longer needed and four Vought Kingfisher reconnaissance seaplanes and a number of Grumman Wildcats were hoisted on to the flight deck. On 16 April, three days after leaving Cape Town, whilst en route to Trincomalee, *Colossus* reduced speed, turned into the wind and catapulted all the Wildcats and Kingfishers into the Indian Ocean. On 27 April, having flown off her own squadrons, she secured to a buoy in Colombo Harbour, having rejoined the East Indies Fleet.

Meanwhile, at home, political discussions were under way between the British and French Governments over the loan of an aircraft carrier to the French Navy, to help it rebuild its Air Arm which had been devastated by the war. Although the discussions did not affect *Colossus'* ship's company in the short term, it was decided that, upon her return to the UK, she would be the carrier to be handed over. During the remainder of her period east of Suez, however, *Colossus* operated out of Trincomalee and, in company with the destroyers *Camperdown* and *Cavalier,* she carried out intensive flying operations. On one occasion she went as far north as Cochin where she

Colossus leaves Cape Town in April 1946. *(Fleet Air Arm Museum, Cars C/84)*

embarked surplus aero-engines, many of which were brand new and still packed in their wooden crates, for ditching at sea. *Colossus* continued to operate from Trincomalee until Monday 24 June, when she left the station and set course for Colombo, Aden and Suez. On 8 July she began her northbound transit of the Suez Canal, and that afternoon she anchored in the Great Bitter Lake for the night. Next morning, at 04.30, she resumed her passage and seven hours later she secured to buoys in Port Said Harbour. Next day, at 12.15, she embarked Crown Prince Paul* of the Hellenes, his wife Princess Frederika of Hanover and a retinue of servants. The Greek Royal Family had been in exile in Alexandria for most of the war, and with a real possibility of the monarchy being restored in Greece they were preparing for a return to the country. At 13.00 on 10 July, as soon as the last of their baggage was on board, the carrier slipped her moorings and set course for Gibraltar where she made a 48-hour stopover. Finally, after a four-day passage north through the Atlantic Ocean and Bay of Biscay, at 04.12 on 22 July, Eddystone Light was sighted and by 06.40 the ship was at anchor in Plymouth Sound, where Crown Prince Paul, his wife and staff were disembarked. Three hours later *Colossus* was steaming up Channel and that evening she flew 12 Corsairs and six Barracudas off to their shore bases before anchoring at Spithead. Next morning, at 06.00 on 23 July, she again weighed anchor and steamed out to the Nab Tower where the remaining Barracudas and a Corsair were launched. *Colossus* had completed her final flying operations for the Royal Navy, and by 08.15 she was firmly secured to Portsmouth's North Corner Jetty.

During the weeks which followed her return, large drafts of men left the ship as her complement was reduced and their places were taken by French ratings who had arrived in Portsmouth on 2 August in the battleship *Richelieu,* which had berthed astern of *Colossus.* Peter Chamberlain, who had been one of the first ratings to join the ship, was now one of the last to leave and his abiding memory of those last few days is of the gradual decline in the cleanliness of the ship, and of the daily ration of wine which was issued to the French sailors. In the City of London the Court of Common Council gave a luncheon for the officers and men of the French Navy who had come to take over *Colossus,* and at 09.00 on Monday 5 August 1946, all the remaining Royal Navy ratings on board were discharged to the naval barracks and *Colossus* was paid off for the first and last time.

At noon the next day a distinguished gathering of VIPs, including the Prime Minister, Clement Attlee, the First Sea Lord, Admiral Sir John Cunningham, the C-in-C Portsmouth, Admiral Sir Geoffrey Layton, Monsieur Maropelli, the President of the French Department of Defence, and Vice-Admiral Lemonnier, the Chief of the French Naval Staff, all mustered on the carrier's flight deck. British and French naval guards, together with a Royal Marines band were mounted and at the stroke of noon a bugle sounded the Alert. The guards presented arms, the company stood at the salute and the band played the

*The future King Paul of the Hellenes, who succeeded his father King George II in April 1947.

National Anthem, while the White Ensign and Union Flag were slowly lowered. Then, with the band playing The Marseillaise, the French Ensign and the Tricolour were hoisted. With this simple ceremony *Colossus* was transferred to the French Navy, with Toulon as her new home port. In an early display of European unity Mr Attlee addressed the guests and told them: 'I am sure we are all glad that with this vessel there will be an opportunity at once for the French Navy to recreate and reconstruct its Naval Air Service. We have learned during the war how close must be the co-operation between men who fight in the air and men who fight on the water. Twice in my lifetime the men of our two nations have been charged with the duty of saving civilisation, and I know that we shall be found fighting side by side whenever it is necessary to defend freedom, justice and right against an aggressor.'

Two months later, in the French naval base at Toulon, *Colossus* played host to the British Ambassador at a reception on board, and in February 1947 King George VI approved a French proposal to rename the carrier FS *Arromanches.* During the late 1940s and early 1950s *Arromanches* played an important role in the French colonial war in Indo-China (Vietnam, Cambodia and Laos), and in August 1952, having been purchased outright by the French Government the previous year, she left Toulon for the third time in four years to take part in military operations against the Vietminh. In November 1956 Clement Attlee's prophecy of ten years earlier came to fruition when, after joining forces with Royal Navy units, including her sisters *Ocean* and *Theseus, Arromanches* took a leading role in the ill-advised and ill-fated Suez campaign. In 1957 she was fitted with an angled flight deck, but a year later she was refitted to carry anti-submarine helicopters. In 1973 *Arromanches* was eventually paid off into reserve at Toulon, and on 31 October 1974 her original ship's bell was returned to the Royal Navy at a ceremony on board HMS *Hermes* at Cherbourg. Finally, in 1978 *Arromanches* was broken up at Toulon and today all that remains of her is the original bell which is on display in the Fleet Air Arm Museum at Yeovilton, a reminder of the first of the light fleet carriers which had served under the Union Flag and the Tricolour.

Commanding Officers:

Captain G. H. Stokes DSC RN — 26 July 1944

Battle Honours:

Groix Island 1795 — Trafalgar 1805
St Vincent 1797 — Baltic 1855
Jutland 1916

FS *Arromanches* leaves Portsmouth Harbour in June 1948. *(Maritime Photo Library)*

Chapter Two

HMS *Vengeance* December 1944 – August 1946

On Monday 16 November 1942, just 12 days after the Battle of El Alamein which, for Britain, marked the turning point in the Second World War, the first keel plates for the second of the Royal Navy's light fleet aircraft carriers were laid at the Tyneside shipyard of Swan Hunter & Wigham Richardson. As building work on the carrier progressed the first naval personnel were appointed to stand by the ship in January 1944, but with the hull still lying on the stocks they were accommodated ashore. Five weeks later, on Wednesday 23 February 1944, the carrier was launched as HMS *Vengeance* - the sixth Royal Navy vessel to bear the name. On Wednesday 27 September 1944, the ship's first commanding officer, Captain D. M. L. Neame DSO RN, was appointed. Captain Neame had entered the Navy at the Royal Naval College Osborne on the Isle of Wight, and he was at sea as a midshipman for most of the Great War. In 1927 he trained as a pilot in the Fleet Air Arm and having been promoted to Captain in 1940, in May 1941 he was appointed to command the anti-aircraft cruiser *Carlisle.* During his time in command he was awarded the DSO and Bar for his leadership whilst taking part in operations in the Mediterranean. Captain Neame was also an accomplished athlete, having represented Great Britain in the Olympic Games in Amsterdam during August 1928, and the British Empire Games of 1930, which were held in Canada.

By mid-December 1944 *Vengeance* was almost ready for sea, and at 06.30 on Friday 15 December a special train carrying the main body of the ship's company arrived at Wallsend-on-Tyne. Half an hour later the men were having breakfast at Swan Hunter's canteen, and at 09.00 they marched to the ship to carry out the routine of being allocated mess decks, finding their action station and generally getting to know the ship. Next day, at 12.00, with all hands mustered in the hangar, there was a Dedication and Commissioning Service, conducted by Captain Neame and the Bishop of Newcastle upon Tyne.

Vengeance in the Pacific early in her career. Note her aircraft are carrying British Pacific Fleet markings.
(Fleet Air Arm Museum, Cars V/136)

Three hours later, at 15.00, with two tugs secured forward and two aft, the mooring ropes were slipped and *Vengeance* was moved downriver to the Tyne Commissioners Quay at North Shields, which had been vacated by her sister *Colossus* only the previous day. *Vengeance* remained alongside at North Shields for Christmas and the New Year, but on Thursday 4 January 1945 she left the River Tyne and escorted by the elderly, four-funnelled, Lend-Lease destroyer *Lancaster* (ex-USS *Philip*) she steamed north to anchor later in the day in the Firth of Forth, off the town of Methil. Next morning *Vengeance* moved up to Rosyth and anchored off the naval base where lighters were waiting with a Supermarine Seafire, a Fairey Barracuda and a Vought Corsair, all of which were hoisted on to the flight deck. There then followed ten days of trials in the North Sea, which included an inspection by the C-in-C, and a dummy torpedo attack by 12 Barracudas from nearby Crail. By 15 January *Vengeance* had steamed round to Greenock, and she was ready to undertake her flying trials in the Firth of Clyde.

For the next seven weeks *Vengeance* carried out flying operations, and during the forenoon of Monday 22 January an aircraft made its first deck landing. The event took place at 11.15 when a Seafire landed safely on board, and an hour later a Barracuda also touched down without incident. Later in the day they were followed by a Corsair and by the end of the afternoon all three aircraft had been launched by means of the accelerator. The three planes continued to practise deck landings and launchings, and a few days later they were joined by a Grumman Hellcat. February was a very busy month for the carrier's ship's company, with the ship operating from the Clyde on a daily basis, with only the occasional break of 24 hours. On Sunday 25 February there were more intensive flying operations, with 14 Corsairs of 1850 Squadron and the Barracudas of 812 Squadron landing on the carrier. Later that afternoon, after the ship had anchored off Greenock, the personnel of both squadrons were embarked. Next day flying operations began again and they continued without a break until the evening of Monday 5 March when *Vengeance* secured to a buoy off Greenock and many members of the ship's company were able to take a few days' leave during the six-day break there. On Sunday 11 March, with the ship ready to sail east with her sisters *Colossus* and *Venerable,* Admiral C. H. J. Harcourt, Flag Officer 11th Aircraft Carrier Squadron, spent the day on board, during which time he inspected the ship's company at Divisions, and the ship herself, before returning to *Venerable.* Next day, at 12.45, *Vengeance* weighed anchor and put to sea to rendezvous with *Colossus* and *Venerable* and the escorts *Assiniboine, Cotton, Escort, Inman, Stockham, Tartar* and *Ulysses,* after which the whole force set course for the Mediterranean. During the passage of the North Channel there was a submarine scare, and while the ship went to Action Stations with the aircrews ready to scramble their aircraft for anti-submarine strikes, the escorts dropped depth charges. Fortunately, it was a false alarm and by next morning the carriers were steaming west into the Atlantic Ocean, before altering course south. *Vengeance* made a one-hour stop in Gibraltar Bay, before she flew off her squadrons to Hal Far in Malta and on 20 March she anchored in Marsaxlokk Bay. Once at anchor lighters came alongside and all the squadron personnel and their stores were disembarked before *Vengeance* left the next day to make the return passage to Gibraltar where, on Friday 23 March she entered No 1 dry dock for maintenance on her underwater hull.

It was Thursday 19 April before *Vengeance* was moved out of dry dock and alongside Gibraltar's detached mole, and next day she left for the return passage to Malta. During the afternoon of 23 April she landed on her Barracudas and Corsairs before anchoring in Marsaxlokk Bay again and re-embarking the squadron personnel. For *Vengeance* the last week of April and the first three weeks of May were spent operating from Malta, with an intensive flying programme as the squadrons completed their work-up, but on 12 May she steamed into Grand Harbour for a nine-day maintenance period which also provided a break for the ship's company. During her time in Malta many members were introduced to the establishments of Strait Street, or 'The Gut' as it was popularly known to the generations of sailors who had passed through Grand Harbour. Finally, however, it was time to head east for the British Pacific Fleet and during the forenoon of Monday 21 May, *Vengeance* left Malta to land on her aircraft and to rendezvous with *Venerable* and *Glory,* the latter having arrived off Malta from the UK that very day. Together with the escorts *Tuscan* and *Tyrian,* the carriers set course for Alexandria, where they arrived three days later. After three days in the Egyptian port *Vengeance* left on Sunday 27 May, together with her sisters *Venerable* and *Colossus* and the escorts, to steam east.

At 07.00 on 28 May she passed the Port Said breakwater and 12 hours later she was at anchor in Suez Bay and ready to steam south through the Red Sea. During the passage all three carriers undertook flying exercises and during the forenoon of 30 May two Corsairs from 1850 Squadron were lost when they crashed into the sea. On 1 June there was a break in Aden, but *Vengeance* spent less than 24 hours in harbour before, at 12.00 on 2 June, along with the remainder of the force, which had now been joined by the battleship *Duke of York,* she left for Trincomalee. Once into the Arabian Sea and approaching the Far Eastern theatre of war, the ship was darkened each night, Action Stations were regularly exercised and anti-submarine patrols were flown. On Saturday 9 June, after flying the serviceable aircraft ashore, *Vengeance* secured to a buoy in Trincomalee Harbour. That afternoon lighters came alongside to unload

At Sydney in late 1945. *(Fleet Air Arm Museum, Cars V/84)*

the remaining planes, and two days later *Vengeance* sailed for Madras where the personnel of 1850 Squadron left the ship for the nearby naval air station at Tamberam. The carrier then steamed back to Ceylon (Sri Lanka), and to the port of Colombo where the men of 812 Squadron went ashore, before the ship returned to Trincomalee. The last week of June was spent operating from the naval base, and carrying out deck landing trials with Grumman Avengers, but on 1 July she was back off Madras to pick up the squadron personnel. Three days later the personnel of 812 Squadron were re-embarked in Colombo and by 6 July *Vengeance* was back at Trincomalee. At 07.20 on Saturday 7 July, together with *Venerable, Colossus,* the battleship *Anson,* and the escorts, she sailed for Australia.

Two days after leaving Trincomalee, at 09.42 on Monday 9 July, one of the Corsairs of 1850 Squadron was badly damaged and the pilot injured, when the machine overturned on landing. The wrecked plane was ditched overboard and that afternoon the flight deck was cleared for the Crossing the Line ceremony. On 11 July *Vengeance* passed the Cocos Islands and five days later, with the rest of the force, she anchored off Fremantle for just over eight hours. The passage from Fremantle to Sydney, by way of Australia's south coast, took seven days and this included most of 22 July at anchor in Jervis Bay. Before anchoring, however, 11 Corsairs and 11 Barracudas were flown ashore, with a further three being accelerated whilst the ship was at anchor. Next morning, after an early start, *Vengeance* set course for Sydney and that afternoon she steamed up harbour to secure alongside No 2 Wharf at Sydney's Woolloomooloo Docks. Once alongside it was clear to the ship's company that their arrival in Australia was very popular with the residents of the city, many of whom were waiting in cars on the quayside ready to whisk them off into Sydney to sample the generous 'Aussie' hospitality. Over the next week, whilst the final momentous events in the Pacific War were taking place, in the words of one member of the ship's company, 'We were too engrossed in the "battle of the barons of Sydney", to be at all conscious of what was to be expected during our coming showdown with the Japs.' On 6 August, the first atomic bomb, a 9,000lb device, was dropped on Hiroshima, to be followed three days later by a second which was dropped on Nagasaki. On 10 August Tokyo announced that the Japanese were willing to surrender, but only if the status of their Emperor remained unchanged. The Allies responded to this by declaring that the Emperor would be subject to Allied authority, and the Japanese then agreed that their surrender would be unconditional. The end came at 09.00 on Wednesday 15 August, and Captain Neame cleared lower deck to address the ship's company and announce the news personally. However, he also told them that the ship would sail as planned that afternoon to assist with the surrender of Japanese forces. So, at 14.15, when *Vengeance* left Sydney and set course for Manus, the main brace was spliced, and the additional tot of rum that evening almost made up for having left the 'fleshpots' of Sydney.

After leaving harbour and landing on her squadrons in Jervis Bay, *Vengeance* rendezvoused with *Colossus, Bermuda, Tuscan, Tyrian* and other units and set course for the

Admiralty Islands, the forward operating base for the British Pacific Fleet. After a voyage of five days *Vengeance* and the rest of the force arrived at the narrow entrance to Manus harbour and during the ten days at the base the carrier made three sorties out to sea for flying practice. On 30 August, however, she sailed for Leyte Gulf and after only a few hours at anchor there she was ordered to sail for Hong Kong. Although Japan had announced its willingness to surrender, nobody knew how individual commanders in the various Pacific and South-East Asian theatres of war, whose large armies were undefeated in battle, would react. With a former Hong Kong Government official, Franklin Gimson, having been released from internment and having virtually taken over the running of Hong Kong single-handedly, and with the Foreign Secretary Ernest Bevin putting a great deal of pressure on the US Administration to allow British naval units to re-enter Hong Kong and take the Japanese surrender, it was eventually agreed that a Royal Navy force could sail into the colony. The first units to steam into Hong Kong were *Indomitable, Venerable* and the cruiser *Swiftsure,* which arrived on 30 August, and six days later, at 09.30 on Wednesday 5 September, having made her way slowly through a very precarious swept channel, *Vengeance* anchored in Hong Kong Harbour. Although no shore leave was granted, armed platoons of both sailors and Marines were landed to keep order in Victoria and Kowloon, and to round up and guard Japanese prisoners of war. The Royal Marines band also went ashore, together with all their musical instruments, to undertake a tour of the various camps to entertain the Allied ex-POWs and civilian internees.

With the help of the ships' companies from *Vengeance, Colossus, Venerable* and *Indomitable,* 3,000 RAF technicians, and between 30,000 and 40,000 labourers, including Japanese POWs, work was started to create some order from the chaos and neglect of almost four years of Japanese occupation, not to mention putting a stop to the widespread looting which had taken place between the announcement of surrender and the arrival of Admiral Harcourt's force. On the day after her arrival in Hong Kong some limited shore leave was granted to *Vengeance's* ship's company, and at 16.30 on Sunday 16 September 1945, with the official surrender ceremony having taken place in Victoria's High Court building on Hong Kong Island, all the naval units in harbour fired a 21-gun salute and for the second time in five weeks the main brace was spliced. During the last few days of September and the first week of October *Vengeance* put to sea on a number of occasions to carry out flying operations, and one of the more unusual duties the aircraft were required to perform was the spraying of the chemical DDT over the colony. During their occupation the Japanese had taken no precautions against malaria, so when British forces returned the disease was rife and urgent anti-malarial measures were needed. Also during *Vengeance's* stay in Hong Kong post-war demobilization of Hostilities Only ratings began, and there was a constant stream of men leaving the ship to await their passage home. On Friday 19 October the Portuguese sloop *Goncala Velho**, carrying the Governor of the neighbouring Portuguese colony of Macau, entered harbour for the first official post-war visit to the newly liberated Crown Colony. During the Japanese occupation Macau had remained neutral under its Portuguese administration, but the residents had been confined to the small area which comprised this very Portuguese Asian colony. The Governor met Admiral Harcourt who, until the return of Sir Mark Young in May 1946, was the head of Hong Kong's British Military Administration. On Saturday 20 October he paid an unofficial visit to *Vengeance,* accompanied by Admiral Harcourt, and two days later, he returned to Macau on board *Goncala Velho.*

On 6 November *Vengeance* had to shift her anchorage in the harbour to allow the battleship *Anson* to berth, and on 21 November her sister *Glory,* which was on POW and internee repatriation voyages, entered harbour. Later in the month *Vengeance* spent two days at sea carrying out flying practice with her squadrons, which were now based ashore at Kai Tak, but by 1 December she was back in Hong Kong Harbour. On 20 December all the aircraft and squadron personnel were embarked by lighter, and four days later, on Christmas Eve, the ship's company held a party on board for the children of Chinese orphanages on Hong Kong Island and Kowloon. Altogether 400 children attended and, thanks to a number of fund-raising events which were held on board, the galley was able to provide a veritable feast, complete with soft drinks, and an improvised 'fairground' for the youngsters, who had never seen so much food. Each child received a small gift, most of which had been hand made by the ship's 'chippies'. That same day Admiral Harcourt visited the ship for an hour, and three days later the C-in-C British Pacific Fleet, Admiral Sir Bruce Fraser, paid a short visit. On 28 December there was a change of role for *Vengeance* when she sailed for Labuan and during the passage the ship's company prepared the hangar for the accommodation of troops. New Year's Eve saw *Vengeance* steaming through the South China Sea and at 07.40 on 1 January 1946 she anchored in Victoria Harbour, Labuan, in North Borneo. That forenoon she embarked 42 officers and 400 men of the Australian Army, all of whom were part of the reoccupation force stationed in North Borneo, now due for demobilization. At 12.35, with the embarkation of the troops and their baggage complete, *Vengeance* weighed anchor and set course for Sydney. During the 11-day passage the troops were

* Built in Britain in the early 1930s, *Goncala Velho* was a modified version of the Royal Navy's Bridgwater class of minesweeping sloops.

employed chipping the paintwork off the flight deck and repainting it, so they were probably quite relieved when, during the early hours of 12 January, the carrier arrived off Sydney Heads and the aircraft were flown ashore. By 09.50 *Vengeance* was passing through Sydney Heads and an hour later she was secured to dolphins in the harbour where the troops were disembarked.

To the relief of the ship's company, before *Vengeance* joined the East Indies Fleet at Trincomalee, the carrier was to undertake an eight-week refit in Sydney and on 19 January she was shifted to the Cruiser Wharf of Cockatoo Island Dockyard. With the ship well and truly in dockyard routine the officers and men were once again able to enjoy the amenities of Sydney and everyone was able to take a week's station leave. Unfortunately, the death of an able seaman, who was drowned whilst swimming on one of Sydney's many beaches, cast a shadow over the visit, and with the prospect of the coming weeks which would be spent at Trincomalee, many drowned their sorrows in the Australian city. During the refit the ship spent nine days in dry dock, and ashore 812 Squadron exchanged their Barracudas for Fairey Fireflies. It was on Tuesday 19 March that the final farewells were bade to Sydney and *Vengeance* sailed for Ceylon (Sri Lanka). The first three days of the passage were spent carrying out flying practice in the Jervis Bay area, with the new Fireflies making their first deck landings. Finally, however, on Friday 5 April, after flying the aircraft ashore, *Vengeance* secured to buoys in Colombo Harbour, where all the squadron personnel were disembarked. During the two days at Colombo, whilst the off-duty watches enjoyed the beaches of Mount Lavinia, surplus aircraft and separate aero-engines were loaded on board, then on 7 April, the carrier left the port to make an overnight passage up India's Malabar Coast to Cochin where she secured alongside and shore leave was granted. For the remainder of the month *Vengeance* was to be employed on ferrying duties and she embarked both Royal Air Force and Royal Indian Air Force personnel for passage

With Sydney Harbour Bridge in the background, in early 1946 *Vengeance* lies in the Captain Cook dry dock undergoing a refit. *(Fleet Air Arm Museum, Cars V/83)*

to Singapore and to Japan, where detachments would form part of the Commonwealth Occupation Force. Also embarked by crane were a number of Spitfire and Auster aircraft, plus more surplus planes which were to be dumped at sea. After leaving Cochin on 9 April, *Vengeance* made a five-day passage to Singapore where, on 14 April, she anchored off the city and the RIAF personnel were landed, following which she steamed round to the naval base on the north side of the island where the Spitfires and men of the RAF's No 11 Squadron were embarked before the carrier sailed for Japan. Six days later, during the early morning of 23 April, the ship's company closed up at their stations and all doors, scuttles and deadlights were closed as the ship steamed slowly through the mined waters of the Bungo Suido and the Hayasui Seto to enter the Inland Sea. That afternoon, at 14.00, *Vengeance* anchored off Iwakuni, from whose airfield the RAF would operate*, and where the Spitfires were loaded on to lighters and ferried ashore. Next day, whilst the RAF working parties were continuing the task of unloading aircraft and stores, some limited shore leave was granted and a few men were given the unique opportunity of visiting the city of Hiroshima, some 30 miles north of Iwakuni. On 26 April, after leaving Iwakuni, *Vengeance* returned to Hong Kong where she secured alongside No 1 Pier at Kowloon, and from there she made her way back to Trincomalee. On Saturday 4 May, whilst steaming across the Bay of Bengal, *Vengeance* passed her sister *Venerable,* which was on passage from Ceylon to Singapore, and on 9 May, once she was secured to No 5 buoy at Trincomalee Naval Base, the squadron aircraft and men were embarked from lighters, while *Vengeance* herself remained there for the rest of the month.

At 06.30 on Monday 10 June, when *Vengeance* sailed again it was at last to take on her true role as an aircraft carrier, but sadly operations got off to an unfortunate start when, at 10.58, with the ship a few miles off Foul Point, one of the Fireflies of 1850 Squadron crashed into the sea astern of the carrier. Although she was stopped immediately and the sea boat was launched within minutes, the plane sank quickly before the pilot, Sub-Lt (A) Smith RNVR, could be rescued. Next day, before *Vengeance* set course for Colombo, a memorial service was held over the spot where the Firefly had been lost. After her short break at Colombo, where squadron stores were embarked, *Vengeance* returned to the Trincomalee area from where, over the following five weeks, she would operate. On Friday 21 June, after returning to Trincomalee Harbour for a 12-day maintenance period, both watches were granted a few days' leave at the Diyatalawa Rest Camp on the island, where advantage was taken of the draught beer which was available, making a welcome change from the bottled variety served in the canteen at Trincomalee. However, being more potent than the bottled beer, it was found that even the barbed wire fences failed to stop some men from 'escaping' the confines of the rest camp. By 3 July, however, the carrier was at sea once again and carrying out flying operations off Trincomalee.

Finally, at 07.15 on Saturday 20 July came the day for which everyone had been waiting, when *Vengeance* left Colombo to set course for Aden, Suez and home. She steamed north through the Suez Canal on Thursday 1 August, and she spent 34 hours at anchor in Gibraltar Bay, but at 12.15 on Sunday 11 August, Ushant was sighted. Soon after this *Vengeance* began her passage up Channel and at 06.00 the next day, whilst off the Isle of Wight and east of the Nab Tower, she flew off ten Fireflies and 11 Corsairs to Lee-on-the-Solent and her Walrus seaplane to RNAS Gosport. At 09.44, having completed the flying-off, the carrier anchored at Spithead for Customs clearance, but to everyone's frustration there was no shore leave. Finally, at 20.50 *Vengeance* weighed anchor to steam back down Channel bound for Devonport. After an overnight passage, at 12.15 on Tuesday 13 August 1946, *Vengeance* passed the breakwater to enter Plymouth Sound and steam up harbour with full ceremony. At 13.40 she secured alongside 6 & 7 wharves of Devonport Dockyard. The first commission was over and ahead lay a five-month refit.

*Iwakuni is now an international airport.

Chapter Three

HMS *Vengeance* August 1946 – September 1952

On Tuesday 20 August 1946, just seven days after her return to Devonport from Trincomalee, there was a change of command when, at 18.15, Captain J. H. F. Crombie DSO RN joined the ship and two hours later Captain Neame left. Captain Crombie had entered the Royal Navy in 1913, and by 1934 he had been promoted to Commander. During the Great War he served in the battleship *Queen Elizabeth* and the destroyer *Oak.* At the outbreak of war in 1939 he was the Executive Officer in the battlecruiser *Repulse,* during which time he was Mentioned in Dispatches. In 1941, after promotion to Captain and in command of HMS *Bramble,* he was the Senior Officer Minesweepers and took part in 12 Russian convoys. For his services in minesweeping in the White Sea during the winters of 1941 and 1942 he was awarded the DSO and, in 1943, the Soviet Order of Alexander Nevsky. Later in the war Crombie was appointed to the Admiralty for duties in the Operations Division, which included liaison with Fighter Command. Following this he became Director of the Minesweeping Division in the Admiralty, and it was from there that he was appointed to command *Vengeance.*

After recommissioning in late November 1946, *Vengeance* remained firmly alongside Devonport Dockyard for the remainder of the year, and on 9 December 1946, whilst she was being warped from No 8 to No 7 wharf, a sudden squall seized the ship and drove her on to the quay. Before the tugs could take control of her the hull had been damaged below the bow anchor hawse pipe, and a large hole was punched into her stem. It took five tugs half an hour to get her safely alongside once again, but the damage was soon repaired, and by 19 December basin trials had been carried out on the main propulsion machinery. The refit was finally completed on Saturday 11 January 1947 and, at 08.15 that day, she sailed to carry out engine trials between Plymouth Sound and St Helen's Roads off the Isle of Wight. On 21 January, with aircraft from RNAS Ford making a number of successful deck landings, she completed her arrester gear trials and next day saw the completion of flying trials. This was followed by four days anchored at Spithead, which pleased the 'Pompey' men, but afterwards she set course for Rosyth. The passage was made by way of the Irish Sea, and the night of 28/29 January was spent at anchor off Lamlash. By Friday 31 January, however, the carrier was at anchor off Rosyth and waiting for her were a number of Fireflies and Seafires which were loaded on board from lighters. With her long refit having been completed and being operational once again, *Vengeance* had been allocated to Rosyth Command for duties as a Home Fleet training carrier.

Vengeance leaves Malta on a cargo voyage to the Far East with aircraft and military transport on her flight deck.
(Michael Cassar)

Throughout the bitterly cold February and March of 1947 *Vengeance* operated from Rosyth, carrying out flying training in the misty, grey waters off Scotland's east coast. During February she was accompanied by the destroyer *Rapid* which acted as planeguard. At 12.41 on Thursday 13 February 1947 came the first fatal flying accident, when a Firefly which was landing on crashed into the port stanchion of the first crash barrier and burst into flames. One member of the flight deck party, Stoker J. E. Snell, was lost overboard and the wrecked aircraft fell into a port side sponson. Fortunately the pilot of the plane was not seriously hurt, but a long and thorough search by both *Vengeance* and *Rapid* failed to find any trace of the missing man. The programme of flying training continued into March, when *Vengeance* was operating in the North Sea and off the north coast of Ireland with Seafires from Eglinton. On 7 March, whilst operating off Rosyth, she met the fleet carrier *Formidable,* which was on her way to the naval base from Portsmouth to be mothballed. Later in the month, escorted by the destroyer *Rocket,* she returned to the Irish Sea and on Saturday 22 March she called at Belfast. Unfortunately, the short visit was overshadowed by the loss of a rating, Stoker W. Slasor, who went missing in the harbour and who was believed to have drowned. Despite a thorough search by the ship's divers no trace of the man could be found, and it was seven weeks before his body was recovered from the sea in Bangor Bay. On 27 March the carrier returned to Rosyth to begin an assisted maintenance period.

When *Vengeance* sailed on Tuesday 6 May she returned to the Irish Sea and Bangor Bay, this time escorted by the destroyer *Fernie,* where she continued her training duties with Seafires and Fireflies making deck landings and launches. On Wednesday 28 May she returned to Rosyth and six days later she hoisted the flag of the First Sea Lord, Admiral Sir John Cunningham, for an official visit to Oslo, which would be politically important as an expression and confirmation of the close friendship between Britain and Norway. Escorted by the destroyers *Cadiz* and *Sluys, Vengeance* left Rosyth at 14.55 on 3 June and two days later, as the three units approached Oslo, they were met by three Norwegian destroyers and an MTB group under the command of Commodore Jacobson, who escorted them through Oslofjord and to their berths in the city. During the visit the Royal Marines Detachment were kept very busy parading numerous Guards of Honour, and mounting various ceremonial occasions ashore. On 5 June they marched through the city, from Pipervika to Studenterlunden, accompanied by hundreds of local people, and next day the Guard and Band paraded in honour of the Norwegian Crown Prince when he visited the ship. On 7 June they paraded once again, this time the occasion was a visit from King Haakon of Norway and later in the day, together with a contingent from the ship's company, they marched through the city, before finally Beating Retreat. After leaving Oslo during the afternoon of 10 June *Vengeance* called at Tromso on 11 June, and at Bergen the following day. Once again there was a ceremonial march past through the town, with the First Sea Lord taking the salute, before *Vengeance* moved on to Trondheim and Tromso where, 200 miles inside the Arctic Circle, the band played at the town's football stadium, spurred on no doubt by the local ladies' gymnastic display team. On Sunday 22 June, having received a most enthusiastic and generous welcome from the people of Norway, *Vengeance* and her escorts weighed anchor and left Tromso bound for Rosyth, where they arrived at 11.35 on 25 June.

Once *Vengeance* had anchored in the Firth of Forth the First Sea Lord struck his flag and that evening the carrier weighed anchor to head for the North Sea, where she rendezvoused with the battleship *Duke of York,* the cruiser *Diadem,* the monitor *Roberts* and the escorts *Blencathra, Fernie* and *Nepal.* For three days the whole force, with Seafires of 807 Squadron flying from *Vengeance,* took part in an air defence exercise, in conjunction with the RAF. On 28 June, after completion of the exercise, *Vengeance* returned to Rosyth where she secured to a buoy in mid-river for a four-day break. *Vengeance* left Rosyth during the evening of Wednesday 2 July and steamed round the Pentland Firth for the Clyde area where, two days later, she anchored at Lamlash for several days of painting, scrubbing and drilling. During the next 14 days, although the carrier did put to sea for flying training, most of the time was spent practising for the forthcoming Clyde Fleet Review. It was to be the first peacetime visit of the Home Fleet to the Clyde since 1912, and it was being staged as a result of a request to the Admiralty by the Lord Provost of Glasgow, to acknowledge the Clyde's contribution to naval strength during the Second World War. Most previous assemblies of a fleet of this size had been at Spithead or in Torbay and, by 1947, as few of the wartime naval resources remained in the area, most of the arrangements had to be improvised.

By Thursday 17 July *Vengeance* had steamed as far south as Morecambe Bay as she carried out flying training with aircraft from Eglinton, but at 14.30 the next day she anchored off Greenock, in her review position. Fortunately, during the nine days the fleet spent at anchor the weather was kind and tens of thousands of people came to view the assembled warships from the banks of the Clyde, or from the small steamers which toured the anchorages on their usual ferry services as well as carrying ships' visitors out to the warships. *Vengeance* was opened to visitors on Saturday 19 July, and two days later there was a full dress rehearsal for the Review. By this time the whole fleet had arrived on the Clyde and the 100 assembled warships included the battleships *Duke of York* (Flagship C-in-C Home Fleet, Admiral Sir Neville Syfret), *Anson* and *Howe,* the fleet

The Sea Otter crashes into the sea off the port side during the passage south to Cape Town. *(George Cashmore)*

A Firefly loses its undercarriage whilst landing on *Vengeance*. *(George Cashmore)*

carrier *Illustrious,* units of the 2nd Cruiser Squadron, led by *Superb* (Flag Rear-Admiral H. A. Parker) and the 4th and 5th Destroyer Squadrons. The highlight of the Review came on Tuesday 22 and Wednesday 23 July, when King George VI, together with Queen Elizabeth and the Princesses Elizabeth and Margaret, visited the fleet. The royal barge put off from Princes Pier, Greenock, during the forenoon of 22 July, and then, to the thunder of a traditional salute of 21 guns, it made its way to the flagship *Duke of York* where the Royal Family were met by the C-in-C and the Prime Minister, Clement Attlee, who had arrived a few minutes earlier. Once on board a Guard of Honour was inspected and from there the Royal Family visited the destroyer *Myngs,* the battleship *Anson,* the fleet carrier *Illustrious* and the destroyer *Solebay.* That evening there was a formal dinner on board *Duke of York,* which was hosted by the C-in-C, and next morning the tour of the fleet continued with more visits to the assembled warships. The day started with a visit to HMS *Maidstone,* from which the Royal Family watched the submarine *Tiptoe* submerge and resurface. In HMS *Superb* they walked round assembled Divisions, in which detachments from all the cruisers took part, and at 11.40 they arrived on board *Vengeance.* After meeting all the carrier's officers the King took the salute of 1,200 officers and ratings from the ship's company, together with detachments representing ships of the Portsmouth, Plymouth and Nore Commands, who marched past to the music of the Royal Marines Band. After leaving *Vengeance* at 12.15 the royal inspection of the Home Fleet culminated that afternoon in a royal procession through the lines of assembled warships. The royal party were embarked in an MTB of the coastal forces, and for over an hour they wove in and out of the ships, all of which were dressed overall and manned by long lines of cheering sailors. Next morning came the welcome signal of 'Splice the Main Brace' from the King, and that afternoon the additional tot of rum was enjoyed.

Vengeance left the Clyde at 18.50 on Saturday 26 July and steamed south to the Channel where, off the Isle of Wight, she landed on eight Barracudas for flying training. This was followed by manoeuvres in the North Sea with other units of the Home Fleet, including *Duke of York,* after which the carrier returned to the Channel to fly off the Barracudas and anchor at Spithead. On Friday 1 August *Vengeance* steamed up harbour to carry out a dockyard assisted maintenance period, which included six weeks in dry dock. It was on Monday 22 September that *Vengeance* left harbour to carry out engine trials and to steam north to the Firth of Clyde, where she landed on the 15th Carrier Air Group, which consisted of ten Seafires of 802 Squadron and 11 Fireflies of 814 Squadron. Having landed on the aircraft the carrier then anchored off Greenock to embark the Air Group personnel and stores and to unload a Seafire which had been damaged in a landing mishap. Following this, during the first three weeks of October, *Vengeance* carried out an intensive period of flying practice with the Air Group, operating on a daily basis out of Greenock or Lamlash. Finally, on Monday 27 October, the carrier steamed up the River Clyde to secure alongside Glasgow's King George V Dock, where more stores, deck cargo and aircraft were embarked. Although *Vengeance* had embarked the Air Group she was not taking up the duties of an operational aircraft carrier, and on the last day of October she left the Clyde and set course for the Mediterranean and the Far East on a cargo and personnel delivery voyage.

On Tuesday 11 November, with the ship off the island of Malta, the Air Group was flown ashore to Hal Far, and stores and personnel were disembarked in Grand Harbour. After leaving Malta on 20 November, *Vengeance* passed south through the Suez Canal four days later and on 28 November she called at Aden for 24 hours. On 6 December she arrived at Trincomalee where large quantities of cargo were unloaded, and smaller amounts taken on board. Seven days later she secured alongside the naval base at Singapore, and once again large quantities of cargo, and some personnel, were disembarked. The final leg of the outward passage took her to Hong Kong and after an extremely choppy passage through the South China Sea, during which some of the cargo was damaged, she arrived in Hong Kong Harbour on 23 December, just in time for Christmas. For the ship's company of this Home Fleet carrier there was the novelty of spending the traditional holiday in the 'fleshpots' of Wanchai, but on New Year's Day work began in earnest when drafts of men who were due for demobilization, along with some cargo, were embarked. On Saturday 3 January 1948 *Vengeance* left Hong Kong to begin her voyage home and at Singapore aero-engines, together with RAF personnel and officers and ratings on draft to the UK, came aboard. At Trincomalee more aircraft, stores and homeward-bound drafts were embarked and after a 24-hour stop at Aden, on 5 February *Vengeance* made her northbound transit of the Suez Canal, with shore leave being granted at Port Said. More drafts of men joined the ship at Malta and Gibraltar and on Monday 23 February, with the ship anchored in Plymouth Sound, all the naval and RAF passengers were disembarked. After leaving harbour that afternoon *Vengeance* steamed north to Glasgow to unload her cargo and aircraft, before sailing south to Portsmouth where she arrived on 1 March.

On Friday 12 March, whilst lying alongside Portsmouth's North Corner Jetty, there was a change of command when Captain J. Terry CBE MVO RN took over from Captain Crombie. After seven weeks alongside in Portsmouth, during which time leave was taken, on 19 April *Vengeance* sailed via the Irish Sea and Pentland Firth for Rosyth where she arrived two days later to begin deammunitioning prior to a long refit. During the refit, whilst *Vengeance* was in dry dock, Captain Terry was detached temporarily to take command of the fleet carrier *Implacable,* but six weeks later he was back on board *Vengeance,* which was almost ready to sail once again. On Thursday 29 July the refit was completed, but the carrier remained at Rosyth for Navy Days during the weekend of 31 July - 1 August, and when she finally sailed on 5 August she steamed via the Pentland Firth for the Western Isles. Once there the 15th Carrier Air Group, which now consisted of the Sea Furies of 802 Squadron and the Fireflies of 814 Squadron, landed on. For the remainder of the month *Vengeance* remained in northern waters as the Air Group carried out their work-up, and she was usually escorted by either *Alamein* or *Barrosa* to act as planeguard. There were minor mishaps during this period of intensive flying activity, but the most serious accident occurred at 15.02 on Thursday 19 August, when a Firefly which was being launched crashed into the sea. Fortunately the pilot was rescued by *Barrosa* and flying operations were quickly resumed. On Friday 20 August there was a break from routine when *Vengeance* and *Barrosa* called at Belfast, where they secured alongside the Airport Jetty. The intensive flying operations continued into September with the carrier

On 17 October 1948, *Vengeance* arrived at Cape Town's Duncan Dock. She and *Theseus* were making a 'flag showing' visit to the Dominion. *Theseus* can be seen forward of *Vengeance* and already alongside her berth.
(Maritime Photo Library)

operating in the North Sea, off the Cromarty Firth, with few opportunities for shore leave, and when *Vengeance* arrived in Portland Harbour on Saturday 18 September she had spent 30 out of the previous 36 days at sea.

With the conclusion of the intensive flying operations of the work-up *Vengeance* had five days of relaxation at Portland before, at 21.50 on Thursday 23 September, she sailed for an unusual autumn cruise which would take her as far afield as Durban in South Africa. Accompanying her during the voyage was her sister *Theseus,* the destroyers *Gabbard, Jutland* and *St Kitts,* and the frigate *Loch Arkaig.* The success of the Royal Tour in *Vanguard* the previous year had led the Government to repeat another, lower profile, naval visit to the country. Although the moderate South African Prime Minister, Jan Smuts, had been voted out of office in favour of the segregationist National Party led by Douglas Malan, it was hoped that the tour would help maintain good British-South African relations. After leaving Portland during the evening of 23 September and rendezvousing with the other units, the whole squadron took part in a Home Fleet air defence exercise with *Illustrious, Duke of York,* and a number of destroyers. On Wednesday 29 September the force was some 600 miles out in the Atlantic Ocean, off the coast of Portugal, when *Vengeance* suffered two flying accidents. The first, at 17.14, resulted in the loss of the ship's Sea Otter when it crashed into the sea, but fortunately the crew were rescued by *Cadiz,* and in the second at 17.55 a Sea Fury crashed into the sea close to *Theseus.* Once again the pilot was rescued safely, this time by *St Kitts.* Once the force had reached the vicinity of the Azores *Illustrious* and *Duke of York* were detached to return to the UK, leaving *Theseus, Vengeance* and their escorts to steam south. On Tuesday 5 October the two carriers and their escorts called at Freetown where shore leave was granted until 18.30. The squadron sailed again on 7 October and next day, at 09.15, there was a full Crossing the Line ceremony on the flight deck. Ten days later, at 08.00, *Vengeance* and the other units anchored off Cape Town. Just over two and a half hours later, at 10.40, *Vengeance* weighed anchor and after flying off the Air Group to nearby Brooklyn airfield, she followed *Theseus* into harbour and secured alongside Cape Town's Duncan Dock. Once the gangways were in place officers and men of all units were welcomed by the overwhelming hospitality of the people of Cape Town which continued for the eight days that they were alongside. *Vengeance* sailed during the forenoon of Tuesday 26 October and before landing on board, the Air Group put on an aerobatics display over the city, after which the squadron set course for the Indian Ocean and the east coast of South Africa. During the morning of 28 October *Vengeance* anchored off East London, but as so often is the case along that part of the African coast, the heavy swell prevented liberty boats from providing a full ship to shore service. As it was, only special parties managed to make the precarious trip into the port. On the last day of October *Vengeance* and *Theseus* put on an impressive fireworks display, and next morning they sailed for Durban where, at 07.50 on Tuesday 2 November, to an operatic welcome from 'The Lady in White', Mrs Perla Gibson, they steamed through the breakwater to secure alongside. Once again the hospitality was overwhelming, although as George Cashmore remembers, there was one disappointment when: 'Local Zulu dancers came on board to perform some of their traditional dances on the flight deck. Unfortunately, however, the steel deck was far too hot for their bare feet and the show had to be cancelled.' Like all members of the ship's company George enjoyed the visit to Durban and he has, 'happy memories of invitations to people's homes, entertainments too numerous to list and playing football matches. I was the

Icy conditions on the flight deck during the Arctic trials, and...

...Flight deck personnel clear away the snow and ice. *(George Cashmore)*

Vengeance dodges the pack ice in Arctic waters. *(George Cashmore)*

goalkeeper for the ship's team and in Durban we won an inter-services tournament and were presented with a trophy which was donated by the De Beers diamond company.'

Vengeance and the other units left Durban early on the forenoon of Monday 8 November, and once again the 'Lady in White' sang as the warships passed the breakwater, a gesture which was appreciated by the ship's company who were manning the flight deck. Once clear of the harbour the Air Group was landed on and, together with *Theseus, Vengeance* set course for Cape Town where she arrived three days later. On 12 November she loaded gold bullion for passage home to the Bank of England's London vaults and four days later, at 09.00 on Tuesday 16 November, with *Theseus* and the escorts, she left Cape Town. As they left harbour the South African Navy's frigate *Natal* (ex-HMS *Loch Cree*) steamed past the squadron and cheered ship. During the northbound passage there was a refuelling stop of 21 hours at Freetown, with shore leave being limited to just a few hours during the afternoon, for even in those days the town was not considered safe after dark. On 3 December, as the ships steamed north through the Bay of Biscay, the 4th Destroyer Flotilla met them and steamed past in salute and next day, for the final leg of the voyage, they rendezvoused with *Duke of York, Illustrious* and the cruiser *Cleopatra.* Finally, at 20.00 on Saturday 11 December, Portland Bill was sighted and *Vengeance* anchored for the night in Weymouth Bay. Next morning after an early start, *Vengeance* weighed anchor to fly off the Air Group to Yeovilton and, at 10.37, she secured to a buoy in Portland Harbour, in plenty of time for Christmas and New Year leave.

An ice-bound HMS *Gabbard* comes alongside *Vengeance* for a jackstay transfer. *(George Cashmore)*

No sooner had she arrived home than her programme for early 1949 was announced by the Admiralty and it had been decided that, together with other units, she would make a six-week experimental cruise in the North Atlantic and Arctic Oceans. During this period they would test new equipment which had been designed for overcoming the difficulties of naval operations in very cold conditions. As far as *Vengeance* was concerned a specially equipped Air Group, including Sea Vampire jets and Dragonfly helicopters, would be embarked. Although the Navy had gained a great deal of experience operating in Arctic waters during the Second World War, much of the equipment used then had been improvised, and arrangements had been rather primitive. During this cruise the effect of very low temperatures on equipment and weapons was to be studied as well as the men themselves who would be testing special Arctic clothing. Prior to this however, *Vengeance* left Portland on 13 December and steamed to Spithead, where she anchored, entering Portsmouth Harbour on 15 December and securing in D lock. No sooner were the gangways in place than the first leave party was on its way home, and those remaining on duty were helping to unload the gold bullion which had been brought from South Africa.

Christmas and New Year were spent at Portsmouth, but on Thursday 20 January 1949, with seasonal leave and the celebrations over, *Vengeance* left D lock and steamed to Portland from where, with the destroyer *Contest,* she carried out daily flying operations. The cruise to Arctic waters began during the forenoon of Saturday 5 February when, with *Gabbard, Loch Arkaig, St Kitts* and RFA *Wave Premier, Vengeance* left Portland to steam north through the Irish Sea and into the Atlantic Ocean where, on 8 February, heavy seas and gale force winds were encountered. Two days later the force was well north of Jan Mayen Island and in the Greenland Sea, but even so, with the weather having moderated *Gabbard* was detached to search for ice floes. On most days flying operations were carried out and during the afternoon of 11 February one of the aircraft which was landing on collided with the island superstructure, fortunately with no serious injuries. By 13 February the force was steaming through severe blizzards, which hampered flying operations, and that afternoon the flight deck personnel were employed clearing snow drifts and ice which had built up. At 14.47 on Friday 18 February there came tragedy when, in a position Lat 70° -

55'N/Long 09° - 37'W, the carrier's Sea Otter crashed into the sea. The observer, CPO Gibbs, was rescued by the frigate *St Kitts*, but with the machine sinking within minutes of hitting the water, the pilot, Lt (A) D. J. Elliot, was unable to escape and he went down with the aircraft. Both *Loch Arkaig* and *St Kitts* carried out a thorough, but unsuccessful search of the area. That evening, with severe gales and heavy seas, the two frigates with the force were ordered to the lee side of Jan Mayen Island. On one calm day three officers took part in a test of new survival suits, which entailed swimming 30 yards in an icy and unpredictable sea to climb into a rubber dinghy. By the end of February the ships were again steaming through severe snowstorms and additional lookouts were posted to watch for large icebergs which were almost invisible during the severe blizzards. The Arctic trials ended on Saturday 5 March, when *Vengeance* and her escorts set course for Rosyth, where they arrived during the early forenoon of 8 March. The trials had been a success, and the icy conditions had not affected the working of any armament or radio and radar equipment. The helicopters which had been aboard during the trials had been able to operate when the fixed-wing aircraft had been grounded by weather conditions, but it was apparent that light fleet carriers operating in pack ice risked incurring serious damage. Once back at Rosyth, however, the 33 scientists who had been aboard for the trip were thankful to be leaving, as for them it had been a very rough few weeks.

With her Arctic voyage completed there was another day at sea on 16 March, when the aircraft were flown off and *Vengeance* returned to Rosyth to begin a long refit and by the end of the month she was high and dry in the dockyard's No 2 dry dock. On Tuesday 28 June, with the carrier still in dry dock, there was a change of command when Captain J. W. Cuthbert RN took over from Captain Terry, who had been a very popular commanding officer. Captain Cuthbert had gone to sea as a midshipman in 1919 and, having been promoted to Captain in 1941, he commanded the cruiser *Glasgow* in 1942 and *Ajax* in 1944. It was on 14 July that *Vengeance* was shifted from No 2 dry dock to the main basin of Rosyth Dockyard, and at the end of July she took part in Navy Days. On Tuesday 23 August she put to sea again, and for several days she underwent engine and machinery trials in the North Sea, off Rosyth. On 30 August she started her flying trials, which took her through the Pentland Firth and as far south as Penzance, but on Wednesday 7 September with these completed, she secured to a buoy in Portland Harbour. At 12.00 next day Rear-Admiral C. E. Lambe, Flag Officer 3rd Aircraft Carrier Squadron, transferred his flag from *Theseus* to *Vengeance* and later that day, in company with the destroyer *Gabbard*, *Vengeance* sailed to carry out flying operations in the South Western Approaches. With just a short break at Portsmouth during the weekend of 16 to 19 September, *Vengeance* continued her flying operations with Sea Furies and Fireflies off Scotland's east coast and off Norway right through until the second week of November, with few opportunities for shore leave. On 6 October, having flown on by Barracuda, the C-in-C Home Fleet, Admiral Sir Rhoderick McGrigor, spent the day aboard, and on 11 November *Vengeance* made a short call at Portland, before putting to sea again. This time she was in company with the fleet carrier *Implacable*, which was operating a small complement of Sea Vampires, and with a number of destroyers she took part in a convoy escort exercise which ended at Portsmouth on 22 November, when she began a dockyard assisted maintenance period.

When *Vengeance* left Portsmouth during the forenoon of Monday 23 January 1950, it was to take up the duties of an operational Home Fleet aircraft carrier, for which she embarked Fireflies and Blackburn Firebrands. On Sunday 29 January she joined the battleship *Vanguard*, the fleet carriers *Implacable* and *Victorious*, the cruiser *Superb* and destroyers which included *Alamein*, *Cadiz*, *Gabbard* and *St James*, for the Home Fleet's cruise to Gibraltar and the Western Mediterranean. For the remainder of the month *Vengeance* operated from Gibraltar and on 1 March, whilst on passage to Palmas Bay, Sardinia, she cross-operated with her sister *Glory* before joining other units of the Mediterranean Fleet including the cruisers *Cleopatra* and *Phoebe* and numerous destroyers, to anchor in Palmas Bay. During the following week she again cross-operated with *Glory* and paid visits to Leghorn (Livorno) and Cagliari. She also operated Italian navy helicopters, and on 18 March she hoisted the flag of Vice-Admiral Sir Reginald Portal, Flag Officer Air (Home), for her return passage to Portsmouth via Gibraltar. On Tuesday 21 March, whilst operating with *Glory* and *Implacable*, there were two flying accidents. The first, at 08.24, saw a Firebrand ditch into the sea astern of *Glory*, with the pilot being rescued by *Alamein*, and just over an hour later, at 09.56, a Sea Fury ditched into the sea shortly after take-off. Once again the pilot was rescued safely, this time by *Chaplet*. Next day *Vengeance* secured alongside in Gibraltar and five days later she sailed for home, carrying out 'Exercise Artful Antic' with *Implacable* and *Superb* on the way. Finally, on the last day of March she secured alongside North Corner Jetty in Portsmouth Dockyard, where seasonal leave was given.

After the usual hustle and bustle of a leave period *Vengeance* left Portsmouth on 8 May, and after hoisting in the Sea Otter at Spithead she prepared to take on board six Sea Hornets and ten Mk V Fireflies of 809 Squadron for night flying exercises. After anchoring in Torbay, which allowed for a run ashore in Torquay, the aircraft landed on during 10 May and thereafter for four weeks the sound of launchings and landings could be heard well into the night as the Sea Hornet and Mk V Fireflies operated in the darkness of the early hours. Between 10 May and 9 June,

With a Sea Vampire and Fireflies on deck, *Vengeance* leaves Portsmouth for night flying trials. *(Fleet Air Arm Museum, Cars V/4)* some 68 night landings were carried out successfully by the Sea Hornets, with only one minor mishap when a Sea Hornet damaged its tail oleo. On conclusion of the exercises it was decided that the Sea Hornet, although possessing good landing characteristics, was too big to operate efficiently from light fleet carriers - which all aircrew and flight deck personnel already knew, since two aircraft could not pass each other in the hangar, thus causing serious delays in movements to and from the aircraft lifts. As for the Mk V Firefly, it was decided that it was not really suitable for night carrier operations, the main problem being 'view', the fact that it proved difficult to line the aircraft up with the flight deck, and when flaring out to land all sight of the deck ahead was lost to the pilot. On Saturday 17 June all the Sea Hornets and Fireflies were flown ashore, and next day *Vengeance* steamed into Rosyth Dockyard for a two-week maintenance period, leaving again on 4 July to land on the Fireflies of 809 and 814 Squadrons. The carrier remained in northern waters with her flying operations taking her up to Scapa Flow, where there was the opportunity of a run ashore at Kirkwall, and at Stavanger where the ship was opened to the public. On her arrival in the Norwegian port *Vengeance* had been secured by bow and stern wires to two buoys, but in high winds on 14 July the stern wire parted and before tugs could get to the scene and get her under control, the carrier's stern had swung round and struck a shore installation causing damage to the port side. Fortunately, before the position got too serious the ship was moved to a nearby anchorage. On 18 July she made a six-day visit to Oslo, and on leaving Norway she took part in a joint Anglo-Dutch exercise in the North Sea, with the cruiser *Jacob van Heemskerck* and the destroyer *Marnix,* which ended on 27 July at Spithead.

Vengeance remained at Portsmouth until 4 September 1950, during which time seasonal leave was taken, the ship spent three weeks in dry dock and there was another change of command. At 10.20 on Thursday 17 August Captain R. Gotto DSO CBE RN joined the ship and took over from Captain Cuthbert, who left half an hour later. Under her new commanding officer *Vengeance* sailed during the forenoon of Monday 4 September to land on the Fireflies of 809 Squadron and a Dragonfly helicopter of 773 Squadron before anchoring in Plymouth Sound. Flying the flag of Rear-Admiral C. E. Lambe, the carrier was to take part in the autumn exercises and cruise of the Home Fleet, during which the C-in-C Home Fleet, Admiral Sir Philip Vian, would fly his flag in the battleship *Vanguard.* Also taking part were the cruisers *Swiftsure* and *Cleopatra,* both from the 2nd Cruiser Squadron, with 11 destroyers, two frigates and two submarines. For *Vengeance* the exercises began on Friday 15 September, when she left Plymouth Sound to rendezvous with *Vanguard, Swiftsure* and escorting destroyers, and set course for Gibraltar. During the passage south the aircraft carried out flying operations to test the fleet's air defences and off Gibraltar on 20 September, *Vengeance* met her sister *Glory* again, with the two carriers entering harbour together. For the rest of September and the first week of October *Vengeance* operated from Gibraltar and after a break of seven days she left with *Vanguard* and two destroyers for a visit to the Portuguese Cape Verde Islands, with the battleship calling at St Vincent and *Vengeance* at Porto Grande. Following this *Vanguard* steamed south to Madeira and *Vengeance* carried out flying practice as she headed for the Moroccan port of Casablanca, where she spent five days before returning to the Gibraltar area on 2 November.

During her stay in Gibraltar the ship's company took part in the fleet regatta, without any success, and on Thursday 9 November, with the cruiser *Cleopatra* and units of the 5th Destroyer Flotilla, *Vengeance* left for home. Once into the Atlantic Ocean and off Cape St Vincent, she carried out a night exercise with the Canadian aircraft carrier *Magnificent* and her two escorts *Huron* and *Micmac,* before setting course for Plymouth Sound where, on 14 November, she embarked 15 Customs officers. Next day, with everyone's wallets feeling a little lighter, *Vengeance* sailed for Portsmouth, securing at South Railway Jetty during the forenoon of 16 November. The break at Portsmouth lasted for only an extended weekend, however, and during the afternoon of Monday 20 November the carrier was at sea once again, carrying out flying operations off Portland. These exercises, with Sea Furies and Fireflies, continued into the second week of December with little opportunity for shore leave, but during the afternoon of 8 December *Vengeance* returned to Portsmouth for Christmas and the New Year.

With the holiday celebrations and a short maintenance period over, flying the flag of the new Flag Officer 3rd Aircraft Carrier Squadron, Rear-Admiral C. John, *Vengeance* left Portsmouth on 15 January 1951 to take over the duties of trials and training carrier from *Illustrious* which was undergoing a three-month refit. After landing on the aircraft of No 53 Training Air Group she steamed north for the Irish Sea and Bangor Bay and in wet, cold and windy weather she operated in the North Channel and off the coast of Northern Ireland for ten days. During the afternoon of 29 January there was the opportunity of a run ashore at Penzance before she returned to the Channel to land on five Seafires from Culdrose. For ten days in a misty and foggy Channel *Vengeance* operated her Seafires, anchoring most evenings in Falmouth Bay and once again there were few opportunities for runs ashore. On 6 February 1951 Admiral John transferred his flag to *Indomitable* and four days later there was a weekend break at Portsmouth, following which flying operations in the Channel continued until 23 February when, having flown off all embarked aircraft, the carrier secured alongside

A splendid aerial view of *Vengeance* and her escorts, including HM Ships *St James* and *Matapan*, off Southend Pier in July 1951 for Festival of Britain Week. She has five Sea Furies on deck. *(FotoFlite)*

Portsmouth's Pitch House Jetty for leave and maintenance.

For *Vengeance* the summer cruise began on Monday 16 April, when she left Portsmouth to carry out flying training in Bangor Bay. The weather conditions were fine and the sea calm, and so with no disruption to the programme there was time for a weekend break at Plymouth at the end of the month. When flying got under way again on the first day of May, *Vengeance* landed on eight Mk VI Fireflies of 814 Squadron for night flying exercises in the Channel, between Plymouth and Land's End, with the destroyers *Cadiz* and *Zest* acting as planeguards. For the first two days a Sea Vampire made a number of landings and launches from the carrier's flight deck, before the Fireflies began night flying trials. Once again, with a full flying programme there was little time for shore leave or for deck hockey, but the Royal Marines Band gave weekly concerts in the hangar and on 3 May there was another diversion from the intensive flying programme when a BBC team spent a day on board making recordings for a radio programme called 'Life in a Carrier'.

At 22.35 on Thursday 31 May, whilst *Vengeance* was carrying out night flying exercises off Lizard Point, a Firefly of 814 Squadron crashed into the sea close to the ship. Using searchlights both the carrier and *Cadiz* combed the area and the plane's observer, although seriously injured, was rescued by the destroyer. Although the search continued until 07.15 the next day no trace was found of the pilot, and later that day *Vengeance* secured alongside at Devonport for a weekend break. When she left Plymouth Sound again during the early afternoon of 4 June, in company with *Broadsword* and *Cadiz,* it was to continue the night flying exercises with the Fireflies of 814 Squadron. Four days later, in preparation for a major exercise, a squadron of Dutch Seafires also landed on and *Vengeance* carried out her flying operations in the South Western Approaches. 'Exercise Unite' began on 13 June and, in addition to *Vengeance,* 30 surface ships took part, including the cruiser *Sheffield,* the escorts *Boxer, Corunna, Contest, Fleetwood, Redpole, St Kitts* and *Starling,* together with 18 submarines, two of which were Dutch, and all under the command of Rear-Admiral S. M. Raw, Flag Officer Submarines. It took place in the South Western Approaches and the Irish Sea, and as an escorted convoy approached home waters to make for the Clyde, the submarines simulated attacks on merchant shipping. In turn the submarines were 'attacked' by the anti-submarine screens, aircraft from *Vengeance* and shore-based RAF planes. The exercise ended on 29 June and that afternoon *Vengeance* anchored off Greenock, where some very welcome shore leave was granted.

The first ten days of July 1951 were spent carrying out more flying exercises, on occasions in company with *Indomitable,* in northern waters, but on Friday 13 July there was a four-day break at Portsmouth before the carrier undertook a far more relaxed duty for Festival of Britain Week. The Festival of Britain had been opened on 4 May and it was a Government-sponsored event, described by a minister as, 'the people giving themselves a pat on the back'. It also marked the centenary of the Victorian Great Exhibition, with the main attraction being the site which had been built on 27 acres of derelict bomb-damaged land on London's South Bank, close to Waterloo Station. Today the Royal Festival Hall is the only real reminder of this post-war event. However, in addition to the London attraction, it was decided that a number of Home Fleet units would call at ports and resorts around the country, and for *Vengeance* this entailed a five-day visit to Southend-on-Sea. The carrier left Portsmouth during the afternoon of Tuesday 17 July, to rendezvous with the five destroyers which would accompany her, including *St James, Gabbard* and *Matapan.* Next morning, at just after dawn, *Vengeance* and her escorts anchored south-east of Southend Pier and that afternoon all the ships were opened to visitors, with their boats providing a shuttle service for liberty men and for sightseers to and from the shore. During the week both the ships' boats and local tenders worked flat out to bring members of the public out to the ships, and no fewer than 15,000 people took the opportunity to visit *Vengeance.* Ashore the town's Council arranged free entry to cinemas and theatres for the ships' companies and it was said that some of the pubs almost ran out of beer. A *Vengeance* ship's company dance was held in Southend's famous Kursaal Ballroom, with the Royal Marines dance band providing the music, and needless to say the event was very popular with both the sailors and the local people. The visit ended during the early evening of Wednesday 25 July and after spending the night at Sheerness, *Vengeance* sailed for Portsmouth the next day. During the forenoon of 27 July *Vengeance* completed her final operations as one of the Royal Navy's aircraft carriers, when the embarked Sea Furies were flown off and in the early afternoon the carrier secured alongside at Portsmouth.

Vengeance remained at Portsmouth for the rest of the year, undergoing a refit and being prepared for ferrying duties which would see out her final duties with the Royal Navy. On Wednesday 12 September Captain Gotto relinquished his command, and soon afterwards the ship was moved into dry dock. During the weeks which followed, ship's company numbers were reduced, and it was on Thursday 10 January 1952 that her new commanding officer, Captain H. C. N. Rolfe RN, joined the ship. A few days later, on a dull wintry day, *Vengeance* left Portsmouth bound for Glasgow where she embarked stores and 100 personnel of 809 Sea Hornet Squadron, whose aircraft would fly out to Malta at a later date, men of the Royal Marines 2nd Raiding Flotilla, an advance party for the cruiser *Ceylon* and drafts for HM Ships *Gambia, Glasgow, Kenya* and *Ocean.* She also had on board spare Sea Furies

HMAS *Vengeance* in service with the Royal Australian Navy between 1952 and 1955.
(Royal Australian Navy)

and Fireflies all bound for the Far East and, eventually, the war in Korea. *Vengeance* left Glasgow on Monday 21 January to set course for Gibraltar, Malta, Port Said, Aden, Trincomalee and Singapore. Taking passage from Gibraltar to Trincomalee were two Barbary Apes, which were destined for a zoo in Ceylon, and it is said that volunteers to care for these unusual passengers were hard to find in case they were confused with their charges at any time!

During the carrier's first trooping voyage it was announced that the Government had agreed to lend *Vengeance* to the Australian Navy pending the completion of the half-built light fleet carrier *Majestic,* which had been launched in February 1945, but upon which work had been stopped at the end of the war. Although work on the carrier, which would eventually become HMAS *Melbourne,* had resumed in 1949 when the Australian Government had agreed a contract for its purchase, with numerous modifications to the original design, including a strengthened flight deck, larger aircraft lifts and improvements to the living accommodation, it would not be ready until 1955 at the earliest. Meanwhile, *Vengeance* returned home by the same route and she arrived in Portsmouth on 23 March. On 7 May 1952, before leaving on a second trooping voyage, Captain G. T. Coney RN relieved Captain Rolfe as commanding officer. On 23 May *Vengeance* made a short trooping run to Malta, and in June she left Portsmouth for her final voyage. Embarked was a new complement for the cruiser *Ceylon,* which was recommissioning in Singapore for another stint off Korea. On the return voyage she brought home the cruiser's old ship's company and, flying her paying-off pennant, she arrived in Portsmouth on Thursday 28 August 1952. Her active service with the Royal Navy was over.

On Monday 15 September *Vengeance* left Portsmouth for Devonport to be prepared for handing over to the Australian Navy, and during the weeks which followed the carrier was refitted. On 13 November 1952 she was commissioned with her new Australian ship's company, commanded by Captain H. M. Burrell RAN, as HMAS *Vengeance.* When she sailed for Australia on 22 January 1953 she had on board three Bristol Sycamore SAR helicopters, and when she arrived on 11 March to join HMAS *Sydney,* she embarked 850 (Sea Fury) and 817 (Firefly) Squadrons. During most of her service with the Australian Navy she was used in a training role and in April 1955, with HMAS *Melbourne* having carried out her contractor's trials successfully, it was announced that *Vengeance* would be returned to the Royal Navy. She left Sydney in late June 1955 and, steaming via Singapore and Suez, she arrived back in Portsmouth on Friday 5 August, after which her officers and men, now commanded by Captain O. H. Becher DSO DSC RAN, travelled to Barrow-in-Furness to man and commission *Melbourne.* For *Vengeance* there followed a passage to Devonport where she was refitted and modernized by the addition of a partially angled flight deck. The refit ended in August 1956 and she was then placed in the Reserve Fleet, but it was not for long and on 14 December 1956 she was sold to the Brazilian Government. From Devonport the carrier was sent to Rotterdam where the Verolme United Shipyards Company virtually rebuilt her in a massive three-year refit. The main boilers were retubed and her steam capacity was increased, new lifts were installed, a steam catapult and new arrester wires were fitted and a fully-angled flight deck was added. The work also included the provision of a mirror-sight landing system, a new island superstructure and modern radar equipment. When, on 6 December 1960, she was recommissioned into the Brazilian Navy as *Minas Gerais,* she was unrecognizable as the old Colossus-class aircraft carrier *Vengeance,* but she still had a long career ahead of her.

Used primarily for anti-submarine warfare, her standard displacement had risen to 19,890 tons, and she operated Grumman S-2G Tracker aircraft and helicopters. She received a thorough refit in 1981, and between July 1991 and October 1993 she was further modernized. By 2001, however, *Minas Gerais,* as the last survivor of Britain's wartime light fleet carriers, finally reached the end of her long 58-year career and as this is written it is reported that the Brazilian Government has put her up for sale. During her long career she had served under three flags and in every ocean of the world.

Commanding Officers:

Captain D. M. L. Neame DSO RN	27 September 1944
Captain J. T. H. Crombie DSO RN	20 August 1946
Captain J. Terry CBE MVO RN	12 March 1948
Captain J. W. Cuthbert RN	28 June 1949
Captain R. Gotto CBE DSO RN	17 August 1950
Captain H. C. N. Rolfe RN	10 January 1952
Captain G. T. Coney RN	7 May 1952
Captain H. M. Burrell RAN	2 October 1952
Captain O. H. Becher DSO DSC RAN	25 August 1954

Battle Honours:

Quiberon Bay 1759
Martinique 1794
St Lucia 1796
Crimea 1854

Vengeance at Portsmouth in October 1955 before being placed in reserve; she was later sold to the Brazilian Navy. *(Maritime Photo Library)*

Chapter Four

HMS *Venerable*
December 1944 – May 1948

In December 1944, just two years after the first keel plates were laid on 3 December 1942, the third aircraft carrier of the Colossus class, HMS *Venerable,* was commissioned at Birkenhead. Not only was this a vindication of the decision to use merchant ship standards in the construction of light fleet aircraft carriers, but it was a credit to the strength of her design and Cammell Laird & Company's shipbuilding expertise. Like her sister *Vengeance, Venerable* would have a career of over 50 years and she would serve under three flags.

On 22 November 1943 *Venerable's* first key naval personnel, under the command of Cdr (E) S. T. Stott RNR, were appointed to the ship and a few weeks later on Thursday 30 December, the carrier was launched. For 12 months she remained alongside Cammell Laird's fitting-out berth off Birkenhead's Chester Road, and on 16 October 1944 her first commanding officer, Captain W. A. Dallmeyer DSO RN, joined the ship. A few weeks later, in December 1944, *Venerable* was commissioned with a full complement, following which the task of storing and ammunitioning began. At 11.00 on Sunday 14 January 1945 *Venerable* slipped her mooring ropes and, in company with the corvette HMS *Pimpernel,* she steamed down the River Mersey and set course for the Firth of Clyde. During the passage north the anti-aircraft guns, six four-barrelled 20mm pom-poms, were fired and the main propulsion machinery was put through its paces, with full-power trials and several runs over the Skelmorlie measured mile. Finally, at 16.45 on Monday 15 January, *Venerable* anchored at the Tail o' the Bank, off Greenock. The following days saw further machinery trials, with the ship being run at full power for long periods before, on 20 January, she returned to Greenock for an 11-day break prior to starting her flying trials.

At 08.00 on Wednesday 31 January, *Venerable* left her buoy off Greenock to steam into the Firth of Clyde and just over three hours later, at 11.25, a Fairey Barracuda became the first aircraft to land on her flight deck. During the next hour three more aircraft, a Vought Avenger, a Supermarine Seafire and a Grumman Hellcat, all made

Venerable at sea soon after her completion. *(Fleet Air Arm Museum, Cars V/1)*

successful deck landings. That afternoon all four aircraft were launched by means of the accelerator, and in the evening *Venerable* returned to Greenock for the night. During the whole of February and into the first week of March *Venerable* carried out a busy programme of flying operations as she completed the first phase of her work-up, in preparation for service with the British Pacific Fleet. On 10 February there was an unusual visitor in the shape of a Fairey Swordfish torpedo-bomber, but fortunately the carrier would not be operating this sturdy, but obsolete biplane. A few minutes later the Corsairs of 1850 Squadron, which belonged to her sister *Vengeance,* landed on, to continue the flying trials at the start of an intensive period of flying operations. At 09.00 on Thursday 1 March Rear-Admiral C. H. J. Harcourt, Flag Officer 11th Aircraft Carrier Squadron, of which *Venerable* would form a part, hoisted his flag in the carrier, and two hours later he was piped aboard. Between midday on 6 March and the afternoon of 8 March all the personnel and the aircraft of 1851 (Corsair) Squadron and 814 (Barracuda) Squadron, who together would form *Venerable's* Air Group, were embarked. Flying operations then continued, with only the occasional break, until 12.55 on Monday 12 March when, in company with her sisters *Colossus* and *Vengeance,* and the escorts *Assiniboine, Cotton, Escort, Inman, Stockham* and *Ulysses,* she left to steam into the Atlantic before altering course for Gibraltar, which was reached on Saturday 17 March. Here *Venerable* took a break of just over three hours as she anchored in Gibraltar Bay, but by 15.00 she was under way and heading for Malta.

At 09.30 on Tuesday 20 March *Venerable* arrived at Malta's Grand Harbour and the scene as she steamed past the breakwater is described by Geoffrey Ellison: 'It was a marvellous sight, the sun shining overhead, all hands manning the flight deck and the band playing. The view of the harbour as we entered was lovely, with the sun showing up the white buildings to their best effect. The harbour was dotted with brightly painted dghajsas and the whole scene was like a picture from a travel book.' On this occasion, however, *Venerable* did not spend long in harbour and three hours later, at 12.30, she was steaming out to sea once again. That afternoon, at 14.40, as a range of Corsairs was lining up on the flight deck to fly off to Hal Far, one of the flight deck personnel, AM (E) 'Ginge' Thompson, who had climbed up on to one of the aircraft to speak to a pilot, lost his footing and was blown back in the slipstream right into the revolving propeller of the following aircraft, causing grave injuries. The injured man was rushed straight to the sickbay and, in the words of Bill Cooper, 'It was not long before a pipe was made over the tannoy requesting blood donors to go to the sickbay, and I think all the ground crews from both squadrons went straight down there.' Sadly, it was to no avail and AM (E) Thompson died of his injuries. That afternoon when *Venerable* returned to Grand Harbour his body was taken ashore for burial, with the funeral service taking place on 22 March.

Venerable remained in Grand Harbour for the next four weeks as essential maintenance was carried out, which gave the ship's company an opportunity for some shore leave. Bill Cooper remembers his run ashore: 'We set off through Valletta, or what was left of it. All the streets had been cleared of rubble so that traffic could flow freely, but the damage wrought by the wartime bombing was extensive.' For many members of the ship's company there was an introduction to Strait Street, more familiarly known as 'The Gut', and Bill Cooper remembers that, 'During daylight hours it was a quiet place, but after dark it really came to life and was almost a different place. One evening a crowd of us visited every bar from one end of "The Gut" to the other. In one bar there was a man dressed up in drag, who played a piano and, being encouraged by the sailors, it was funny to watch.'

At 10.00 on Monday 16 April, after almost four weeks in Grand Harbour, *Venerable* sailed to land on her squadrons for a period of intensive flying operations which would complete their work-up and prepare for operations against the Japanese in the Pacific Ocean. Each morning at just after 06.00 the carrier would weigh anchor and leave Marsaxlokk Bay for deck landing practice which continued until well into the dog watches, when the carrier would anchor for the night. At 10.15 on Friday 20 April there came another fatal accident, which is described here by Bill Cooper: 'Landing on was going very well. We watched "Bats" giving instructions to the pilots, and he was indicating to one of our Corsairs that he was flying too low and should gain some height. For some reason the pilot was not able to do so even though he was well astern of the ship. The "Bats" officer was waving frantically to get him to pull up, but he slowly lost altitude and was almost down to sea level. We were all waiting to see the pilot pull back his hood, and we were willing him to do so as it was clear that he would never be able to land on. Inevitably the plane ditched into the sea and although the escorting destroyer was not far away, the Corsair vanished beneath the waves taking the pilot, Sub-Lt Lowden, with it.'

Next day *Venerable* returned to Grand Harbour for the weekend, but she was back at sea on the following Monday morning, when flying operations began again. By the end of April the carrier was undertaking night flying exercises and it was not until 20.00 on 4 May that this programme was completed and the ship anchored in Marsaxlokk Bay. Next morning she entered Grand Harbour and six days later she was high and dry in Malta Dockyard's No 4 dry dock. On Tuesday 8 May came VE-Day and Geoffrey Ellison, who went ashore on a make and mend, remembers the experience: 'There were scenes of great rejoicing throughout Valletta and big processions all through the town. So vast were the crowds that one could only move about the streets with great difficulty. There were more flags being waved than I thought existed, and there were drunken matelots everywhere. We all enjoyed it and I am sure everyone had a great time.' Next day another make and mend was granted when Geoffrey Ellison went ashore with a swimming party, but it was not long before it was 'business as usual' for *Venerable's* ship's company, for the war against Japan in the Pacific appeared far from over.

At 13.40 on Monday 21 May *Venerable* left dry dock and steamed straight out to sea, where the squadrons were landed on and the ship set course for Alexandria, arriving there three days later. At the Egyptian base *Venerable* rejoined her sisters *Colossus* and *Vengeance,* and to make up the four light fleet carriers of the 11th Aircraft Carrier Squadron, *Glory* had also arrived in the Mediterranean. The stay in Alexandria lasted for three days, and most of the ship's company were able to get ashore. When, at 17.25 on Sunday 27 May, with *Vengeance* and *Colossus,* she set course for the Suez Canal, red Fez hats were much in evidence on the mess decks. At 06.00 on 28 May the entrance to Port Said Harbour was reached and shortly afterwards, at 06.45, with *Venerable* leading the way, the three carriers began their southbound transit of the canal, with *Venerable* anchoring in Suez Bay ten hours later at 16.45. Later that evening, at 23.00, she was under way again and steaming down the Red Sea, bound for the inhospitable port of Aden. During the passage south flying operations took place and at 09.59 on Wednesday 30 May there was a tragic accident when two Corsairs from 1851 Squadron collided in mid-air, with the loss of both pilots, the commanding officer, Lt Cdr (A) McDonald and the senior pilot, Lt (A) Malins RNVR. Bill Cooper watched the whole incident, which he remembers thus: 'The pilots were flying against the ship's AA defences to give the guns' crews some practice in meeting the expected kamikaze attacks. They were flying in at a low level from different angles and only lifting in order to clear the flight deck, before dropping down low on the other side of the ship, where they appeared almost to skim the water. For the guns' crews they were certainly realistic exercises. On that particular morning the two Corsairs were coming in from amidships in opposite directions and hurtling over the flight deck, just missing each other and the ship. On the final pass they again came in from opposite sides of the ship when, suddenly, meeting in mid-air at very high speed they collided and span off into the sea. Both pilots must have died on impact. It was terrible to watch and it was a major loss to the squadron.' Next morning at 19.10, just after flying operations had been completed for the day, a memorial service was held on the quarterdeck.

At 14.05 on Friday 1 June *Venerable* anchored in the outer harbour off Aden, where only very limited leave was granted to one watch. Next forenoon, having been joined by the battleship *Duke of York, Venerable* left Aden to make her passage across the Arabian Sea, to Colombo Harbour where, at 13.55 on 8 June, she secured to head and stern buoys. During the three days in harbour the personnel of 814 Squadron disembarked, together with their stores. As *Venerable* left harbour the Barracudas were flown off and the carrier set course for Madras where, during the forenoon of Wednesday 13 June, the personnel of 1851 Squadron were disembarked to RNAS Tambaran, just outside the city. Back on board leave was granted to one watch only and, once again, it was White Watch, who had been the only ones to get ashore in Aden. Next day, after getting under way and flying off the Corsairs, *Venerable* set course for Trincomalee where she arrived during the forenoon of 15 June. Since the fall of Singapore in 1942 Trincomalee had been the headquarters for the East Indies Fleet, and although it was a natural and picturesque harbour, its facilities were limited. Sited on the north-east coast of Ceylon (Sri Lanka) and separated from Colombo by the heavily forested central mountain range, it was, in the 1940s, quite isolated. However, Geoffrey Ellison remembers that, 'Although the place was little more than a village of huts made from palm fronds, there was a good NAAFI shop and naval canteen, and the swimming was good. There were also some rather ramshackle cinemas and the Elephant House Cafe, which served delightful banana fritters.'

Venerable's stay at Trincomalee lasted for only three days before she put to sea with *Colossus* for joint manoeuvres, but by the end of the day she had returned for two more days in harbour before sailing for Colombo where, on 21 June, stores of all kinds were taken on. Following this *Venerable* returned to Trincomalee for one more week before she sailed for Madras to embark both the aircraft and ground crews of 1851 Squadron. From Madras she steamed to Colombo where the men and aircraft of 814 Squadron rejoined the ship, and two days later she left for Australia where she would join the British Pacific Fleet. Once at sea *Venerable* rendezvoused with *Vengeance, Colossus,* the battleship *Anson* and destroyer escorts as they steamed south-east across the Indian Ocean. During the forenoon of Sunday 8 July a Corsair crashed into the sea on launching, but fortunately the pilot was rescued by the destroyer *Tuscan.* That same afternoon the Crossing the Line ceremony was held on the flight deck, which is recalled by Bill Cooper: 'King Neptune, with a mass of long green hair, wearing a crown and accompanied by his "wife", was welcomed on board. Following them came the lather man carrying a bucket full of soap suds with a large brush, and the barber with a huge wooden razor. Suddenly, as we all stood round the makeshift canvas pool, men ran round from the stage and grabbed anyone who had not crossed the line before. The victims were carried up to the stage and, having been liberally lathered, they were tossed into the pool.' Three days later North Keeling Island

Undergoing flying trials in February 1945, with two Fairey Barracudas on deck.
(Fleet Air Arm Museum, Cars V/162)

(Cocos Islands) was sighted, and at 08.15 on Monday 16 July *Venerable* anchored off Fremantle to embark mail and Australian currency, but by 18.30 she was heading for Sydney.

During the afternoon of Saturday 21 July the squadrons were flown ashore and next day, at 09.00, *Venerable* steamed through Sydney Heads to secure alongside Cruiser Wharf at Garden Island Naval Base three-quarters of an hour later. For the ship's company the three weeks spent at Sydney were to be a pleasant interlude before the expected action with the enemy forces which were defending the main islands of Japan, and there were queues of kindly Australians waiting to give them a taste of the city's hospitality. Those who took advantage of this could enjoy the home comforts offered by their hosts, and Geoffrey Ellison stayed with a family at Warawee, some 12 miles from Sydney. For others there was dancing at the Trocadero Ballroom in Sydney's George Street, or swimming at the renowned Bondi Beach. Meanwhile, back on board there were the grim reminders of the action to come as the 20mm, four-barrelled pom-poms were exchanged for larger 40mm guns. A plan had also been put forward for Rear-Admiral Sir Philip Vian, Flag Officer Commanding Aircraft Carriers (AC1), British Pacific Fleet, to hoist his flag in *Venerable,* but the problems of accommodating his large staff and the sudden end to the war meant that this was not implemented. On Sunday 12 August Admiral Harcourt transferred his flag to the fleet carrier *Indomitable* and that same day, following the dropping of the atomic bombs on Hiroshima and Nagasaki the previous week, it was announced to the public that Japan had declared its willingness to surrender. Geoffrey Ellison, who went ashore that day, recorded in his diary: 'Everyone in Sydney was going mad with excitement. Thousands of Australians and British servicemen thronged the streets, shouting, dancing and singing. I was in Martin Place where people joined hands in great circles and sang until they were exhausted. Traffic was brought to a standstill, traffic signs were pushed over, windows were broken and waste paper bins set on fire. The police tried vainly to control the enormous crowds, but it was a hopeless task. Girls were being kissed by everyone and I have never enjoyed myself so much.'

Venerable's holiday however, was short-lived and on 13 and 14 August she put to sea for six hours each day to land on her aircraft and carry out flying practice. Although she returned to Sydney Harbour and secured to a buoy each evening, shore leave was much more limited. At 09.00 on Wednesday 15 August came the official announcement that Japan had surrendered and that the Second World War was finally over. At 11.00 on board *Venerable,* Captain Dallmeyer addressed the ship's company and an hour later the main brace was spliced, with the welcome additional tot of rum being issued. A few hours later, at 15.15, *Venerable* slipped her mooring ropes and left Sydney Harbour to rendezvous with a Task Group led by Rear-Admiral Harcourt in *Indomitable.* Among the other units were *Colossus, Vengeance,* the battleship *Anson,* the cruiser *Bermuda* and a destroyer screen. Together, the whole force steamed to the British Pacific Fleet's forward operating base at Manus, one of the Admiralty Islands, but *Venerable* stayed only long enough to embark a Supermarine Walrus seaplane before she set course for Leyte Gulf where, during the afternoon of 25 August, she anchored in San Pedro Bay. At that time Olongapo in Subic Bay was not the enormous US naval base it subsequently became in the 1950s and 60s, and liberty men from *Venerable* were landed on

Flying operations en route to the Pacific in 1945.
(Fleet Air Arm Museum Cars V/79)

Grande Island. Geoffrey Ellison recalls that it was a, 'grim place, crowded with noisy American sailors playing baseball.' Bill Cooper, however, remembers that, 'We went ashore on one of these islands which was occupied by American troops who were playing baseball. We were made welcome and offered some cans of American beer, which were readily accepted. Sitting down with them we watched the game and drank our cans of beer.'

By this time it was becoming clear that *Venerable* was likely to be employed in taking the Japanese surrender somewhere in the South-East Asian theatre, and on board armed landing parties were being organized and drilled in preparation for future operations. At 16.20 on Monday 27 August, with an agreement having been reached between the British and American Governments for a Royal Navy Task Force to re-enter Hong Kong and take the surrender of the Japanese garrison there, *Venerable* weighed anchor to rendezvous with the other units involved. Led by Admiral Harcourt in *Indomitable,* the force included *Venerable, Vengeance,* the battleship *Anson,* the cruisers *Black Prince* and *Swiftsure,* and a destroyer screen. They arrived in the waters off Hong Kong during the early hours of Wednesday 29 August and at first light, to provide air cover for the force, aircraft were launched from the three carriers. In response to air reconnaissance sightings and intelligence reports, air strikes were made on Japanese suicide boats which had been massed for raids on the fleet. *Venerable,* escorted by the destroyer *Quadrant,* remained at sea off Hong Kong for three days with the squadrons continuing to provide air cover and during the forenoon of 31 August an Avenger from *Indomitable* landed on to pick up a prisoner of war liaison officer and to fly him to Kai Tak, Hong Kong's only airfield. At 20.19 on Saturday 1 September *Venerable* anchored some ten miles off Lamma Island, just out of sight of Hong Kong Island, and next morning she put to sea again to provide air cover for the task force. Finally, during the morning watch of Monday 3 September, *Venerable* closed Hong Kong Harbour and at 09.40 she passed the boom into the Lei Yue Mun Channel, to anchor in the harbour half an hour later. That afternoon she weighed anchor and at 15.15 she secured alongside Holt's Wharf, Kowloon.

Venerable had been given the task of occupying the Kowloon peninsular and Kai Tak Airport, and by 17.55 the first armed landing parties had left the ship. To the Royal Marines Detachment, commanded by Captain R. J. McGarel-Groves RM, there fell the unusual tasks of occupying the San Miguel Brewery on the outskirts of Kowloon, and of setting up a prisoner of war camp at Whitfield Barracks on Kowloon's Nathan Road. The barracks had been built before the war to house some 700 Indian troops, but Captain McGarel-Groves found himself the commandant of a camp containing approximately 16,000 Japanese, Korean and Formosan military and civilian personnel. Having ringed the camp with coils of barbed wire, the Royal Marines patrolled the perimeter on commandeered bicycles. Some of the problems encountered are recalled by Brigadier McGarel-Groves: 'I summoned the leading Japanese to meet me and formed a committee of Heads of Departments, such as food, water, sanitation and health. We seemed to have births and deaths each day, and a local undertaker, equipped with a four-berth, two-wheel hearse, solved the problem of corpses and I never enquired to where. I formed a garage repair unit in the camp, to which we towed the many broken-down vehicles which were littering the area. When these were repaired we started the first post-war vehicle registration system, using the prefix MAK (Military Administration Kowloon). One of our success stories was the repair of a green Vulkan diesel bus, with which we started the first bus service running up and down the length of Nathan Road. Starting was always a problem, so the bus was parked at the top of Nathan Road each night. When the bus filled with passengers in the morning everyone had to get out and push, and when the engine started thick black smoke billowed out. So it continued until dusk and the curfew to await the start of another day. Initially I found one big problem, namely removing all arms from the camp. Eventually, having collected in all the Japanese swords, I passed 600 back to *Venerable* for safe-keeping and later distribution to the ship's company. In my area was a Japanese destroyer which was alongside a berth which was required by the large liners on repatriation duties. I was ordered to "get rid of it". I found a Chinese tug which towed my destroyer out into Kowloon Bay until it ran aground, where we dropped anchor and abandoned ship. No sooner had we left than hordes of sampans converged on the ship and, like locusts, the boat people removed everything that was portable. A few days later the propeller shaft, with propeller still attached, was reported to be "walking" towards China. The occupation of the San Miguel Brewery ensured that my Detachment received a regular supply of beer, and it is to their credit that they never abused this privilege. Outside the camp there were other problems, one of them in the form of a potent alcoholic drink called Golden Dragon Brandy which unwary soldiers and sailors bought. I remember sitting on the edge of Nathan Road breaking confiscated bottles of the brew and pouring it down the drain.'

Geoffrey Ellison was in a landing party which disarmed Japanese military personnel and guarded factories. He remembers the Japanese being used in working parties and initially receiving some, 'pretty rough treatment', until it was pointed out that they had all volunteered for these duties. At 16.30 on Sunday 16 September the formal surrender ceremony was signed in Hong Kong's High Court building and, as well as Splicing the Main Brace, that evening there was a firework and searchlight display over the harbour. Next day *Venerable* was shifted to an anchorage in the harbour, and on 24 September she put to sea with *Anson, Vengeance* and a destroyer screen, but 24 hours later she was back in harbour again. There were further forays to sea in early October, but when *Venerable* finally left Hong Kong it was to take up duties as a prisoner of war repatriation ship.

At 10.15 on Thursday 18 October, in company with the destroyer *Wager, Venerable* left Hong Kong to make a two-day passage into the Gulf of Tongking and to the port of Haiphong in French Indo-China (Vietnam). During the passage all the aircraft were moved onto the flight deck and the hangar was prepared for the reception and accommodation of Allied ex-prisoners of war. It was during the afternoon watch of 20 October that the carrier anchored off Haiphong and a few hours later embarkation began, to continue into the early hours of the following morning. Most of the ex-prisoners were men of the Indian Army who had been taken prisoner at Singapore in February 1942 and Bill Cooper, who now had no aircraft to look after remembers them thus: 'We took on about 300 men at Haiphong, and they were shown to the hangar where they were allocated a bed space. The hangar had been converted to a much more pleasant space than I thought possible, with mattresses laid out at intervals over the full length of the deck. There was plenty of food, but some of the soldiers were so emaciated that at first they were unable to eat anything.' At 05.00 on 21 October *Venerable* left Haiphong to make a six-day passage to Madras, where all the passengers left the ship and she sailed for Trincomalee, arriving there at 09.30 on 28 October. Although the POW repatriation voyage from French Indo-China was over, it was not the end of *Venerable's* trooping career and on Saturday 3 November, after several days of storing ship, she left for Bombay (Mumbai), where she anchored three days later. After two days at anchor she went alongside at Alexandra Dock where RAF and Army personnel of the Royal Engineers and Royal Signals were embarked for passage to Singapore. After leaving Bombay on 11 November *Venerable* arrived alongside the Singapore Naval Base six days later to discharge her passengers. From Singapore the carrier steamed back to Ceylon and the port of Colombo, then on to Bombay where, once again, she secured alongside the Alexandra Dock. Once alongside the troops and transport of a Gurkha Regiment were embarked, and on 27 November the carrier sailed for Batavia (Jakarta) in the Dutch East Indies (Indonesia). There was a short stop off Colombo to pick up mail and a few more passengers, before *Venerable* sailed by way of the Indian Ocean and the Sunda Strait, where everyone had an excellent view of the island of Krakatau, to Tanjong Priok, the port for Batavia where, at 09.15 on 4 December, she went alongside. Once the mooring lines had been secured the Gurkhas, together with all their stores, ammunition and transport, were disembarked. They were to become involved in a vicious war to pacify the country's nationalists who, shortly before the Japanese surrender, had been given independence, thus fanning the flames of nationalism in the country. For the British and Indian troops involved it was a bloody and thankless task which would last until April 1946, when Dutch troops arrived to take over.

For *Venerable* there was another mission of mercy to complete, and at 08.30 on 6 December she began embarking the first of 650 Dutch refugees, all of whom were ex-internees of the Japanese who had suffered a great deal of cruelty and neglect during their years of internment. Before the arrival of British and Indian troops they had also suffered at the hands of nationalists who were desperately trying to consolidate their hold on the country before Dutch forces arrived. The refugees were mostly women and children, with only a few men, and once again some of them were in a very emaciated condition. After moving to an anchorage later in the day, *Venerable* left Tanjong Priok at 06.30 on Friday 7 December and, in the words of Geoffrey Ellison: 'This short voyage was the happiest period of my naval service. All the ship's company did everything possible to keep the Dutch refugees entertained, particularly the children. We made swings and see-saws, and organized children's sports days. We held dances, the engine room concert party was a great hit, and the lads of 20 Mess gave a fantastic party for the children. Our efforts were clearly appreciated and one of the ladies gave a moving speech of thanks over the ship's tannoy.' On 11 December *Venerable* arrived in Colombo where her passengers were disembarked, and after a short stop at Trincomalee came the reward for all the hard work - Christmas and New Year in Australia.

Venerable left Trincomalee during the forenoon of Saturday 15 December and she arrived alongside G berth of Fremantle Docks eight days later, at 10.30 on 23 December. For the officers and men of *Venerable* the three-day break, which included Christmas, was enjoyed by all and on 26 December the carrier sailed for Sydney where she was to undergo a dockyard assisted maintenance period. The squadron aircraft were flown off and the personnel disembarked, then at 14.30 on New Year's Eve the carrier secured alongside No 6 Wharf of Woolloomooloo Docks, which housed the Navy's repair facilities. There was plenty of time for the off duty watches to celebrate the New Year in the city of Sydney.

A seven-week refit lay ahead for *Venerable* which included dry docking, while station leave was granted to all the ship's company. There was, however, still time for the formalities of naval routine, and on 6 January 1946 Vice-Admiral Vian took the salute at Divisions and a march past on the flight deck. Some members of the ship's company were married at Sydney, and many new faces appeared on board as time-expired men were discharged to await their passage home and new personnel took their places. Ashore, meanwhile, the Barracudas of 814 Squadron had been replaced by new Fairey Fireflies. Finally, however, during the forenoon of 22 February, in company with the destroyer *Armada, Venerable* left Sydney to land on her squadrons before returning to a buoy in Sydney Harbour to complete storing and to embark the squadron ground crews. When the carrier left Sydney again on 26 February, it was to rendezvous with the fleet carrier *Implacable* and the destroyers *Armada* and *Tyrian,* for flying operations with the new Fireflies in the area of Jervis Bay followed by a passage to Melbourne. After five days alongside she moved round the coast of Victoria to anchor in Twofold Bay, off the town of Eden, but with a heavy swell running she sailed earlier than scheduled to Jervis Bay where, on 10 March, she started flying training. This was brought to a sudden halt on 13 March by engine trouble, and she limped to Sydney on one main engine for repairs. After leaving Sydney on 19 March *Venerable* steamed into the Pacific Ocean for a 'flag showing' cruise into the Pacific Ocean, with flying training en route. On Monday 25 March, when the ship was off the island of Fiji, there was a tragic accident when a Corsair rolled off the flight deck onto a gun sponson, killing Able Seaman Burfitt and seriously injuring two other men. Later that day *Venerable* anchored off Suva, but with torrential rain the image of an idyllic tropical paradise seemed to be lost. Although the carrier put to sea for a 24-hour flying programme, by Saturday 30 March she had returned to Suva where the ship's company, led by the Royal Marines Detachment, carried out a grand march past through Suva. Judging by the turnout of local people, the event was a great success.

After leaving Fiji on the last day of March, *Venerable* returned to Sydney by way of Norfolk Island, the tiny Pacific island situated half way between New Caledonia and New Zealand, to which in 1856 the descendants of Fletcher Christian's *Bounty* mutineers had been relocated from Pitcairn Island. At 11.00 on Wednesday 3 April *Venerable* anchored in the island's Sydney Bay, but with a heavy swell running no shore leave was granted and only a few boat trips were made between the ship and shore. Geoffrey Ellison remembers manning the cutter which took the Executive Officer, Cdr Crawford, ashore where several members of the reception committee were named Christian. Seven hours after her arrival, at 17.55, the carrier weighed anchor and set course for Sydney where, after flying off the squadrons, she secured to the Bradley Head dolphins at 08.45 on 6 April. Once again *Venerable* was to undergo a change of role, for the escort carrier HMS *Speaker,* which was carrying out trooping and transport duties, had suffered serious mechanical problems with her main boilers and had left for the UK. Her duties were to be taken up by *Venerable.* For the immediate future, however, the ship's company had another welcome respite in Sydney and, for many members of the ship's company, there was the prospect of at least weekend leave in the city.

The carrier's first trooping voyage began at 11.30 on Monday 15 April when she left Sydney for Colombo, via Fremantle, with a draft of 600 ratings from Sydney's shore base, HMS *Golden Hind,* which was being moved to Ceylon as the British Pacific Fleet ran down its Australian base. During the trip there was plenty of PT on the flight deck and musical entertainment from the Royal Marines Band. The pause at Fremantle lasted for only seven hours and, after flying off her aircraft, *Venerable* arrived in Colombo during the forenoon of 26 April to disembark her

At Sydney in August 1945. *(Fleet Air Arm Museum, Cars V/164)*

Venerable in Hong Kong Harbour shortly after the liberation of the colony from the Japanese. On top of the Peak, to the left of the picture, can be seen the Japanese War Memorial which was soon demolished. *(Fleet Air Arm Museum, Cars V/229)*

draft of passengers who would set up a new barracks and manning depot, HMS *Gould.* Before leaving Colombo the carrier embarked another draft of 400 ratings, and she sailed east, through the Bay of Bengal and into the Strait of Malacca. During her passage south, between Penang and Singapore, a Stoker Petty Officer was lost overboard; during the following forenoon, at 10.00 on Friday 3 May, the carrier anchored in Singapore Roads, south of the city. Most of her passengers were disembarked here and more men joined the ship for passage to Hong Kong, where she arrived on 6 May to go alongside one of the main wharves at Kowloon. At Hong Kong more passengers joined the ship and *Venerable* retraced her route to Colombo where they disembarked and the carrier steamed round to Trincomalee for a two-week maintenance period.

At 17.45 on Monday 3 June, with *Venerable's* maintenance programme completed, Vice-Admiral Sir Denis Boyd, the C-in-C British Pacific Fleet designate, embarked in the carrier for the voyage to Hong Kong and a quarter of an hour later she left Trincomalee. During the passage across the Bay of Bengal flying practice was undertaken by both squadrons and on 6 June she called at Georgetown, Penang, where the Governor of the newly formed Malayan Union called on Admiral Boyd. Next day *Venerable* sailed for Singapore and during the evening of 8 June she anchored in Singapore Roads. Next morning, at 09.00, the battleship *Duke of York,* carrying the outgoing C-in-C, Admiral Sir Bruce Fraser, steamed into the anchorage. At midday the handover of the command was executed and four hours later *Duke of York* sailed for home, leaving *Venerable* as the Fleet Flagship. On 12 June, with the destroyer *Camperdown* as escort, the carrier left Singapore and set course across the South China Sea for Hong Kong where, to the salutes of all units in the

On 18 March 1947, *Venerable* made a smart entry into Malta's Grand Harbour during her passage home from the Pacific.
(Michael Cassar)

harbour, she arrived three days later. After leaving Admiral Boyd in Hong Kong, on 21 June *Venerable* sailed from Hong Kong and although flying practice took place en route to Singapore, her days as a troop transport were not yet over. At Singapore, as well as taking on stores, she embarked a UK-bound draft of officers and ratings for passage to Trincomalee where, on the last day of June, they were disembarked.

With her trooping duties now completed, *Venerable* once again assumed the role of an operational carrier of the British Pacific Fleet, but the whole of July was spent at anchor in Trincomalee Harbour. The engineering department had become aware that, with the ship's speed having dropped by almost two knots, the underwater hull was fouling up and the Engineer Commander recommended that the carrier be dry docked at the earliest opportunity. On the brighter side, however, the spell at Trincomalee allowed the ship's company to take some leave at the naval rest camp situated at Diyatalawa, some 2,359 feet up at the southern edge of the island's central mountain range, which as Geoffrey Ellison remembers was reached by a very rickety mountain railway. On Monday 15 July, Captain J. L. Storey DSO CBE RN arrived on board to relieve Captain Dallmeyer, who left the ship two days later to await a passage home. Three weeks after taking command, Captain Storey took *Venerable* to sea for the first time when, at 08.15 on 6 August, she carried out flying practice off the island, but by the end of the day she was safely back at her buoy. On Monday 12 August the carrier steamed round to Colombo for stores, before returning to Trincomalee. Monday 19 August proved to be a strenuous day for the flight deck personnel when over 30 surplus aircraft, including Corsairs, Defiants and Swordfish, were embarked from lighters and next morning the carrier sailed to a point just outside the harbour where, with the ship steaming astern for two hours, they were all ditched over the forward end of the flight deck. Following this *Venerable* spent the rest of the day carrying out deck landing training with her Fireflies. The remainder of August was spent operating from Trincomalee and although a number of the new planes were damaged in landing accidents, there were no serious injuries.

On Sunday 1 September, Rear-Admiral A. R. M. Bridge, Flag Officer (Air) BFP, hoisted his flag in *Venerable* for three days during which time he watched flying operations before leaving the ship by air. For most of the month *Venerable* operated out of Trincomalee and on 21 September she operated with her sister *Glory* as both carriers and their escorts headed for Singapore. After 24 hours alongside at the Singapore Naval Base, on 27 September *Venerable* sailed for Hong Kong, where she arrived five days later after flying exercises off the colony. The following 19 days were spent operating from Hong Kong with the destroyers *Camperdown* and *Lagos,* but during the forenoon of Thursday 24 October she was secured in the King George VI dry dock at Singapore Naval Base. For seven days the ship's company lived ashore in the relatively spacious and comfortable accommodation of HMS *Terror,* but by 1 November they were back on board. On Friday 15 November, after leaving the naval base for machinery trials, *Venerable* operated in the South China Sea for five days, but at 16.15 on 26 November, having completed an anti-submarine exercise, she arrived in Hong Kong once again from where, flying the flag of Flag Officer

Venerable laid up at a buoy in the Hamoaze in September 1947, before her sale to the Royal Netherlands Navy. Brunel's Saltash Bridge can be seen in the background. *(Maritime Photo Library)*

(Air) BPF, she operated until 19 December. Christmas Day was spent at Hong Kong, with the Royal Marines Band performing an evening musical concert in the hangar. On Thursday 2 January 1947 the 'holiday' came to an end when *Venerable* left harbour to carry out flying training in company with *Glory* and the escorts *Alert* and *Widemouth Bay.* These exercises continued throughout January with six days being spent at sea on the manoeuvres, with the ships either returning to Hong Kong Harbour, or anchoring in Junk Bay at the end of each day.

In February 1947 *Venerable's* long commission east of Suez came to an end when, at 10.35 on Friday 14 February she slipped her mooring ropes at A2 buoy and set course for Singapore and home. After a mock attack by RAF Beaufighters, the carrier spent two days in the naval base before, at 10.00 on 20 February, she left for Trincomalee. On 1 March she left the base at Ceylon and during a 24-hour refuelling stop at Aden her sister *Theseus* arrived at 07.00 on 8 March and officially took over her duties. *Venerable* then sailed for Suez and she made her northbound transit of the Suez Canal on 14 March before experiencing an extremely rough three-day passage through the Eastern Mediterranean to Malta. At Grand Harbour *Venerable* met her younger sisters *Ocean* and *Triumph* for the first and last time and after a short stop at Gibraltar she sailed for home. During the morning watch on Wednesday 26 March, many members of the ship's company had their first sighting of Britain's south coast for two years. At just before 09.00 *Venerable* anchored in Plymouth Sound, where the squadron personnel were disembarked and Customs clearance was obtained. Later that evening she sailed for Glasgow where, during the dog watches of Friday 28 March, she secured alongside Glasgow's King George V Dock. As the squadron stores and unserviceable aircraft were unloaded, the off duty watches had their first run ashore on home soil since the ship left Greenock on 12 March 1945. During the afternoon of 29 March, having spent less than 24 hours alongside, *Venerable* left Glasgow to return to Plymouth Sound, where she arrived the following evening, and at 14.15 on Tuesday 1 April she steamed slowly up harbour to No 1 buoy at Devonport's battleship trot in the Hamoaze. Her operational service with the Royal Navy was over.

During the afternoon of Tuesday 20 May *Venerable* was moved to Devonport's No 6 wharf, and two days later the ship was cleared of personnel whilst the dockyard carried out 'Operation Rats', a three-day fumigation of the ship. On 27 May Captain Storey relinquished his command and Commander R. B. Jennings DSO DSC RN took over, but by now the ship's complement was reducing drastically as men were drafted away from *Venerable.* In June the carrier was moved back to a buoy in the Hamoaze, but in January 1948, with negotiations under way for her sale to the Royal Netherlands Navy, she was moved into No 10 dry dock to start a long refit. Four days later Commander Jennings left the ship, which was placed in dockyard hands, and on 11 March the Dutch aircraft carrier *Karel Doorman,* ex-escort carrier HMS *Nairana,* which had been loaned to the Dutch Navy in March 1946, arrived in Devonport. That same day *Karel Doorman's* commanding officer and Vice-Admiral Berrings of the Royal Netherlands Navy made the first of many visits to *Venerable.* By the end of March working

RNNS *Karel Doorman* at sea in the mid-1960s. She is unrecognizable as the former *Venerable*, and she later went on to serve as the *Veinticinco de Mayo* in the Argentine Navy. *(FotoFlite)*

parties from *Karel Doorman* were cleaning up the accommodation on board *Venerable* and by mid-May the ship's company from the old *Karel Doorman* had moved on board *Venerable.* Finally, with the sale having been completed, on 28 May *Venerable* was commissioned into the Royal Netherlands Navy as the second *Karel Doorman,* with the first ship of the name having been returned to the Royal Navy, but she was quickly sold for scrap.

In service with the Royal Netherlands Navy *Karel Doorman* operated an Air Group of Sea Furies and Fireflies, but in 1954 she was placed in dockyard hands at the Wilton-Fijenoord Shipyard and given a refit which completely changed her appearance. The flight deck was strengthened and enlarged to allow for an 8° angled landing area. She was fitted with a mirror landing sight, a steam catapult, new arrester gear, her island superstructure and funnel were rebuilt and she was given new and very distinctive radar aerials. Following the refit she operated Sea Hawk, Avenger and Tracker aircraft, together with ASW helicopters. She regularly exercised with Royal Navy units, but not with any of her sisters as only *Triumph* remained, as an escort maintenance ship based in the Far East. In 1966 she was given new steam turbines and boilers, with the machinery having been removed from the Majestic-class aircraft carrier *Leviathan.* Having been launched by the Duchess of Kent in June 1945, *Leviathan* had never been completed and, having been towed to Portsmouth in July 1946, she languished in No 3 basin until 1961 and then at a buoy in Fareham Creek, giving rise to all sorts of rumours about her seaworthiness. Unlike her sisters a foreign buyer was never found for her and over the years she had been constantly raided for spare parts. However, with the removal of her main propulsion machinery she was rendered unseaworthy and in the summer of 1968 she left Portsmouth for the breaker's yard.

In 1968 one of *Karel Doorman's* engine rooms was damaged by fire and she was laid up, but it was not for long as she was soon purchased by the Argentine Navy. On 12 March 1969 she was commissioned into the Argentine Navy as *Veinticinco de Mayo,* and after a major refit she sailed for Argentina on 1 September that year. Initially she operated Skyhawks and Tracker aircraft, but in 1981 she was equipped with Super Entendards which had been purchased from France.

During the Falklands War in 1982 she was the flagship of the Argentine Navy and although she did make one foray out to sea to steam in towards the Task Force from the north, the sinking of the cruiser *General Belgrano* saw her head straight back home, never to venture out again. For Geoffrey Ellison, who had served in *Venerable* for the whole of her career with the Royal Navy, there was the irony of seeing his old ship at war against HMS *Hermes,* in which his son Philip was serving as a Leading Rate. Thankfully, no harm came to *Hermes.* Today, the only relic from *Venerable's* service with the Royal Navy is the ship's bell which, having been acquired by the Church Warden, hangs in the Parish Church at Ash Vale, Hampshire, on the outskirts of Aldershot.

Commanding Officers:

Captain W. A. Dallmeyer DSO RN	16 October 1944
Captain J. L. Storey DSO CBE RN	15 July 1946

Battle Honours:

Camperdown 1797	Belgian Coast 1914-15
Gut of Gibraltar 1801	Dardanelles 1915

Chapter Five

HMS *Glory*
February 1945 – January 1948

The last of the light fleet aircraft carriers to be completed in time to join the British Pacific Fleet at the end of the Second World War was HMS *Glory*, and she was to play an important role in the surrender of Japanese forces in the Pacific. After *Colossus* she was the second of the carriers to be ordered and on Thursday 27 August 1942, the first keel plates were laid at Harland & Wolff's Belfast shipyard. In September 1943 the first naval personnel travelled to Belfast to stand by the ship as she lay on the stocks. A few weeks later, on Saturday 27 November 1943, Lady Cynthia Brooke, the wife of the Prime Minister of Northern Ireland, launched the ship into Belfast's Musgrave Channel, from where she was towed to the nearby Thompson Wharf for fitting out. On 1 November 1944, *Glory's* first commanding officer, Captain Sir Anthony W. Buzzard DSO OBE RN, joined the ship and three months later, on Wednesday 21 February 1945, she was commissioned by the officers and men who were standing by the ship. That same afternoon the small complement commenced watchkeeping duties and 24 hours later the main drafts, who had travelled by special trains and ferries, joined the carrier. Within 24 hours the process of loading stores and ammunition had begun, and on 27 February the first aircraft, in the form of three Vought F3 Corsairs, were hoisted on board, having been folded and towed alongside by tractors. As *Glory* was made ready for sea she was opened to the public and Belfast residents flocked to see the latest warship built in their city. During the afternoon of 19 March the ship's sponsor, Lady Brooke, visited the ship and, addressing the ship's company over the tannoy, she wished them luck for the future.

Like her three earlier sisters, *Glory* was destined for the British Pacific Fleet and in early 1945, unlike the war in Europe, there seemed to be no end in sight to the hostilities in that area. Having been formed in January 1945 the British Pacific Fleet was spearheaded by the fleet carriers of the Illustrious and Implacable classes and they had borne the brunt of what was, as far the Royal Navy was concerned, an air war led by the Allied aircraft carriers. The first four light fleet carriers, fully worked up, were due to arrive in Australia in the summer of 1945 and they would go into action to relieve the operational pressure on the larger aircraft carriers. At 08.07 on Friday 23 March, *Glory* slipped her mooring ropes and, looking resplendent in her Pacific Fleet camouflage paintwork, she steamed down the River Lagan, into Belfast Lough and Bangor Bay to begin her initial trials. Next day, escorted by HMS *Westcott*, she steamed across to the Firth of Clyde for two days of machinery trials, anchoring off Greenock each evening. During the early afternoon of Friday 30 March, with the carrier in the Firth of Clyde, 'Flying Stations' was piped and at 13.12 the first deck landing was made by a Seafire. During the rest of the afternoon three Seafires and the three Corsairs which had been embarked at Belfast made a series of landings and launchings from the accelerator. Finally, after a busy day of trials, *Glory* anchored off Greenock for a weekend break.

When flying trials resumed on 2 April, the three Corsairs were flown off and during the next day Barracudas of 837 Squadron landed on to carry out two weeks of flying practice. At 10.05 on Wednesday 18 April came the first fatal flight deck accident. *Glory* had left her Greenock anchorage at 08.47 that forenoon and as the Barracudas were being ranged to start the day's flying, two aircraft handlers were slow to react and they were caught by the blade of a propeller. One man, Able Seaman Emerson, was killed outright and the second, Able Seaman Mason, was seriously injured. With flying temporarily suspended the ship steamed in close to Largs Pier where the injured man was rushed to hospital and the body of AB Emerson was landed for burial. That evening, when the ship anchored off Greenock, there was an 18-day break, with leave being given to both watches before the final preparations were made to embark her two squadrons, together with all their personnel and stores. During the afternoon of Sunday 6 May, after leaving Greenock, *Glory* landed on three Barracudas, three Blackburn Firebrands and a Grumman Wildcat, all seven of which remained with her for two days carrying out an intensive programme of flying. During the evening of 7 May, with the aircraft having left, the personnel of 837 Squadron were embarked and four days later *Glory* steamed upriver to Glasgow's King George V Dock to embark the personnel of 1831 Squadron, together with some of their Corsairs and large quantities of stores. Finally, after a long weekend alongside, on Monday 14 May, together with the destroyers *Hotspur* and *Icarus*, *Glory* set course for the Mediterranean.

After leaving the Clyde she landed on the Corsairs of 1831 Squadron and the Barracudas of 837 Squadron, and during the passage anti-aircraft exercises were carried out with the carrier's own Corsairs providing the attacking force. There was a short stop off Gibraltar and on Monday

Glory is launched on 27 November 1943, at Harland & Wolff's Belfast shipyard by Lady Cynthia Brooke, the wife of the Prime Minister of Northern Ireland. *(Neg 8874, Ulster Folk & Transport Museum)*

21 May she joined her sister *Vengeance* at Malta's Marsaxlokk Bay, with *Venerable* arriving soon afterwards. That afternoon Rear-Admiral C. H. J. Harcourt, Flag Officer 11th Aircraft Carrier Squadron, paid a short visit, and next morning *Glory* weighed anchor and set course for Alexandria. Shortly after leaving she experienced her first aircraft loss, when a Corsair crashed into the sea following an accelerated take-off, but fortunately the pilot was recovered safely and all three carriers carried out flying exercises as they steamed south-east. On 24 May they arrived at Alexandria and for *Glory,* once secured, the task of disembarking squadron personnel and stores began. The carrier herself was to undergo an essential maintenance period, including a week in dry dock, and five days later she put to sea to fly off the squadrons. On Saturday 16 June, when she moved back to her buoy, she was the only carrier left at Alexandria as the others had sailed for Trincomalee. On the following Monday she was ready to complete her work-up and she set sail with the cruiser *Cleopatra.*

Each day until the end of June *Glory* operated out of Alexandria, with the squadrons carrying out up to ten hours' intensive flying practice each day and on 29 June the Flag Officer Eastern Mediterranean carried out both sea and harbour inspections. During the evening of Sunday 1 July *Glory,* escorted by the destroyer *Wizard,* left Alexandria and set course for Port Said, making their southbound transits of the Suez Canal during 3 July. With the other carriers having arrived at Trincomalee in mid-June, *Glory* made her best speed across the Arabian Sea and during the early evening of 16 July she anchored in the picturesque harbour, which was the main base for the East Indies Fleet.

However, as *Glory* was due in Sydney for mid-August there was little free time for the ship's company and it was not long before she and *Wizard* were at sea and involved in intensive exercises, practising night encounter exercises and anti-aircraft measures designed to shoot down kamikaze bombers. There was a visit to Colombo, which proved to be a livelier and more popular run ashore than Trincomalee, but on Friday 3 August *Glory* and *Wizard* left Colombo for a passage across the Indian Ocean, bound for Fremantle. During the passage there was time for the Crossing the Line ceremony, during which Captain Buzzard was deposited in the makeshift canvas pool on the flight deck. Three days into the passage, however, the first atomic bomb was dropped on the city of Hiroshima, and three days later a second bomb was dropped on Nagasaki. These momentous events signalled the end of the Pacific War, and on 10 August *Glory* and her escort arrived in Fremantle, where they went alongside for a 20-hour stopover.

After leaving Fremantle during the forenoon of 11 August the two vessels made a fast passage to Sydney and by the morning of 15 August they were just 24 hours steaming from Sydney Heads. At 09.00 that forenoon there came the very welcome news that Japan had surrendered and, at 10.00 on Thursday 16 August, after flying off her squadrons, *Glory* secured alongside No 3 Wharf of Sydney's Woolloomooloo Docks, in a world which was at peace. That day, with the main brace having been spliced, 'sippers' and 'gulpers' were being generously handed out.

With the end of the war against Japan having come suddenly and unexpectedly, all over the Pacific and South-East Asia Japanese armies, which had not been defeated on the field of battle, still occupied vast areas and controlled thousands of Allied prisoners of war who had suffered horribly at the hands of their captors. On 2 September the official surrender ceremony took place aboard the battleship USS *Missouri* in Tokyo Bay, and this paved the way for similar ceremonies in Japanese-occupied territories, such as Singapore, Hong Kong and the Japanese South-Eastern area, which included New Britain, Bougainville and New Ireland. It had been agreed that the surrender of Japanese forces in the latter area would be taken by the Commander of the 1st Australian Army, Lt-General V. A. H. Sturdee, whose troops had fought a gruelling campaign in New Guinea in the steaming rainforests over the Kokoda Trail, right across the Owen Stanley Range of mountains. The Australian Government, however, required the assistance of the Royal Navy and *Glory* was ordered to fulfil the role of General Sturdee's base off New Britain. In the immediate future, however, the carrier's ship's company had two weeks in Sydney, enjoying the lavish hospitality of the people of the city. Each watch was granted station leave and on 26 August the ship was opened to visitors. The holiday atmosphere ended at 08.00 on Saturday 1 September when General Sturdee embarked and shortly afterwards *Glory's* mooring ropes were slipped and she left harbour to land on her squadrons. Once this had been completed she set course for Jacquinot Bay on the south side of the island of New Britain, accompanied by her escorts, *Amethyst and Hart.*

Because it was not known how individual Japanese garrisons would react to the news of their country's surrender, to guard against last-ditch suicide attacks during the passage Beaufort aircraft from the Royal Australian Air Force provided long-range air reconnaissance cover for the force. As *Glory* and her escorts neared their immediate destination, anti-aircraft guns were manned and the ship went to the third degree of readiness before anchoring well offshore in Jacquinot Bay during the forenoon of Wednesday 5 September. That afternoon General Sturdee went ashore to organize surrender parties, who returned to the ship with him, then at 17.55 *Glory* and her escorts weighed anchor to make an overnight passage through St George's Channel to Rabaul on the north side of the island. Next morning, at 07.50, with all her gun crews closed up at 'Action Stations', and with *Amethyst* and *Hart* stationed one mile on either side of the carrier, *Glory* arrived off Rabaul. It had been decided that, with the possibility of enemy attack, she would not anchor, so instead, the main engines were stopped, with the engine rooms remaining at immediate notice for steam, and she drifted offshore with the engines being used occasionally to keep her position. There were a few worrying moments when, soon after stopping, an unusual vibration was felt throughout the ship, but it was soon realized that this was caused by an earthquake in the area. Clearly the forces of nature had no sense of occasion that day.

At 10.40 the duty watch was placed at a third degree of readiness, and all those members of the ship's company who were off watch were ordered to fall in on the flight deck by divisions. Twenty-five minutes later the Japanese military officers of the surrender delegation, led by Lt-General H. Imamura and Vice-Admiral K. Kusaka, arrived on board, their uniforms still wet, after what had been a choppy boat ride from Rabaul. After preliminary discussions below decks about the Japanese military installations ashore, at 11.30, with the ship stopped in a position Lat 04° - 32'S/Long 152° - 34'S, Lt-General Imamura, Vice-Admiral Kusaka and their staff were marched under escort along the flight deck, in front of the assembled ship's company, to a small table covered by green baize on which were arranged the surrender documents, pens and ink, and behind which stood General Sturdee and his staff. After first laying down their ceremonial swords as a symbol of surrender, both senior Japanese officers signed the document surrendering the Japanese South-Eastern Army and the naval forces. As soon as this had been completed the whole delegation was again escorted below

Immediately after her launch *Glory* is towed to her fitting-out berth. *(Neg 8876, Ulster Folk & Transport Museum)*

decks for further talks on the military dispositions in the area. While these talks were under way *Glory* and her escorts steamed slowly at ten knots off the northern coast of New Britain. Finally, at 14.51, with the surrender complete, the ship stopped close in to Rabaul and both Japanese and Allied delegations were disembarked by boat to HMS *Hart,* after which *Glory* set course back to Sydney. With flying practice, the return passage took six days and it was during the late forenoon of Wednesday 12 September that *Glory's* squadrons were flown off. A few hours later she entered Sydney Harbour where she secured to a buoy.

Having taken the surrender of the Japanese South-Eastern Area, the next major task for the Allied forces was to rescue and repatriate all the Allied prisoners of war who were being held in prison camps all over South-East Asia. Meanwhile, during her 13-day stay in Sydney in the second half of September, dockyard workers swarmed over *Glory* as the ship was fitted to carry ex-prisoners of war on the first stage of their journey home. In the main hangar 200 beds were constructed, with a complete mobile hospital at the after end. The forward hangar was fitted out as a dining hall and recreation centre, with refectory tables and benches. In the forward lift well a mobile cinema, complete with two projectors and a full-size screen, was set up. With the squadrons ashore their mess decks were emptied and prepared for the new passengers, with some cabins in the wardroom flat being reserved for 36 nursing sisters who had volunteered to join the ship for this mercy mission.

When *Glory* left Sydney during the afternoon of Wednesday 26 September, she was initially ordered to the Pacific Fleet base at Manus, and after refuelling there she was sent to Leyte Gulf in the southern Philippines where she arrived during the forenoon of 6 October. After only a brief stay she left, arriving in Manila Bay at 08.37 on 8 October. During the day lighters came alongside with new army uniforms for the passengers, and next day, at 09.00, the first relay of LCIs came alongside with the initial batch of men who were all serious hospital cases. They were followed by the main body of over 1,100, mainly British, ex-POWs, most of whom had been taken prisoner at Singapore and it was not long before the hospital was full of men who, after years of ill-treatment, were literally walking skeletons. Finally, at 18.24 on 9 October, with the embarkation complete, *Glory* weighed anchor and set course for Pearl Harbor. With the sea calm for the Pacific voyage the officers and men put on a well-planned programme of sports and amusements for the passengers. Deck hockey and 'horse racing' proved popular, with the cinema, improvised concerts and tombola heading the list of favourite pastimes. Sadly, at 05.50 on 15 October, six days out from Manila, Sapper William Owers died from tuberculosis and that evening, in a position Lat 11° - 32'N/Long 163° - 05'E the funeral service was held for him. At 05.15 on Saturday 20 October land was sighted on the starboard beam as *Glory* approached Oahu, and later that forenoon she berthed at Ford Island Naval Base, Pearl Harbor, where shore leave was granted.

After refuelling *Glory* left Pearl Harbor the following day and no sooner had Hawaii slipped over the horizon than the air temperatures got noticeably cooler and the ship's company changed into blue uniforms. On Friday 26 October the Pacific voyage came to an end when, at 10.35, *Glory* secured alongside the Canadian naval base at Esquimalt. She had been greeted by a cacophony of noise from bells, hooters and suchlike, and even two very loud brass bands on the jetty. That afternoon, shortly before disembarkation began, the lower deck was cleared and the Officer Commanding the troops presented an inscribed silver bugle and a mace to the ship as a token of thanks for the way the ship's company had looked after them during their first weeks of freedom. That evening, the ship's hangar was deserted, and the ship's company were enjoying a run ashore in the small town of Esquimalt. Next morning *Glory* slipped her mooring ropes to steam through the Juan de Fuca Strait and under the Lion's Gate Bridge, to berth in Vancouver. The ship's company had nine days to enjoy the hospitality of the Canadian city, but on the morning of Monday 5 November *Glory* set sail and course was set for Hong Kong.

For the return crossing of the Pacific Ocean the weather was not so kind and for the first few days not many ventured onto the flight deck. The nurses had little to do during the 16-day non-stop voyage and *Glory* arrived in Hong Kong Harbour during the forenoon of 21 November, having missed 13 November altogether when she crossed the International Date Line. With the colony having been reoccupied by British forces for only three months, leave was limited to afternoons and evenings until 22.30. With both Hong Kong and Kowloon still recovering from the privations of the Japanese occupation, the establishments of Wanchai were unusually quiet. After 48 hours in Hong Kong, *Glory* was ordered to Manila Bay and after a 36-hour passage she anchored off the city at 18.30 on 24 November. Once again she was to repatriate ex-prisoners of the Japanese, but this time they were Dutch civilian internees, including women and children. Having embarked her passengers *Glory* left Manila Bay, but this time she made only a short two-day passage to Balikpapen on the south-east coast of Borneo in the Dutch East Indies (Indonesia). On arrival in the harbour she was able to go alongside, but this time Japanese prisoners of war, in a reversal of roles, provided the working parties to land all the passengers' baggage. During the two days the carrier was alongside, because of the threat of civil unrest ashore and nationalist opposition to the returning Dutch authorities, leave was severely restricted, then on her departure from Balikpapen *Glory* made a short overnight passage north to the island of Tarakan, where she anchored offshore. The 'buzzes' that Christmas was to be spent at

Sydney were confirmed when troops of the Australian 7th Division, who had been involved in some of the fighting against the Japanese in Borneo, were embarked for the passage home. After spending two days embarking the troops and their equipment, at 16.15 on 2 December *Glory* weighed anchor and left Tarakan bound for Manus. For the troops aboard, who were all eager to return home, the short break at the Admiralty Islands was frustrating, but five days later, during the morning watch of Wednesday 12 December *Glory* arrived off Sydney Heads, where she was met by the Australian destroyer *Queenborough* for her final passage up harbour. At 09.55 she secured alongside No 7 wharf of Woolloomooloo Docks, where her passengers were disembarked. With her errands of mercy over *Glory* was to undergo a maintenance period during which her temporary passenger accommodation would be removed and she would be refitted to carry and operate her aircraft once again.

Glory's officers and men spent the Christmas and New Year of 1945-46 enjoying the beaches and surfing at Bondi and Manly, with plenty of ice-cold lager and the traditional Christmas and New Year festivities. On 9 January 1946 *Glory* entered the Captain Cook dry dock on Cockatoo Island, where she spent five days for essential maintenance on her underwater hull. On 15 January, however, she was ready for sea again and at 09.20 that day she left harbour and set course for Jervis Bay. During the afternoon of 15 January the Corsairs of 1831 Squadron and the Fireflies of 837 Squadron, which had replaced the Barracudas, landed on safely. For four days, together with the destroyers *Armada* and *Tumult,* and the fleet carrier *Implacable, Glory* exercised in the Jervis Bay area. On 20 January she returned to Sydney, but only for a few hours, for at midday she weighed anchor to leave in formation with the fleet carriers *Implacable* and *Indefatigable* (flag Vice-Admiral Sir Philip Vian), and the destroyers *Armada* and *Tuscan.* The squadron was bound for Melbourne to show the flag in the state capital of Victoria, which had not seen any Royal Navy warships since the outbreak of war in September 1939. During the passage the three carriers carried out joint flying operations, and in the early hours of 23 January the force arrived off the mouth of the Yarra River. At just before 06.00 pilots were embarked for the passage up harbour and by 10.00 the three carriers were secured alongside Station Pier, Melbourne. During the visit the combined ships' companies marched through the city and the Royal Marines' ceremony of Beating Retreat was broadcast throughout the country. On Thursday 31 January 1946 the visit came to an end, and after leaving Melbourne Admiral Vian transferred his flag to *Implacable,* before *Indefatigable* set course for Fremantle, Cape Town and home. For *Glory, Implacable* and their escorts there was the return passage to Jervis Bay for joint flying exercises, during which they were joined by *Anson* and *Bermuda.* Both carriers remained in the area for most of February, with *Glory's* Corsairs and Fireflies cross-operating with *Implacable's* Avengers. On 15 February there was a four-day break in Sydney, during which all the squadron personnel were landed as *Glory* was about to become a troop transport once again. After leaving Sydney on 25 February and flying off her aircraft, she set course for Auckland. After the hectic flying programme of early February off the coast of New South Wales, the passage to Auckland was quiet and after seven days at sea she arrived at her destination. *Glory* had been ordered to embark a contingent of No 14 Squadron, Royal New Zealand Air Force, together with some aircraft, transport and stores, and deliver them to Kure at the south end of Japan's main island of Honshu. There they were to form part of the Commonwealth Occupation Force in Japan. Although the new passengers were very eager when they embarked in the carrier, the 15-day passage saw the carrier steaming into some very rough weather which kept many of them confined to their mess decks, and reduced the food consumption on board. On the morning of Saturday 23 March, however, *Glory* steamed into Japan's Inland Sea to make a daylight crossing of the picturesque waterway, and that evening she secured to a buoy in Kure harbour, close to the battleship *Duke of York.*

For most of *Glory's* officers and men the visit to Kure was their first sight of Japan, which was now very different from the neat and tidy pre-war days. One member of the ship's company recalls his memories of the city: 'The Japanese fleet showed no signs of life as we entered harbour, owing to the fact that it was lying on its side on the beaches after repeated visits of the US Air Force. Life on shore seemed to be just an existence, with labour gangs clearing away the rubble of what was once a first-class naval base. There were curios for sale in the shops, but food was clearly more important to people than money and it was surprising how many nutty bars one could exchange for Japanese yen. Most of us went to the small naval canteen on the jetty, which became very popular with the ship's company.' *Glory* left Kure during the morning of Friday 29 March, to set course for Sydney. During the passage south there was a full Crossing the Line ceremony, complete with Neptune, Aphrodite and the Bears, which was combined with an inter-departmental sports day. Finally, on Friday 12 April, after an absence of over six weeks, *Glory* arrived back in Sydney Harbour.

With *Glory* about to begin an eight-week maintenance period there was a large turnover of personnel, and all members of the ship's company due for demobilization left the ship to await a passage home. The refit began on 17 April when *Glory* was shifted to Garden Island Naval Base, which meant ten days' station leave for the ship's company. At 11.00 on 5 May, the lower deck was cleared and the ship's company cheered *Implacable* and *Duke of York* as they left for their voyage home via Trincomalee and Suez.

Glory and her escort on their way east. She is painted in the British Pacific Fleet camouflage colours.
(Fleet Air Arm Museum, Cars G/126)

With the ship's company having fallen in by Divisions and with armed Marines escorting them, Japanese officers wait to sign the surrender documents on *Glory's* flight deck as Lieutenant-General H. Imamura and Vice-Admiral K. Kusaka surrender their Army and Naval Forces in the South-Eastern area of operations.
(Fleet Air Arm Museum, Campaigns/585)

An aerial view of *Glory* as she enters Melbourne in January 1946.
(Fleet Air Arm Museum, Cars G/62)

Twelve days later *Glory* was towed into the Captain Cook dry dock for maintenance to the underwater hull, and the ship's company took part in the Sydney Victory Parade. On Friday 14 June, with her refit completed, *Glory* left Sydney with the cruiser *Euryalus* to land on the aircraft and to visit the town of Newcastle, some 125 miles north of Sydney, where they secured alongside Lee Jetty. The visit coincided with the England Rugby Team's tour of the area, so the ships' companies were able to turn out in force to support the national team. On Monday 17 June, after 48 hours in Newcastle, *Glory* and *Euryalus* were at sea again and flying operations were under way. On the last day of the exercises there was a tragic accident when one of the carrier's aircraft handlers, Able Seaman Sherley, was killed when he was hit by the rotating propeller blades of an aircraft. Next day, at 08.35 on Thursday 20 June, in a position Lat 33° - 50'S/Long 151° - 26'E, just off Sydney Heads, his burial service was held. Just over an hour later *Glory* secured alongside a berth at Woolloomooloo Docks. After only 48 hours alongside in Sydney *Glory,* together with the destroyer *Finisterre,* sailed once again to make a well-publicized visit to Adelaide in South Australia. After anchoring off the port overnight, the two ships steamed up harbour during the forenoon of 27 June to secure alongside the main jetty in the outer harbour. During the seven-day visit the carrier was opened to the public and, to the delight of the residents of Adelaide, the ship's company marched through the city. When they sailed from the port on 3 July, however, they left Australian waters, setting course for the East Indies Fleet and the less attractive prospect of Trincomalee.

During the passage flying practice was undertaken and at 10.20 on Thursday 11 July, a Firefly of 837 Squadron got into difficulties some miles away from the ship. Fortunately the pilot was able to bale out and he was picked up by *Finisterre.* Despite having a fractured leg he was transferred to *Glory* by jackstay. Five days later, having flown off the aircraft, *Glory* secured to No 1 buoy in Trincomalee Harbour. On Monday 29 July 1946, Rear-Admiral A. R. M. Bridge, Flag Officer (Air) of the joint British Pacific and East Indies Fleets, hoisted his flag in *Glory,* and next day the carrier and her escort sailed for flying practice in the exercise areas off Ceylon (Sri Lanka). This routine continued during August and into September, with a short break at Colombo. At 09.00 on Saturday 7 September 1946, when *Glory* was at Trincomalee, there was a change of command when Captain W. T. Couchman DSO OBE RN relieved Captain Buzzard. Captain Couchman, having entered the Navy in the early 1920s, specialized in aviation in 1928 serving in *Hermes* on the China Station, and *Courageous* in the Mediterranean. On 21 September *Glory* and *Finisterre* rendezvoused with *Venerable* and her escort *Lagos,* and all four vessels set course for Hong Kong. During the passage both carriers cross-operated their aircraft, but on 26 September *Venerable* stopped off at Singapore Naval Base, whilst *Glory* continued on her way to Hong Kong. At 09.05 on Friday 27 September there was another fatal accident on the flight deck, when Air Mechanic J. F. Adams was killed by the rotating airscrew of a Firefly. Later that day, at 17.10, with the ship in a position Lat 06° - 12'N/Long 107° - 45'E, his burial service was held on the quarterdeck. Finally, during the forenoon of 1 October, *Glory* secured to a buoy in Hong Kong Harbour, to be joined by *Venerable* next day.

During the first three weeks of October, both *Glory* and *Venerable,* escorted by the destroyers *Comet* and *Contest,* carried out flying operations off Hong Kong. On completion of each day's flying programme they would anchor in Junk Bay, and at weekends they would return to their respective buoys in the harbour. On Sunday 20 October the C-in-C British Pacific Fleet, Vice-Admiral Sir Denis Boyd, inspected the ship's company at Divisions on the flight deck, and during the following week *Glory* put to sea for the ship's Sea Otter to carry out landing practice. That week the carrier returned to harbour on 23 October to prepare for a ceremonial Beating Retreat by the massed bands of the Royal Marines from *Glory* and the cruisers *Belfast* and *Bermuda.* The event took place during the evening of Friday 25 October on *Glory's* flight deck and, as well as Vice-Admiral Boyd, it was attended by the Governor of Hong Kong, Sir Mark Young, together with the commanding officers of the Army and RAF units in the colony. For the last few days of October and the first two weeks of November *Glory* operated out of Hong Kong accompanied by *Constance* and *Contest* and, on occasions by the cruiser *Belfast* (flag Vice-Admiral Boyd). On Wednesday 13 November, accompanied by *Lagos,* the carrier left Hong Kong to set course for Singapore where, five days later, she entered the King George VI dry dock, which had been recently vacated by *Venerable.* The run ashore in Singapore meant a pleasant change of scenery for the ship's company, and the dockyard canteen was always well stocked with ice-cold Tiger beer.

It was Monday 9 December when *Glory* left Singapore Naval Base to recover her aircraft and to carry out exercises with the RAF. That afternoon a Corsair of 1831 Squadron was forced to ditch in a bay on the east coast of Malaya, but fortunately the pilot escaped with only minor injuries. Four days later *Glory* was heading for Hong Kong and after a four-day passage and a night at anchor off Junk Island she rendezvoused with *Venerable.* The two carriers then operated in local waters before they entered Hong Kong for the Christmas and New Year celebrations. *Glory's* ship's company spent Christmas Day secured to No 1 buoy, but at one hour's notice for steam after a number of typhoon warnings were received, which restricted the engine room department's shore leave. By New Year's Eve this had been extended to four hours and all but the duty watch were

Framed by coconut palms *Glory* lies at anchor in Trincomalee Harbour, the base for the East Indies Fleet.
(Fleet Air Arm Museum, Cars G/88)

able to join in the festivities ashore.

At 08.15 on Thursday 2 January 1947 *Glory* and *Venerable,* escorted by *Alert, Finisterre* and *Widemouth Bay,* left Hong Kong to operate in the local exercise areas off the coast. During the afternoon of the seventh day a Corsair from *Glory* ditched in the sea, about 13 miles from the ship. Fortunately, the injured pilot was rescued by *Finisterre* and taken directly to Hong Kong, and later that day both carriers returned to harbour to undergo maintenance. On board *Glory* there was the extra workload as the ship was prepared for inspection by Admiral Bridge on 21 January. Both carriers left Hong Kong on 28 January to continue their flying practice, which continued into February, but on 14 February *Venerable* set course for Trincomalee and home. Four days after her departure *Glory* and *Finisterre* followed her through the South China Sea, bound for Trincomalee. There were joint exercises with RAF Beaufighters and Sunderland flying boats off Singapore, and the two ships arrived in Trincomalee on 27 February, where Admiral Bridge transferred to *Venerable,* which promptly left for Devonport. *Glory* undertook further flying off Trincomalee, in company with *Contest* and the cruiser *Jamaica,* before setting course north for Bombay (Mumbai). During the passage tragedy struck on the afternoon of 7 March, when Firefly 272 crashed during flying operations, killing the pilot, Lt-Cdr Bates, and the observer, Lt Mayne. Next day *Glory* anchored in Bombay Harbour, close to the Gateway of India. The carrier had been sent to Bombay, not only to show the flag during the dying months of Britain's Indian Empire, but to mark the arrival of the incoming and last Viceroy, Lord Mountbatten. Although he had flown direct from London to New Delhi, where he met the outgoing Viceroy, as far as *Glory* was concerned the changeover day, 20 March, began at 08.10 when 160 VIP guests embarked in the carrier, which then weighed anchor and put to sea to give a flying demonstration. Following this the carrier's Air Group rendezvoused with RAF aircraft to stage a fly-past over the port and city of Bombay. Next day, with the viceregal duties having been completed, *Glory, Jamaica* and *Contest* left Bombay to make the passage south back to the naval base on Ceylon's north-east coast.

After arriving at Trincomalee on Tuesday 25 March, *Glory* met her younger sister *Theseus* for the first time, and

Rear-Admiral Creasy, the Flag Officer (Air) for the newly designated Far East Station, transferred to *Glory* having travelled out from the UK in *Theseus.* During the carrier's stay at Trincomalee the Corsairs of 1831 Squadron were exchanged for the Seafire FX Vs of 806 Squadron, with the personnel joining the ship during the afternoon of 1 April. Next day *Glory* left harbour to begin a busy programme of flying, which would continue each week, with weekends being spent at Trincomalee. On 22 April she took part in manoeuvres with *Theseus* and the cruisers *Glasgow* and *Jamaica* and the destroyer *Contest.* Next day, whilst launching a range of Seafires for a mock raid on Fort Frederick, a member of the flight deck personnel, Able Seaman Taylor, was struck by the wing of a Seafire and killed. Later that afternoon, shortly before the ship anchored off Trincomalee, his burial service was held. Six days later, at 11.48 on Tuesday 29 April, with the ship in a position Lat 08° - 05'N/Long 81° - 54'E, Seafire SW 821 piloted by Lt-Cdr (A) Thurston, crashed on deck whilst landing on and went over the port side of the ship and into the sea. The main engines were immediately stopped and the seaboat was lowered, but there was no sign of the pilot or the aircraft. Next day saw the final flying operations before *Glory* was prepared for a maintenance period.

During the first two days of May, with the carrier secured to a buoy at Trincomalee, all the aircraft were loaded into barges to be taken ashore and Admiral Creasy transferred his flag to *Theseus.* On 12 May *Glory* weighed anchor and set course for Singapore Naval Base, where she arrived five days later. Shortly after her arrival she was shifted into the King George VI dry dock and the ship's company moved into shore accommodation. During the few weeks that the carrier remained high and dry a large number of her officers and men left for their passage home, with their places being taken by fresh personnel from the UK. It was Thursday 19 June before *Glory* was ready for sea again and she sailed that morning to embark her aircraft, before carrying out a mini work-up off Singapore. Four days later, having rendezvoused with *Theseus, Cockade* and *Contest,* she set course for Australia. Once off the Australian coast *Theseus* and *Cockade* parted company and set course for Tasmania and a visit to Hobart. *Glory* and *Contest* meanwhile, headed for Adelaide, arriving off the port on 4 July. At 07.15 as the two ships steamed towards the harbour, 11 Fireflies and nine Seafires were launched to make an early morning fly-past over Adelaide, and once alongside there was a substantial programme of entertainment for the ship's company, including sightseeing tours, dances, private parties and a full sports programme. When the visit ended on 9 July, 60 VIP guests boarded the carrier to be taken to sea for a forenoon flying display, after which they rendezvoused with *Theseus* off Melbourne. The two carriers then steamed into harbour to secure alongside the city's Station Pier for a nine-day visit, which was broken for a few hours on 15 July when they put to sea to rehearse for a mass fly-past over the city. The visit ended at 10.00 on 20 July, when the carriers and their escorts left for Sydney, but the fly-past that afternoon was marred by the collision in mid-air of two Fireflies from *Theseus,* killing all four crew members. Meanwhile, on board *Glory,* the aircraft were giving a flying demonstration to a group of RAAF officers, but at 14.50, as the Seafires were landing on, one aircraft crashed on deck, seriously injuring two of the flight deck personnel. One of the men, N/A T. Saddler, was gravely injured and he was quickly transferred to *Contest* which steamed at full speed for Melbourne where he was transferred to hospital. Sadly, later that evening it was learned that he had died from his injuries and a memorial service was held on the quarterdeck.

After exercising with the RAAF off the coast of New South Wales, the two carriers entered Sydney Harbour during the forenoon of 24 July and as *Glory's* long commission east of Suez was now nearing its end she took on board a large quantity of stores under the 'Food for Britain' scheme, which was designed to ease the austere conditions at home where the country was slowly recovering from the devastation of the Second World War. Finally, after putting on two well-attended ship's company dances in the hangar, during the afternoon of 5 August both *Glory* and *Theseus,* together with the two escorts, left Sydney for Brisbane, where they spent ten days. On 18 August, after leaving Queensland, *Theseus* and *Cockade* parted company, leaving *Glory* and *Contest* to set course for Singapore. It was the first stage of the carrier's voyage home.

At Singapore over 100 passengers, consisting of naval, army and RAF personnel were embarked, together with the Colours of the 1st Battalion of the King's Royal Regiment, for passage to Devonport. After leaving the naval base on 2 September, *Glory* called at Trincomalee and Aden, and by the afternoon of 23 September she had left Port Said and was heading for Malta. During her three-day stay in Grand Harbour she met her younger sister *Ocean* for the first time, and after leaving Malta there was only a five-hour stopover in Gibraltar Bay before, at 08.10 on Monday 6 October 1947, she anchored in Plymouth Sound. The commission was not quite over, however, for after clearing customs and disembarking her passengers, she left the Sound to arrive alongside Glasgow's King George V Dock on 8 October. During her two days alongside all the squadron personnel, aircraft and the 'Food for Britain' were disembarked before, at 08.20 on 10 October *Glory* left for Devonport. After a slow voyage south, and three hours at anchor in Plymouth Sound, Glory steamed up harbour during the forenoon of 13 October, and at midday she was manoeuvred into North Lock dry dock. During the weeks that followed the ship's company was steadily reduced, and on 15 January 1948 Captain Couchman relinquished his command. For *Glory* long months in reserve lay ahead.

In September 1947, on a homeward-bound trooping voyage, *Glory* lies at Grand Harbour. She is carrying a deck cargo as well as aircraft. She also had Navy, Army and RAF personnel embarked. *(Author's collection)*

Chapter Six

HMS *Glory* January 1948 – October 1951

In early 1948 *Glory* was towed into Devonport's No 5 basin where, under a small care and maintenance party, she remained until the summer of 1949. For a time in 1948 she was used as an accommodation ship for the Australian ship's company of HMAS *Sydney,* the Majestic-class light fleet carrier which had been launched in September 1944 as HMS *Terrible.* With the commissioning of *Sydney* in December 1948 *Glory* was again left without a role, but in the early summer of 1949 she was brought out of reserve and refitted for further operational service. During the refit the arrester gear was modernized, her bridge was rebuilt and pom-pom anti-aircraft guns were replaced by 16 single 40mm Bofors guns.

On Monday 15 August 1949 her new commanding officer, Captain E. H. Shattock OBE RN, joined the ship, and by the end of that month the carrier was once again alongside the sea wall in Devonport Dockyard. On 2 September the elderly cruiser *Leander,* which was under tow, collided beam on to *Glory,* but apart from some dents and minor abrasions to her paintwork the carrier was not seriously damaged. At 10.00 on Monday 17 October 1949, *Glory* was recommissioned and two days later she left Devonport to begin her post-refit trials. During the first two days the carrier underwent full-power trials in the Channel and when these were completed she anchored in St Austell Bay. At 21.15 on 25 October, whilst the carrier was at anchor, a distress message was received from a small coaster, SS *Yew Park,* which was in difficulties off Land's End. The boiler rooms were immediately ordered to raise steam, but before this could be completed other vessels had gone to the aid of the merchantman and *Glory* was stood down. At 07.30 on 26 October she resumed her sea trials and next day, at 07.57, the first landing on the flight deck for two years was made by an Avenger. Half an hour later the aircraft was launched from the catapult, and at 10.50 there was an even more dramatic landing when a Vampire jet touched down safely. For the remainder of the day the Avenger continued to carry out landing trials on board, and the Vampire was successfully launched, then at 17.15

After recommissioning at Devonport and carrying out her post-refit trials, on 31 October 1949 *Glory* left Portsmouth for Glasgow and the Mediterranean Fleet. *(Author's collection)*

Glory anchored in Sandown Bay, off the Isle of Wight. Next day saw the carrier undergoing another ten hours of flying trials, before she made a ceremonial entry into Portsmouth Harbour for a weekend break.

Whilst she was in Portsmouth 150 ratings joined *Glory* and the Duke of Edinburgh's yacht *Coweslip* was loaded aboard before, at 13.47 on Monday 31 October, she sailed for Glasgow where, two days later, she secured alongside King George V Dock. During the next 24 hours the stores, equipment and some aircraft for the 14th Carrier Air Group, which consisted of the Sea Fury FIIs of 804 Squadron and the Mk 6 Fireflies of 812 Squadron, were embarked. Most of the aircraft were already in Malta, having left in *Ocean* the previous month. *Glory* left Glasgow during the forenoon of Thursday 3 November to make an eight-day passage to Marsaxlokk Bay, where she arrived on 11 November. Next day she entered Grand Harbour where she took *Triumph's* place in the Mediterranean Fleet, the latter having sailed for the Far East. On 15 November, just a few days after her arrival at Malta, *Glory's* work started in earnest and she was at sea with the Sea Furies and Fireflies of 804 and 812 Squadrons beginning two weeks of intensive flying. On 29 November, having flown off the aircraft, *Glory* entered AFD 35 in Grand Harbour, for maintenance on the underwater hull. It was 7 December before the carrier left the floating dry dock to be shifted to Parlatorio Wharf and then to No 8 buoy close to Customs House Steps. On 14 December, whilst moored at the buoy, *Glory* received a royal visitor, HRH Princess Elizabeth, who at that time was a serving officer's wife as the Duke of Edinburgh was stationed in HMS *Magpie* at Malta. At 08.00 the ship was dressed overall and half an hour later detachments from other units in harbour arrived on board to represent their various ships. At 11.30 *Glory's* saluting guns crashed out a royal salute and three minutes later Princess Elizabeth arrived on board where she was met by the C-in-C, Admiral Sir Arthur Power, and Captain Shattock. After inspecting the ceremonial Divisions on the flight deck, the Princess reviewed other units of the Mediterranean Fleet, before leaving the carrier at 12.10. Next day came the most popular part of the proceedings when, at noon, the main brace was spliced.

On Monday 19 December *Glory* was at sea again with the squadrons engaged in busy flying programmes and during the afternoon of Friday 23 December she returned to her buoy in Grand Harbour for a five-day break over Christmas. On Tuesday 27 December, Captain Shattock fell ill and he was taken ashore to RNH Bighi. In his place Captain H. Traill CBE RN was appointed to command the carrier temporarily, and no sooner had he settled in than *Glory* was at sea for a full three-day flying programme, which ended on 30 December when she returned to Grand Harbour for the New Year celebrations.

At 08.13 on Wednesday 4 January 1950 *Glory* slipped her moorings and left harbour to carry out a full day's flying south of Malta, with the Indian Navy's destroyer *Ranjit* (ex-HMS *Redoubt*) acting as planeguard. At 15.38, with the carrier some eight miles off Delmira Point, Firefly 204 crashed into the sea from *Glory's* starboard side. Within two minutes *Ranjit* was at the scene of the accident, but her sea boat's crew were only able to recover the body of the pilot, Lt G. W. Turney. Of the observer, Lt T. O. Brigstock, there was no trace, nor could any wreckage be found. Just over half an hour later *Glory* anchored in Marsaxlokk Bay for the night and a memorial service was held for Lt Brigstock. Next day, after a full flying programme, the carrier returned to Grand Harbour and on 7 January the colours were lowered to half mast for the funeral of Lt Turney. During the period at Malta the Flag Officer (Air) Mediterranean, Rear-Admiral G. Grantham, hoisted his flag in *Glory,* which would remain his flagship until December that year. On 10 January *Glory* sailed for three more days of flying, but this was followed by a ten-day maintenance period in Grand Harbour.

When *Glory* left Malta on 23 January she set course north to make her first 'foreign' visit of the commission and two days later, after an extremely rough passage, she arrived at Naples. During her five days in the Italian port there was plenty of ceremonial and on one day the Royal Marines provided nine ceremonial guards and bands in the space of just three hours. *Glory* left the port on 30 January and as she steamed towards Tripoli she rendezvoused with the US Navy's carrier *Midway* to carry out joint manoeuvres. Next day *Glory* anchored off Tripoli and on 2 February, off the Libyan coast, the carrier undertook manoeuvres with the destroyers *Cheviot* and *Vigo,* returning to Tripoli the following morning when shore leave was granted. After three more days off Libya *Glory* returned to Malta and during flying operations on the forenoon of 8 February one of the carrier's Sea Furies ditched into the sea some miles away from the ship. Fortunately, the pilot baled out safely and he was rescued by *Cheviot.* During the afternoon of 10 February *Glory* returned to Grand Harbour.

During her long weekend at Malta, on Sunday 12 February, Captain Shattock returned to duty and the following afternoon Captain Traill left the ship. *Glory* left harbour on 14 February to land on her Air Group and to carry out a three-day flying programme in local waters with other units of the Mediterranean Fleet. This was followed by a ten-day maintenance period in Grand Harbour, and after leaving Malta on 27 February she rendezvoused with *Chequers, Gravelines, Teredo* and *Vigo,* the cruiser *Liverpool* and, from the Home Fleet, the aircraft carrier *Implacable,* and *Vengeance.* After carrying out manoeuvres off Malta the fleet put in to Palmas Bay, Sardinia, the first stop on the spring cruise. From there they steamed west to exercise with French units and to anchor off Golfe Juan on the

In Grand Harbour, with the ship dressed overall, Ceremonial Divisions are held on *Glory's* flight deck.
(Fleet Air Arm Museum, Cars G/98)

Steaming into heavy seas in the Mediterranean.
(Fleet Air Arm Museum, Cars G/95)

Côte d'Azur, close to Cannes. With sea temperatures rising 'Hands to bathe' was piped each day and the ship was opened to the public on one afternoon. After leaving the French Riviera during the evening of 13 March *Glory* took part in a night encounter exercise, and an air defence exercise with *Vengeance,* during which Sea Hornets from *Implacable* 'attacked' the two smaller carriers. The next port of call on the cruise was Algiers, and *Glory* anchored in the Old Port during the forenoon of 16 March for a four-day visit. After leaving Algiers there were further manoeuvres, before the whole fleet put in to Gibraltar on 22 March. *Glory's* first cruise of the year ended on the last day of March when, together with *Liverpool* and the destroyers, she entered Grand Harbour for a maintenance period which was to last until mid-May. On 31 March the Admiralty announced that in December 1950, having been refitted in Malta, *Glory* would return to the UK and recommission with a Chatham ship's company. Following this, it was stated, the carrier would return to the Mediterranean, but might, in May 1951, relieve *Theseus* on the Far East Station. On 13 April the Prime Minister of Malta paid a visit to *Glory,* and on 24 April the carrier was

Glory anchored off the coast of southern France in March 1950. *(Peter Cook)*

shifted to AFD 35 where she remained until 4 May.

Glory left Malta on Tuesday 16 May to land on her aircraft, and for the rest of the month most weekdays were spent at sea. At 13.35 on 24 May, when the carrier was some nine miles south of Filfa Island, there was a tragic accident when Sea Fury 106, flown by Lt Mudford, crashed over the port side of the ship when attempting to land on. Although the motor cutter was away within minutes, there was no trace of the pilot. Later that day a memorial service for him was held on the quarterdeck. Flying operations and fleet exercises continued for three weeks, but on 12 June, *Glory,* together with other units of the fleet, including *Gambia* (flag C-in-C Med Fleet) and units of the 3rd Destroyer Flotilla, left Malta for Corfu, in readiness for exercises with the Royal Hellenic Navy, which included four Greek destroyers and three submarines. The British squadron entered Corfu on 14 June for a five-day break before the start of the exercises. After leaving Corfu *Glory* formed part of 'Green Force', with the British and Greek destroyers, and steamed south where they were to be intercepted by the four submarines of 'Blue Force'. At 18.35 on the first day, the last aircraft in a serial of Fireflies crashed through the barrier when landing on and before it came to a halt it hit a number of planes in the forward park, seriously injuring three ratings. In view of the men's injuries *Glory* was detached from the exercise and, with *Chivalrous,* she returned to Malta to land the casualties and the damaged aircraft. On 21 June *Glory* rejoined the exercise and two days later, with the first phase completed, the fleet anchored off Skiathos Island in the Aegean Sea. During the six days at anchor the Korean War broke out on 25 June, but at the time it was not thought that *Glory* would be affected by what seemed, at first, to be a localized conflict. Before the second phase of the exercise began *Glory* made a 36-hour passage to Piraeus for a five-day visit before moving to the Turkish port of Marmaris, and from there to Larnaca in Cyprus, where she anchored in the bay. On 18 July, after leaving Larnaca, *Glory* rejoined the fleet and phase two of the Anglo-Greek naval exercises began with the ships operating from Khrysokhou Bay. The

A Sea Fury lands on during flying operations in the Mediterranean. *(Fleet Air Arm Museum, Cars G/102)*

manoeuvres ended during the evening of 20 July, when *Glory* set course for Egypt and next morning she moored in Alexandria Harbour. It was her first visit here since July 1945, and it was one of the last 'foreign' visits of the commission. After five days in the port *Glory* left harbour and set course for Malta where, on the last day of July, the aircraft were flown off and the carrier was secured to buoys in Grand Harbour.

During August only seven days were spent at sea, with flying operations being carried out in local waters, but in early September there was a short cruise which took the carrier to Marseilles, Tangier and Gibraltar. These were very brief calls however, and by 26 September *Glory* was at sea carrying out a programme of flying in the Western Mediterranean. On the afternoon of 27 September a Sea Fury from 804 Squadron was lost at sea, and despite a lengthy and extensive search by *Glory* and the destroyer *Saintes,* there was no sign of the pilot. By the end of September the carrier was back in Maltese waters, and on 1 October she secured in Grand Harbour to begin a two-month refit.

At 08.03 on Friday 8 December, with the refit completed, *Glory* left Grand Harbour with the destroyer *Saintes* to embark the squadrons and to set course for Gibraltar. That afternoon Admiral Grantham hauled down his flag and transferred to *Saintes* by jackstay, and three days later the carrier arrived in Gibraltar. Twenty-four hours later she was at sea again and heading for Devonport, but it was a rough passage as Force 11 winds and enormous seas battered the immaculate paintwork of her hull. In the Bay of Biscay all the carley floats were washed away by the huge waves, but relief came on 15 December when the carrier anchored in Plymouth Sound. Next day she steamed up harbour where, at 10.55, she secured alongside Devonport Dockyard.

Soon after her arrival *Glory* had paid off and at 08.00 on 28 December 1950 her new commanding officer, Captain K. S. Colquhoun DSO RN, joined the ship to relieve Captain Shattock. Two days after the change of command a draft of 250 ratings, the first contingent of the Chatham ship's company, joined and by the second week of January 1951 the complement was up to strength. At 13.15 on Thursday 25 January *Glory* was ready for sea and she left Devonport to carry out a full-power trial and to embark her Sea Otter, after which she anchored in Weymouth Bay for the night. Originally it had been intended that *Glory* would rejoin the Mediterranean Fleet, before sailing east to relieve *Theseus,* but by early 1951 the war in Korea had become a major commitment for British troops and naval forces, and it was decided that she would steam east earlier than had originally been anticipated. On 26 January *Glory* left home waters for Malta, which she reached on 2 February to embark the stores and personnel of the 14th Carrier Air Group. Then, after an intensive work-up period, she slipped out of Grand Harbour at midnight on 18 March and set course for Port Said, escorted by the destroyer *Gravelines.* By the afternoon of 22 March she had cleared the Suez Canal and after a short stop at Aden she set course east across the Arabian Sea. When she was off Ceylon (Sri Lanka) she took part in training manoeuvres with the East Indies Fleet and during these exercises, at 06.27 on 3 April, the first flying accident of the commission occurred. *Glory* was in company with the cruiser *Mauritius* and a number of destroyers, when a serial of two Sea Furies and four Fireflies was being launched by catapult. Unfortunately, the last Firefly crashed into the sea, but *Gravelines* was quick off the mark and her sea boat recovered the aircrew and returned them safely to the carrier. Three days later *Glory* arrived at Singapore Naval Base.

After only 24 hours at Singapore, *Glory* was at sea again and bound for Hong Kong where, after flying off the aircraft to Kai Tak, she arrived on 11 April. During the eight days in Hong Kong the opportunity was taken to carry out a large programme of maintenance, while ashore the aircraft were able to continue flying. However, with persistent fog in the area, in order to avoid the possibility of the ship's departure being delayed, on 19 April the aircraft were embarked from lighters. Next day, at 08.30, *Glory* left Hong Kong and after exercises in local waters she set course for Japan. At 10.40 on 23 April, after a foggy passage, at 10.40 on 23 April, *Glory* and her escort *Consort* arrived at Sasebo, on the western side of Kyushu, which

Flying her paying-off pennant, on 8 December 1950, *Glory* leaves Grand Harbour to return to Devonport. *(Peter Cook)*

was the forward operating base for units of the fleet involved in the Korean War. Also in harbour was *Theseus* which had just completed a seven-month tour of duty off Korea and all her officers and men were pleased to see *Glory*, for they were waiting to start their passage home. Two days after *Glory's* arrival, when all stores and a US Navy Sikorsky S51 helicopter and its crew had been transferred, *Theseus* left harbour and set course for the UK.

Glory's arrival had coincided with the joint North Korean and Chinese spring offensive, which started on 22 April, and which involved British Army units. It was the start of the Battle of the Imjin River, which delayed the enemy advance and ensured that the South Korean capital Seoul did not fall. *Glory's* first Korean Patrol began on 26 April, when she left Sasebo with a destroyer escort to steam to the operational area in the Yellow Sea, west of the port of Kunsan. Initially poor visibility prevented flying, but at 13.31 on 28 April, the first of 15 sorties was able to take off. The loss of Sea Fury 103 and its pilot, Lt E. P. L. Stephenson, on the first day was a bitter blow. Lt Stephenson was flying on combat air patrol (CAP) duties in a position Lat 36° - 39'N/Long 125° - 26'E when, at 14.27, after following his leader through a cloud layer at between 800 and 1,500 feet, he lost control and dived into the sea. Despite a thorough search of the area, just a few items of wreckage and an oil slick were found. *Glory's* aircraft operated in close support of the UN ground forces ashore, interrupting the Communist supply routes, acting as spotters for bombarding ships, and continually reconnoitring the coast to ensure that no supplies reached the Communist forces by sea. Once operations were well under way an average of 50 sorties was flown daily, roughly two-thirds of them being Sea Furies armed with cannon and 60lb rockets, the remainder being Fireflies, with cannon and 500lb bombs. Owing to the large number of aircraft being carried, there was always a large deck park so the planes were catapulted, or launched by rocket-assisted-take-off-gear (RATOG), which was an awe-inspiring sight. Flying would begin at dawn, and strikes would then take off at approximately two-hourly intervals until sunset. As soon as a strike sortie and CAP were airborne the previous one landed, and there was then considerable activity refuelling and rearming before they were due to be launched again. By day the ship's company would be at Defence Stations, and at night they would go to Cruising Stations, with all the defensive armament manned. During this first patrol two more aircraft from *Glory* were lost, but the pilots were rescued and the patrol ended at Sasebo on 7 May.

As a run ashore Sasebo was always popular, although the town, in the words of one member of the ship's company, looked, 'derelict and decrepit, with shops little more than shacks, and houses all monotonous, unpainted, drab wooden bungalows, with dingy grey slate roofs. In the main street the shops opened straight out on to the narrow roadway, looking like a cross between an Indian bazaar and one of the back streets of Port Said.' There was, however, a

On 22 March 1951, *Glory* steamed south through the Suez Canal to join the Far East Station.
(Fleet Air Arm Museum, Cars G/107)

Glory off Korea. Note that the aircraft are painted with their Korean War markings in order that they could be distinguished as belonging to Commonwealth Forces. *(Fleet Air Arm Museum, Cars G/44)*

fleet canteen for Commonwealth servicemen and for those who wished to travel further afield there was a pearl farm and a bone china factory, both of which were happy to open their doors to organized parties, to whom they would sell their products at, 'very special price'.

On 10 May, together with her escort, *Glory* left Sasebo for her second patrol, where she relieved USS *Bataan* and flying operations began. The Fireflies attacked bridges at Wontan and Yonan, enemy troops in the area from the Han River to Chinnampo and villages which were reported to be harbouring hostile forces. They also attacked supply lines, railway tunnels and ammunition dumps. Monday 14 May was replenishment day and at 11.00 *Glory* went alongside RFA *Wave Premier* to refuel, an operation which lasted until 14.40. However, at 14.22, one of the carrier's refuelling personnel, AB J. McPherson, caught his foot in a bight of rope and, clad in oilskins and sea boots, he was thrown overboard. As it happened the ship's helicopter was airborne and the pilot, Lt O' Mara USN, saw what had happened and he was quickly over the struggling rating who, in his heavy clothing, was almost exhausted. Fortunately, he was rescued by the helicopter and flown back to *Glory* and, although carried out by a US Navy helicopter and pilot, it was the Royal Navy's first SAR rescue by a ship's helicopter. During the patrol a Sea Fury and a Firefly were lost, but the aircrews were rescued safely, and the patrol ended at Sasebo on Sunday 20 May, when the carrier was dry docked.

Glory's third patrol began on 3 June when she left Sasebo, and flying operations against supply junks at the ports of Hanchon and Kumsan-ni began next day. At 18.00 on 4 June, when returning from the final sortie of the day, a Sea Fury was forced to ditch, but fortunately the pilot was rescued. Next day, however, at 14.45, when a Firefly which had been hit by flak was attempting to land on, it ditched ahead of the ship and sank quickly, with the loss of Pilot 3 S. W. E. Ford. On 7 June another Firefly which had been hit by anti-aircraft fire was forced to ditch, but on this occasion the crew were rescued by a shore-based helicopter. On 9 June, after replenishing from RFA *Wave Premier,* the aviation fuel in *Glory* was found to be contaminated and although reports of sabotage appeared in newspapers, it was found that the problem lay in *Wave Premier's* cast-iron discharge pipes which were badly corroded. During the forenoon of 11 June, whilst *Glory's* aircraft were returning from an armed reconnaissance mission, an enemy twin jet aircraft was spotted. It was the first such sighting during the carrier's patrols, but it made no attempt to interfere with *Glory's* planes. The patrol ended at 08.50 on Friday 15 June, but this time at Kure where an intensive maintenance programme was to be carried out.

Although the town was smaller than Sasebo, the ship's company found it more colourful and with a cheaper shopping centre. According to one member of the ship's company it was more 'permanent looking', and it was not long before the mess decks started to fill up with silks, musical boxes, sets of cultured pearls, damascene work and amazingly ingenious small clockwork animals. Kure also boasted a large grass playing field, and on most days there would be cricket being played at one end, football at the other and a game of hockey in between. During the forenoon of 21 June, *Glory* left Kure to return to the operational area, and next day she embarked Rear-Admiral Scott, the Flag Officer, Second in Command, Far East Station (FO2 FES). Flying operations began soon afterwards and over the course of four days the aircraft carried out their bombing and armed reconnaissance missions over North Korean positions, during which time they clocked up their 1,000th operational sortie. At 14.30 on 28 June a serial of six Fireflies and six Sea Furies was launched to carry out bombing raids in the Chinnampo area, but an hour later when they were over their target, one of the Fireflies was shot down with the loss of its crew, Lt J. H. Sharp and A/C1 G. B. Wells. Next day came a regrettable incident when a Sea Fury sank what turned out to be a friendly junk, which was being used by a secret intelligence organization. Five men, including two intelligence agents, were killed, but it was agreed that the pilot had acted entirely within his briefing. During the afternoon of 30 June a Sea Fury, which was being launched, ditched ahead of the ship, but fortunately the pilot was rescued safely. However, the incident rendered the catapult unserviceable and all further launchings were carried out by RATOG. The patrol ended on 3 July when, after a choppy passage on the edge of typhoon 'Kate', *Glory* returned to Sasebo.

During the break maintenance work was carried out on *Glory's* catapult and all the aircrew were granted five days' leave, but on 10 July the carrier left to begin her fifth patrol. During the final days of the patrol *Glory* operated further north of her usual position, in order to provide close air support during the recovery of an enemy MiG 15 jet fighter. The first confirmation of this top secret Soviet plane came from one of *Glory's* pilots on 11 July, when he spotted its tail in a position Lat 39° - 12'N/Long 125° - 22'E, just off the coast and over 100 miles behind enemy lines. Divers from HMS *Cardigan Bay,* assisted by US Navy personnel, managed to retrieve the wrecked MiG in an operation which was one of the West's most valuable intelligence coups of the 1950s. The presence of *Glory's* low-flying close air support was described as having been, 'of the greatest moral value to the recovery teams'. At 11.51 on 16 July a Firefly was lost to anti-aircraft fire, when it crashed to the ground in flames in a position Lat 38° - 32'N/Long 125° - 44'E, with the loss of its crew, Lt R. Williams and Sub-Lt I. R. Shepley. Next day two Sea Furies were hit by enemy fire and although one pilot was rescued from the sea, the second plane crashed in flames with the loss of Commissioned Pilot T. W. Sparke. Sadly, Captain Colquhoun had to report the loss of a third officer during the patrol, which ended at Kure on 22 July.

Although the carrier's stay in Kure was scheduled for seven days, and was to include a maintenance programme, including cleaning the main boilers, in the early hours of 25 July *Glory* was ordered to sea to provide a show of force in support of peace talks which had started. There then followed an extremely strenuous night as liberty men were recalled and the engineers worked hard to close the boilers and raise steam. To their credit they managed to prepare the main machinery for sea in just seven hours. *Glory* left Kure at 09.18 on 25 July, and rendezvoused with USS *Sicily* in the operational area. Flying operations during this unexpected and extended patrol were hampered by poor weather conditions, and there was a submarine scare which was put down to the presence of a large wreck in the area. On 1 August air cover was provided for HMS *Mounts Bay,* which had been attacked and bombed by a twin-engined jet plane. During the patrol 312 sorties had been flown, and some 40,000 rounds of 20mm ammunition, over 1,000 rocket projectiles and over 100, 500lb bombs had been fired at North Korean targets, with no aircraft having been lost to enemy action. On 5 August *Glory* arrived at Sasebo to embark spares and replacement aircraft, before sailing for Kure where she arrived six days later.

Glory's next patrol began on Monday 13 August and once again poor weather limited flying operations. During the patrol two aircraft were forced down, but the crews were uninjured and after transferring FO2 from the cruiser *Ceylon,* the carrier had to make a passage which took her into the Tsushima Strait, within 70 miles of the Chinese coast and on to Okinawa in order to avoid typhoon 'Marge', but on 24 August she arrived at Kure for a seven-day break. Flying operations for the next patrol began on 2 September, with junks, railway lines and villages being attacked. During seven full days of flying an average of 50 sorties a day was maintained, and on 9 September a total of 84 sorties was flown. Captain Colquhoun reported it as, '...an achievement of which all concerned can be proud.' During the patrol a new junk landing site south of the Chong Chon River was attacked and this was followed up by successful strikes on warehouses and the junks themselves. Although three aircraft were damaged, no aircrew were lost and on 9 September the burnt-out hulk of a junk which had been intercepted by USS *Hanna* was sunk by *Glory's* Fireflies. The patrol ended on Tuesday 11 September when the carrier returned to Kure.

After a five-day break *Glory's* next patrol began on 16 September and this time there was a change of scenery as she operated with other units as Task Group 95.9 on Korea's east coast. A faulty catapult meant that *Glory* had to return to Sasebo to collect more RATOG equipment before flying operations could be resumed. At 11.30 on 22 September, with the aircraft being launched by RATOG, a Firefly's rockets failed to fire and the aircraft ditched ahead of the ship. Although it sank immediately, the pilot managed to escape and he was rescued, but the observer, Sub-Lt R. G. A. Davey, was lost. On 24 September a Sea Fury was hit by flak and forced to ditch, but the pilot was recovered safely and the next day saw the final flying operations before, on 27 September, *Glory* returned to Kure where HMAS *Sydney* was waiting to take over from her.

The three days following her arrival at Kure were spent turning over her duties to *Sydney* while the US Navy helicopter and its crew received a rousing farewell. On 30 September Vice-Admiral Sir Guy Russell, the C-in-C Far East Station, visited the ship and inspected Divisions, after which he congratulated everyone on their fine war record. *Glory* was now scheduled for a refit in Sydney, and at 16.30 the same day, escorted by HMAS *Anzac,* she left Kure for Hong Kong. After only 48 hours in Hong Kong she set course for Singapore, and from there she left for Australia. On 12 October, despite wet and windy weather, King Neptune held court and five days later *Glory* arrived in Fremantle for a brief refuelling stop. On 22 October the aircraft were flown off and two days later, at 09.00 on 24 October, she secured alongside a berth at Garden Island Naval Base, Sydney. While *Glory* underwent her refit the ship's company could look forward to two months of rest and relaxation.

Chapter Seven

HMS *Glory* November 1951 – August 1961

While *Glory* underwent her two-month refit at Sydney her officers and men could enjoy some rest and relaxation after their busy tour of duty in Korean waters and when the dockyard workers descended upon the ship, which spent two weeks in the Captain Cook dry dock, the ship's company was granted 14 days' leave. Accommodation was no problem as the residents of Sydney were queuing up to offer hospitality, and many men were able to see something of life in the outback. On Christmas Eve the ship went to sea for just over seven hours, to carry out full-power and gun functioning trials, but by 16.00 she was back alongside her berth at Woolloomooloo. Next day, in sweltering hot temperatures, the ship's company enjoyed a full Christmas dinner, complete with roast turkey and Christmas pudding.

On Wednesday 2 January 1952, with the Christmas and New Year celebrations over, *Glory* left Sydney to steam round to Jervis Bay where she landed on the Air Group. On 4 January, after two days of deck landing practice, she returned to Sydney but this time it was only for the weekend. On Monday 7 January, with final farewells having been said, *Glory* was back at sea again and after four more days of flying in the Jervis Bay area, she set course for Fremantle and Singapore. She remained at the former port just long enough to refuel, and she spent three days at Singapore embarking winter clothing before proceeding to Hong Kong where she arrived on 30 January. Waiting for her as she secured to No 2 buoy in the harbour was HMAS *Sydney* and over the next two days stores and equipment, including the US Navy S51 helicopter and its crew, were transferred. At 08.45 on 2 February, with the handover

Glory at Sydney during her refit which lasted for over two months, between late October 1951 and early January 1952.
(Fleet Air Arm Museum, Cars G/105)

complete, *Glory* left Hong Kong to set course for Sasebo, where she arrived three days later. Her stay in the Japanese port was limited to just 16 hours before, at 07.00 on 6 February, *Glory* left for the operational area in the Yellow Sea, off Korea's west coast. During this deployment of five patrols her main task would be to provide air defences for the friendly islands situated off the coast in the area of the front line. Flying operations began on 7 February and soon the squadrons were averaging 50 sorties a day. Once again the aircraft were kept busy on bombing and armed reconnaissance missions, and also spotting for the cruiser *Ceylon* and the destroyer *Porterfield.* During the patrol she lost only two aircraft and both pilots were rescued safely, the second by a South Korean minesweeper. With the final sorties being flown on 15 February, next day *Glory* arrived at Sasebo. During her eight-day break two replacement Sea Furies were transferred from *Unicorn* and, in freezing winter conditions, ammunition was embarked. Captain Colquhoun left the ship for medical treatment, and the Executive Officer, Cdr R. L. Alexander DSO DSC, temporarily assumed command until shortly before the ship sailed, when Captain Colquhoun returned.

Glory's second patrol began on Sunday 24 February, when she left Sasebo for the operational area, where she relieved USS *Bairoko.* Flying operations began on 25 February, with rocket attacks on troop concentrations near Chinnampo and next day attacks were made on ammunition convoys and railway installations. During this patrol the 5,000th deck landing was recorded and after replenishment, flying operations began again on 1 March. Next day a Sea Fury returning from a combined CAP and armed reconnaissance mission was forced to ditch astern of the carrier but, already airborne, the ship's helicopter rescued the pilot in exactly one minute. Two days later a catapult failure and shortage of RATOG equipment reduced the number of sorties flown, and on 5 March *Glory* set course for Kure, where she arrived at 15.30 the next day. The carrier's third patrol began on Wednesday 12 March when, with her escorts, *Glory* sailed for the operating area. Once again the air strikes targeted enemy troops and communications, but on 15 March Lt R. J. Overton was lost in a fatal accident when his Sea Fury which had been strafing in the Chinnampo area, was hit by anti-aircraft fire and crashed into a hillside. On 17 March, with reports of an impending Communist attack on Sok-to Island, *Glory* mounted a full-scale air offensive on enemy targets in the area. During a day of intensive flying a total of 106 sorties was launched, which was a record for a light fleet carrier and demonstrated a magnificent effort by aircrews and maintenance personnel. Next day congratulations were received from the C-in-C at Singapore, and from the Admiralty. With the rest of the patrol being hampered by poor weather, during the evening of 22 March *Glory* left the operational area and next day secured to her buoy at Sasebo.

On Monday 31 March, after an eight-day break, *Glory* left Sasebo for her next patrol. This time she was carrying a Royal Navy Dragonfly helicopter and crew, which was to work with the US Navy machine. Steaming into heavy seas and gale force winds, speed was reduced in order to allow the escorts to maintain station. At 06.15 on 1 April, with the force still 52 miles south of its operating position, flying operations were commenced, with bombing missions being mounted on targets at Simpo and Kyomipo. Air cover was provided for minesweeping operations in the Chinnampo Estuary and spotters were provided for *Ceylon* and *Chevalier,* which were bombarding enemy gun positions on the Amgak Peninsular. Despite strong winds some 59 sorties were flown, and next day when the catapult broke down several times, 54 sorties were achieved. On 4 April, despite persistent fog, 56 sorties were flown, some providing close air support for the 1st US Army Corps. On 6 April operations against shore targets were resumed, with the aircraft attacking railways and bridges and next day sorties were flown in support of British troops of the 28th Commonwealth Brigade. On 8 April 61 sorties were flown, and at the end of the day the popular US Navy helicopter and its crew left the ship. The loan of the helicopter had been of the utmost value, and it demonstrated the advantages of the helicopter over any other form of SAR aircraft. On 11 April, when *Glory* secured at her berth in Kure, she had steamed some 80,000 miles since the start of the commission, and accomplished over 6,000 deck landings.

Glory's fifth patrol began at 07.00 on Thursday 17 April, when she left Kure for the operational area. During the first four days fog reduced the number of sorties flown, but once again troop concentrations and lines of communication were attacked. At 15.30 on Tuesday 22 April *Glory's* new commanding officer, Captain T. A. K. Maunsell RN, arrived on board in a US Navy Avenger, and next day Captain Colquhoun transferred by jackstay to HMNZS *Rotoiti* for passage to Sasebo. On 24 April *Glory's* aircraft were again attacking enemy targets, and although a Sea Fury was lost on 28 April there were no further casualties. Tuesday 29 April was *Glory's* final operational day of the deployment, and once the aircraft had landed safely on board, she set course for Sasebo. It had been decided that *Ocean* would relieve her on station in order to provide a break from the intensive flying operations, but this time there was to be no refit in Australia for she had to take over *Ocean's* duties with the Mediterranean Fleet. Since leaving the UK in January 1951, *Glory* had steamed some 85,000 miles, had operated off four continents and had recorded more than 6,000 aircraft landings. During operations off Korea she had lost nine crew members and 27 aircraft, with 140 having been damaged. On the plus side, 24 aircrew members had been rescued after their

Winter conditions on the flight deck, and...

...Heavy weather during *Glory's* second tour of operations off the Korean coast.
(Fleet Air Arm Museum, Cars G/84 & Sea Fury/145)

An aerial view of *Glory* during operations off Korea.
(Fleet Air Arm Museum, Cars G/69)

planes had been shot down.

On 1 May *Glory* left Sasebo for Hong Kong, where she arrived two days later to find *Ocean* in harbour and during the next three days stores and aircraft were transferred to *Ocean.* On Monday 5 May, the C-in-C FES visited *Glory,* and next day the carrier set course for Malta. There were brief stops at Singapore and Aden before, on 23 May, *Glory* began her transit of the Suez Canal and three days later she arrived in Malta, where she was taken into dockyard hands and placed in the floating dry dock. Shortly after her arrival in Malta the personnel of the 14th Carrier Air Group, together with the remaining aircraft, were disembarked to *Theseus* for the passage home. The spell in Malta made a pleasant change for the ship's company, but on Thursday 3 July, with the maintenance work completed, *Glory* and the destroyer *Chevron* left Grand Harbour for Port Said, where they arrived three days later. During the five hours spent in harbour stores and 100 members of the ship's company who had been landed at the British Suez Canal base in May were embarked before the carrier returned to Malta. On 21 July Vice-Admiral R. A. B. Edwards, Flag Officer Second-in-Command, Mediterranean Fleet, hoisted his flag in *Glory* and the carrier left Malta. Once at sea the Sea Furies of 807 and 898 Squadrons were flown on and *Glory* rendezvoused with the cruiser *Cleopatra,* the Canadian aircraft carrier *Magnificent* and the destroyers *Chevron* and *Chivalrous,* for a visit to Istanbul. The squadron arrived in the Bosporus during the forenoon of 24 July, to anchor off the Turkish capital for what was scheduled to be a six-day visit.

Two days before the ships arrived in Istanbul, however, political events were taking shape which would cut short the fleet's summer cruise. A group of Egyptian Army officers led by Colonel Gamal Abdul Nasser and Anwar-el-Sadat were plotting to take over the country's government and they were known to be opposed to any British military presence in Egypt. Their immediate concern, however, was the corrupt administration of King Farouk and his refusal to dismiss his own favourites as government ministers. Events came to a head in July 1952 when Farouk made known his intention of appointing his brother-in-law as War Minister, which led to a coup by the Army officers. They acted during the evening of 22 July, and by 26 July Army tanks surrounded Farouk's palace in Alexandria. That same day Farouk abdicated and left Egypt in his luxury yacht. The coup had been swift and efficient and although Farouk had asked for British troops to occupy Cairo, the Prime Minister Winston Churchill wisely demurred but, in case of widespread civil unrest in the country, the Government ordered naval units to move closer to Egypt.

While *Glory* and the other units lay at Istanbul, the evening of 26 July saw a sudden recall of liberty men and steam was ordered to be raised immediately. In the event the squadron, including *Glory,* left Istanbul at 04.00 on 27 July bound for North Africa and the coast of Libya. At the same time other units of the Mediterranean Fleet left Malta, with the official communiqué describing their mission as being, 'in connexion with safeguarding British interests in Egypt, should the necessity arise.' After a fast passage south *Glory* arrived in Tobruk's outer harbour during the afternoon of 28 July, but by then it was clear that there was no immediate threat to Britain's interests in Egypt and that evening the force was ordered north to Cyprus. During the evening of 30 July *Glory* anchored off Larnaca, remaining in the vicinity until 15 August, when she returned to Grand Harbour.

Glory remained at Malta until Monday 1 September, when she left harbour to land on nine Sea Furies of 801 Squadron and eight Fireflies of 821 Squadron, which were to form her new Air Group. For ten days the carrier carried out an intensive period of flying training off Malta, during which there was only one major mishap when, at 07.37 on 10 September, Sea Fury 162 was lost over the side when launching. Fortunately the pilot was rescued by *Chieftain,* and two days later *Glory* returned to Grand Harbour. On 12 September, flying the flag of Vice-Admiral F. R. Parham, Flag Officer (Flotillas) Mediterranean, and accompanied by the destroyers *Chequers, Chevron* and *Chieftain, Glory* left Malta on 12 September to pay a five-day official visit to Spain's second city, Barcelona. Diplomatically the visit was very important for it was the first time since before the start of the Spanish Civil War that Royal Navy units had visited the port. At a diplomatic level there were receptions in honour of senior Spanish Government ministers, while the ships' companies were treated to a programme of entertainment by the city's authorities. The visit ended on 20 September, when the force sailed for Grand Harbour, and on her return *Glory* completed a seven-day maintenance period, before undergoing more flying training in the exercise areas off Malta.

Accompanied by the destroyer *Daring, Glory* left Malta during the afternoon of 9 October, being seen off by aircraft from Hal Far and Luqa which flew past in formation. They were also saluted by units of the 1st Destroyer Squadron, which steamed past *Glory* with farewell signals flying. By the evening of 13 October both *Glory* and *Daring* had completed their Suez Canal transit, and in the northern area of the Red Sea flying practice was resumed. On 15 October *Daring* detached to Port Sudan, after which she returned to Suez, while *Glory* continued her voyage east. South of Ceylon the carrier's aircraft practised reconnaissance flights over the island and on 27 October, as she steamed south through the Strait of Malacca, her aircraft flew 30 sorties to attack a Communist terrorist gang who were hiding in thick forest in the south-western part of the Malayan state of Selangor. The attacks were co-ordinated with a troop of No 93 Field Battery, Royal

Artillery, who also shelled the terrorists. *Glory* arrived in Singapore on 28 October, and three days later she was bound for Hong Kong. Once off the coast of Hong Kong the carrier took part in 'Exercise Taipan', to test the naval and air defence capabilities of the colony. On 3 November a Firefly ditched on take-off, but fortunately the pilot and his passenger were rescued by *Comus.* At 04.30 on Tuesday 4 November *Glory* rendezvoused with *Ocean,* and after transferring five Sea Furies, three Fireflies and two Dragonfly SAR helicopters from *Ocean* to *Glory* both carriers entered Hong Kong Harbour. Once in harbour *Glory* took over from *Ocean* and during the afternoon of 6 November *Glory* left for Sasebo, arriving there on Sunday 9 November after a rough passage. Captain Maunsell was able to report: '801 Sea Fury Squadron and 821 Firefly Squadron are now fully worked up and the ship is ready to start her third tour of duty with the United Nations Forces.'

On Monday 10 November, flying the flag of Rear-Admiral E. G. A. Clifford, FO2 FES, *Glory* left Sasebo for her patrol off the west coast of Korea. During the initial three days it had been intended that the squadrons would carry out as much reconnaissance as possible over the operational area in order to familiarize aircrews with the area and provide up-to-date target information. However, first low cloud and rain, and then gale force winds, restricted flying for the first four days, so when operations did get under way the aircraft were engaged in attacks on coastal guns, as well as spotting for the cruiser *Birmingham.* Armed reconnaissance missions of coastal areas were carried out to detect any build-up of troops which might indicate an invasion of the friendly western islands. In addition systematic attacks were carried out on railway and road bridges, as well as railway tunnels, rolling stock and convoys of ox-carts, which were being used to carry ammunition. On most days the Sea Furies carried 500lb bombs, but during the armed reconnaissance missions they were armed with 20mm ammunition only. The Fireflies carried eight rockets fitted with 60lb high explosive warheads, but on occasions they were armed with four rockets or two 1,000lb bombs per aircraft. On 13 November came the first fatality when a Sea Fury being flown by Lt R. Newell-Jones was hit by anti-aircraft fire whilst on a dive-bombing mission south of Sariwon. Later that day a Firefly was forced to ditch in the sea, but the pilot was rescued safely. The patrol ended at Sasebo on 20 November, and six days later FO2 transferred his flag to *Unicorn,* which had arrived from Singapore with aircraft from *Ocean.*

When *Glory* left Sasebo on Friday 28 November to return to the operational area, Captain Maunsell was suffering from an attack of gastritis, and command of the ship was taken over by the Executive Officer, Cdr D. E. Bromley-Martin. Although Captain Maunsell returned to duty the next day, on 30 November he was again taken ill and transferred to *Consort* for passage to Sasebo. In the meantime Cdr Bromley-Martin was appointed Acting Captain and he resumed command of *Glory.* During this second patrol flying had to be cancelled on three days, but attacks were made on rail and road bridges, transport and troop concentrations, while close air support was provided for Commonwealth troops. During the patrol a number of aircraft were damaged by flak and one plane was forced to ditch, but the pilot was picked up from the sea, some 26 miles from the ship. *Glory's* second patrol ended at Kure during the afternoon of 9 December.

On Sunday 14 December, whilst the carrier was at Kure, Captain E. D. G. Lewin DSO DSC* RN relieved A/Captain Bromley-Martin, who resumed his duties as Executive Officer. Captain Lewin was a distinguished Fleet Air Arm officer, who had flown the Sea Fox from HMS *Ajax* during the Battle of the River Plate, for which he was awarded the DSC. *Glory* left Kure for her third patrol on 15 December and once again the aircraft targeted road and rail transport, troop concentrations and stores depots, with the Sea Furies directing their main efforts at railway bridges. On Tuesday 16 December one of the Dragonfly SAR helicopters, having been caught in a crosswind, crashed into the sea, with the loss of its two crew members, Lt A. P. Daniels and A/C1 E. R. Ripley. *Glory* spent Christmas Day at sea, with flying operations beginning at 08.45 and continuing until 17.30. That day a Firefly being flown by Lt R. E. Barrett was shot down west of Haeju, with the loss of the pilot. With the final operations taking place on 27 December, after flying on replacement aircraft off Iwakuni, *Glory* arrived in Sasebo on 29 December, for belated Christmas celebrations and in time to see in the New Year.

Glory's fourth patrol began on 4 January 1953, with atrocious weather conditions, including gale force winds and blizzards, disrupting the flying programme. Although reconnaissance was difficult, railway lines were attacked, as well as supply dumps and troop concentrations. Spotting missions were flown for the battleship USS *Missouri,* and on 5 January Lt (E) D. G. Mather successfully baled out of his Sea Fury after being shot down, but he was captured by Communist troops and spent eight harrowing months in captivity. Not knowing what fate had befallen Lt Mather, a Sea Fury which was escorting a rescue helicopter crashed while on its rescue mission with the loss of the pilot, Sub-Lt B. E. Raynor. That afternoon a Firefly was seen to crash with the loss of its pilot, Sub-Lt J. M. Simmonds. The day's flying had taken a heavy toll. Next day, 6 January, flying started early, and that afternoon there was a visit from Rear-Admiral Clifford, the Commander of the US 7th Fleet, Vice-Admiral J. J. Clark USN and the Commander of Task Force 95, Rear-Admiral J. E. Ginnrich USN, who all spent the day on board watching flying operations. That afternoon a Firefly was forced to ditch in the sea, but the pilot was rescued safely. Sunday 11 January saw the final day of operations, and two days later *Glory* returned to

Kure to carry out maintenance.

On Monday 19 January *Glory* left Kure to relieve USS *Badoeng Strait* and to begin her fifth patrol in waters which were virtually frozen over in the coastal areas. During the patrol no aircraft were lost and by 29 January the carrier was safely back at her buoy in Sasebo Harbour. *Glory's* sixth patrol began on 5 February, with the main air effort being directed against troop concentrations and stores dumps. Attacks were also made on troop concentrations and railway lines, and on 6 February four Sea Furies were attacked by two enemy MiG 15s, but no damage was caused. On 9 February a damaged Sea Fury was forced to ditch in the sea, but the pilot was quickly rescued by helicopter, and that same day a Firefly ditched in the sea whilst attempting to land on. Fortunately both the pilot and his Army passenger were rescued. Next day another Firefly ditched immediately after launch, but once again the aircrew were rescued. On 11 February, however, a Sea Fury was shot down and the pilot Lt C. A. MacPherson, was killed. On 14 February a total of 75 sorties was flown, which was the greatest number achieved on one day since the carrier returned to Korean waters in November 1952. Sadly, that day saw another fatality when a Sea Fury which suffered an engine failure as it attempted to land on, crashed into the sea with the loss of its pilot, Sub-Lt R. D. Bradley. Next day *Glory* left the operational area and returned to Kure.

A Sea Fury mishap on the flight deck.
(Fleet Air Arm Museum, Sea Fury/215)

The carrier's seventh patrol began on 24 February, and despite fog, rain, snow and gale force winds, the main air effort was again directed against troop concentrations and stores dumps. With the last sorties being launched on 6 March, *Glory* arrived in Sasebo the next afternoon for an eight-day break. The eighth patrol began on 15 March and lasted for 12 days, until 27 March, when *Glory* returned to Kure to berth adjacent to the maintenance carrier *Unicorn*. *Glory's* ninth period of operations began on 2 April and despite the fact that fog hampered flying, on 5 April the carrier launched 123 sorties, which equalled a record set by *Ocean* in the summer of 1952. The patrol ended on 12 April at Sasebo, and six days later she sailed for her tenth patrol. With an exchange of prisoners of war taking place *Glory's* target areas were more limited than usual, but her pilots prevented enemy troop movements down the west coast. On 25 April two Sea Furies were shot down with the loss of two more pilots, Lt J. T. McGregor and Sub-Lt W. J. B. Keates, but four days later the patrol ended when, at 10.45 on Wednesday 29 April, the carrier secured alongside at Kure. *Glory's* eleventh, and final, patrol began on 4 May and happily there were no casualties. The last operational sortie ended at 14.39 on 14 May when a Firefly flown by Lt B. V. Bacon landed on and *Glory* set course for Iwakuni. That evening, at 18.00, the lower deck was cleared and a memorial service was held for all the officers and men who had lost their lives. After flying off some aircraft to Iwakuni, *Glory* arrived in Sasebo at 17.10 on 17 May, some 20 minutes after *Ocean* had arrived from Hong Kong. During the handover period congratulations were received from Vice-Admiral Clark USN and from FO2 FES, as *Glory* had completed the longest period of air operations of any Commonwealth carrier during the Korean War. Since leaving the UK in January 1951 she had spent 530 days at sea and steamed 157,000 miles. During that period she had completed 15 months' war service and spent 316 days at sea in Korean waters. Of a total of 13,700 flights from her deck over 9,500 had been operational sorties over North Korea. Her aircraft had taken a constant toll of enemy troops and a wide range of military targets had been attacked. During two Korean winters ice and snow had repeatedly been cleared from the flight deck, while operations had been sustained in some of the worst weather experienced by naval aircrews.

With everyone eager to start the passage home, *Glory* left Sasebo on 19 May, steaming by way of Hong Kong, Singapore and Aden. On 22 June she made her Suez Canal transit, and after calling at Malta and Gibraltar, on Tuesday 7 July, after two and a half years away from home, she anchored in Falmouth Roads for Customs clearance. That night she steamed up Channel to receive a tremendous welcome as she entered Portsmouth Harbour and secured alongside North Corner Jetty at 11.30. It was not quite the end of the commission, however, and on Friday 24 July *Glory* left Portsmouth to set course, via the Dover Strait, for Rosyth, where she arrived three days later for a refit.

Glory spent the summer of 1953 in dry dock at Rosyth, and on Thursday 3 September her new commanding officer, Captain R. T. White DSO** RN, was appointed. On Wednesday 23 September, with a new ship's company having joined the ship, *Glory* was shifted from the dry dock and secured to the basin wall at Rosyth Dockyard. Five weeks later, on 22 October, she left Rosyth to carry out engine trials, and to set course for Portsmouth where she arrived on 27 October. She was recommissioned on Saturday 31 October, and two days later she put to sea to land on the Sea Furies of 801 Squadron, the Fireflies of 826 Squadron, three Skyraider AEW1 aircraft of 849C Flight and the two Dragonfly helicopters of the ship's flight. For three days the aircraft were put through their paces before, on 6 November, she left Plymouth Sound and set course for the Mediterranean. *Glory* was taking the place of *Theseus* in the Mediterranean Fleet, and she arrived in Grand Harbour during the afternoon of Friday 13 November. Five days later she left harbour to continue the work-up training which had been started off Portland, but on Saturday 21 November, with the carrier having returned to Grand Harbour for the weekend, there was a fatal accident on the flight deck. As one of the Dragonfly helicopters was operating, Commissioned Air Engineer F. G. Bradbrook was killed instantly by the tail rotor of the machine. The last week of November was spent operating off Tripoli, and on 29 November, having returned to Grand Harbour, the C-in-C Mediterranean Fleet, Admiral Lord Mountbatten, inspected the ship's company at Divisions on the flight deck.

The first three weeks of December were spent mainly at sea, but on 17 December *Glory* entered Grand Harbour to celebrate Christmas and the New Year. On 4 January 1954, with the festivities over, the carrier left Malta to take part in exercises with other units of the fleet, including *Bermuda, Glasgow, Daring* and *St Kitts.* On 22 January there was a visit to Naples, but during the first week of February, whilst the ship was in Grand Harbour, a number of minor acts of sabotage were discovered on board. Although the ship's operational capability was not affected, there was a full investigation and a rating was subsequently convicted of malicious damage and sentenced to a period of imprisonment. After taking part in 'Exercise Febex' with the cruisers *Gambia* and *Glasgow,* on 15 February *Glory* left the Mediterranean to return home via Villefranche and Gibraltar. During the passage home she exercised in the Western Mediterranean with the fleet carrier *Eagle,* and on the last day of February she carried out her final fixed-wing flying operations as all her aircraft were launched to Lee-on-the-Solent. On Monday 1 March, after flying off the helicopters, she entered Portsmouth Harbour to spend two weeks at a buoy in Fareham Creek. Between 9 and 13 April she steamed out to Spithead, returning to Portsmouth for Navy Days where some very popular helicopter flying displays were staged from the flight deck.

In mid-May *Glory* was placed in dry dock and she remained there until 2 June, when she was shifted to

Replenishment at sea between *Glory* and a Colony-class cruiser. *(Fleet Air Museum, Cars G/131)*

Middle Slip Jetty. On Wednesday 7 July Captain H. W. S. Sims-Williams took command of *Glory* and in early September she was prepared for her final operational role, as a transport ship. Between mid-September and early December 1954 she made a passenger and cargo voyage to Singapore, carrying Whirlwind and Sycamore helicopters for use in the Malayan Emergency, together with RN and RAF personnel. On 30 September, whilst making her southbound transit of the Suez Canal she ran aground and it took eight hours to refloat her. During the passage home she carried a cargo of Sea Hawk aircraft for which there were insufficient trained pilots in the Far East, and Christmas and the New Year of 1955 were spent at Portsmouth. In January 1955 the winter weather in Scotland took a hand in prolonging the carrier's career when severe snowstorms cut off many villages and isolated communities. To assist with the emergency two Navy Whirlwind helicopters were operated from the airport at Wick, being supplied with fuel by the destroyer *Urchin,* which anchored in Wicks Bay. Meanwhile *Glory* had steamed north from Portsmouth to Glasgow in order to unload her cargo of Sea Hawks and she was in an ideal position to assist with 'Operation Snowdrop', the delivery of food, animal fodder and medical supplies to areas which were cut off. On 18 January *Glory* left the Clyde and steamed north to Loch Eriboll, where she anchored to provide a co-ordination and refuelling centre for the naval helicopters operating from Wick. Finally, however, after a week of intensive flying operations, more permanent supply routes were organized and *Glory* continued her passage round Scotland's north coast for Rosyth Dockyard where she arrived in the last week of January, to begin a refit before being placed in reserve. On Tuesday 22 February, with the ship having been taken over by the dockyard, *Glory* was paid off.

On 5 April 1956, after 14 months in dockyard hands during which time the ship was given a complete overhaul, *Glory* was recommissioned at Rosyth for sea trials, with a much reduced ship's company. Five days later Captain T. N. Masterman OBE RN arrived to take command and by the weekend of 5 May the ship was ready for sea. On 8 May *Glory* left Rosyth to carry out full-power trials and six days later she arrived at Devonport and secured to a buoy in the Hamoaze. On 4 June the C-in-C Plymouth visited the ship and seven days later she left harbour to carry out speed trials before setting course for the Bristol Channel, where she embarked observers for an air control exercise. During the exercise two Whirlwind helicopters used *Glory* as their base, and after disembarking the visitors later in the day she set course for Rosyth. During the forenoon of 14 June *Glory* met the newer light fleet carrier *Bulwark,* and that afternoon Captain Masterman was able to visit her by helicopter. During the morning of 15 June *Glory* arrived back at Rosyth, and by 08.15 she was secured in the main basin. She had completed her final voyage under her own steam, and at 12.00 on Friday 22 June 1956 she was finally paid off. *Glory* remained in reserve at Rosyth and in 1957, having been joined on the disposal list by her sisters *Ocean* and *Theseus,* she was put up for sale. There were rumours about her eventual fate, and a question was tabled in Parliament as to whether she might be used as a troop transport. *Glory* lay moored and rusting in the Firth of Forth for the best part of five years, but finally, in August 1961, she was towed the short distance to Inverkeithing where she was broken up.

Commanding Officers:

Captain Sir A. W. Buzzard OBE DSO RN	1 November 1944
Captain W. T. Couchman DSO OBE RN	7 September 1946
Captain E. H. Shattock OBE RN	15 August 1949
Captain H. Traill CBE RN	27 December 1949
Captain E. H. Shattock OBE RN	12 February 1950
Captain K. S. Colquhoun DSO RN	28 December 1950
Captain T. A. K. Maunsell RN	23 April 1952
Acting Captain D. E. Bromley RN	30 November 1952
Captain E. D. G. Lewin DSO DSC* RN	14 December 1952
Captain R. T. White DSO** RN	3 September 1953
Captain H. W. S. Sims-Williams RN	7 July 1954
Captain T. N. Masterman OBE RN	10 April 1956

Battle Honours:

The Glorious First of June 1794 — Martinique 1809
Guadeloupe 1810 — Dardanelles 1915
Korea 1950-53

Chapter Eight

HMS *Ocean*
May 1945 – July 1948

The fifth aircraft carrier of the Colossus class to be commissioned was HMS *Ocean* but, unlike her earlier sisters, she was not ready for operational service before the end of the Second World War. The contract for building the ship went to the Glasgow company of Alexander Stephen & Sons and, with the first keel plates having been laid at their Linthouse shipyard on 8 November 1942, she became Yard No 598. Despite the fact that there was an acute shortage of skilled men and materials, the new carrier's hull was ready for launching in the summer of 1944, and the ceremony took place at high tide during the afternoon of Saturday 8 July. Although the carrier's hull was by no means the heaviest built on the Linthouse slipways, at 690 feet it was the longest by almost 80 feet. Prior to this the longest hull launched at the yard was P&O's luxury liner, *Viceroy of India,* in 1928 and at 612 feet it was thought that this would be the maximum length possible in this particularly narrow stretch of the River Clyde, but clearly the urgencies of war overcame such anxieties. The sponsor for the new aircraft carrier was Lady Olive Willis who, as well as being the wife of the Second Sea Lord, Vice-Admiral Sir Algernon Willis, was in her own right a senior officer of the St John's Ambulance Service. As such a large ship was involved and with such tight margins of clearance, all available Clyde tugs stood by that afternoon, but as *Ocean* took to the water all went well and it was not long before she had been towed to the fitting-out basin in the Linthouse shipyard. In May 1945 *Ocean's* first commanding officer, Captain Caspar John RN, was appointed to the ship, which was nearing completion. Captain John was an experienced Fleet Air Arm Officer who had entered the Navy as a cadet in 1916. As a midshipman he served in the battleship *Iron Duke,* and as a sub lieutenant in the aircraft carrier *Hermes* he was clearly an early convert to naval aviation for he soon qualified as a pilot and returned to *Hermes* as a pilot attached to the RAF. In the 1930s he served in *Argus, Courageous* and the cruiser *Exeter,* and when war broke out in 1939 he was serving as the Executive Officer of the cruiser *York.* Later in the war, having been promoted to Captain, he commanded the trials and training aircraft carrier, *Pretoria Castle,* which was a converted Union Castle Line passenger liner, and it was from there that he was appointed to *Ocean.* A few weeks later, at 08.00 on Saturday 30 June, the ship was commissioned by the advance party and shortly afterwards, at 09.35, the main draft of 58 officers and 346 men arrived by train from Chatham. For the time being the new aircraft carrier would be manned by a much reduced complement.

Over the days that followed more men joined from Chatham and on Sunday 1 July the ship was opened to the employees of Alexander Stephen & Sons, who turned out in force to look round this, the largest, vessel which had been built at their shipyard. Three days later, at 07.50 on Wednesday 4 July the mooring ropes were slipped and with four tugs in attendance *Ocean* made her first passage under her own steam, as she was shifted the short distance from the Linthouse shipyard to the King George V Dock, off the Renfrew Road, where she was secured to await the high tide on the following day. After spending the night in the dock, at 08.06 on 5 July, *Ocean's* mooring ropes were again slipped and, with her four tugs in attendance, she steamed slowly downriver. At just after 10.00 Port Glasgow was abeam and an hour later she was secured in the Admiralty Floating Dock at Helensburgh, where her underwater hull was scraped and painted. *Ocean* remained in dry dock until the afternoon of Monday 16 July when she was refloated and anchored off Greenock. On 19 July she steamed out into the Firth of Clyde to carry out initial machinery trials, but by the end of the afternoon watch she had returned to a buoy at Greenock. Over the next few days two Fairey Fireflies and two Grumman Hellcats were embarked from lighters to give the aircraft handlers some practice, but the carrier remained off Greenock until 1 August when she put to sea for three hours of steaming trials. During the following four days *Ocean* steamed into the Firth of Clyde on three occasions to undergo main machinery trials and on Sunday 5 August she ran full-power trials over the Arran measured mile, achieving a speed of 25.78 knots. Finally, however, at 09.00 on Tuesday 7 August she left her buoy at Greenock to begin her flying trials and at 10.30 'Flying Stations' was piped for the first time. Half an hour later, having turned into the wind, the first deck landing was made by a Fairey Barracuda. This was followed by astern power engine trials and it was not until the afternoon that, with the assistance of the accelerator, the Barracuda was launched. Following this initial flying trials continued with a break on 9 August, until 17.30 on 11 August, with a variety of aircraft landing on and flying off. Sunday 12 August was spent at anchor off Greenock with stores being embarked, and during the evening of 14 August *Ocean* left the Clyde to steam south for the River Mersey where she

Ocean on the slipway at Alexander Stephen & Sons' Linthouse shipyard on the Clyde. With the platform having been erected under her stem it is clear she is being prepared for launching. *(UCS3/16/13/1 University of Glasgow Archive)*

anchored the following afternoon. By the evening of 17 August the carrier was secured alongside the north wall of Bootle's Gladstone Dock and she remained there until the first week of November whilst a new main engine turbine rotor and the latest radar equipment were fitted.

On Friday 2 November, with the refit work coming to an end, the Royal Marines Band from Chatham joined the ship, and two days later *Ocean's* chapel was dedicated by the Chaplain of the Fleet. Finally, at 08.00 on Tuesday 6 November, following the arrival of a draft of 158 ratings from Chatham, *Ocean* was recommissioned, but this time with a full complement and work began to prepare the carrier for sea once again. During the forenoon of 16 November *Ocean* left the Gladstone Dock and the River Mersey to steam north for the Firth of Clyde and that evening she anchored off Greenock. On 21 November *Ocean* began an eight-day period of flying with Barracudas and the Hellcats of 892 Squadron. During the first five days *Ocean* operated in the Firth of Clyde with the destroyer *Anthony*, and as well as operating the Fireflies and Hellcats she made the last operational launch of a Fairey Swordfish biplane. Each evening, on completion of flying, she would anchor in Brodick Bay, but during the forenoon of Monday 26 November she set course south, with flying trials continuing as she steamed through the Irish Sea. By next day *Ocean* was operating in the area off Land's End and at 08.30 she commenced landing on ten Hellcats of 892 Squadron. Just over half an hour later there came the first fatal accident when one of the aircraft crashed and killed one of the flight deck personnel, CPO J. H. Baynton. Later that day, at 16.00, his funeral service took place on the quarterdeck. Next day, after flying off the Hellcats, *Ocean* began her passage up Channel and off Start Point she passed the battleship *Rodney*, with salutes being exchanged. Finally, with her flying trials having been completed successfully, during the morning of 29 November the carrier anchored at Spithead where, for the 'Pompey' men there was the prospect of some time at home before, in early December, *Ocean* made aviation history.

At 09.00 on Monday 3 December, after embarking a number of VIPs, including the chief designer of the de Havilland Aircraft Company, a Government Minister and Admiral Sir Denis Boyd, the Chief of Naval Air Equipment, *Ocean* weighed anchor and steamed into the Channel on what was an overcast day, into a moderate swell and 17-knot south-westerly winds. At 10.05 the ship went to 'Flying Stations' and an hour later at RNAS Ford, Lt-Cdr Eric M. Brown RN, who was the Royal Navy's Chief Test Pilot, took off in a prototype de Havilland Vampire jet fighter, bound for *Ocean* where he was to make the first pure jet carrier landing. Captain Brown describes his experience: 'In overcast conditions I found *Ocean* ploughing along rhythmically, and screeched over her with a low pass and roll to announce my arrival. Unknown to me at that precise moment the ship's loudspeakers were announcing that the Vampire had been ordered to return to Ford because the boffins felt the flight deck was pitching excessively. However, Caspar John had been captain of *Pretoria Castle,* the trials carrier, when I was in Service Trials Unit, so he knew me well and he immediately decided to accept me for landing. The combined ship's speed and wind speed over the deck was given to me by radio as 38 knots with the flight deck pitching 12 feet at the stern and rolling five degrees.' Lt-Cdr Brown's landing circuit was begun at 1,000 feet, at 200 mph, with the Vampire's engine well throttled back. His final turn-in was a fairly wide sweep made in nose down attitude at 115 mph, losing 100 feet in height so that his straight approach was begun from 300 feet. Once again he takes up the story: 'Speed was reduced gradually to 100 mph, until a position about 150 feet aft of the round down and 30 feet above the flight deck was assumed. From this position the throttle was cut and no further movement on the elevators made until the round down was crossed at 95 mph, then the stick was eased back fairly sharply until the aircraft stalled completely as felt by the kick on the port aileron as the port wing dropped. Although I aimed for No 4 arrester wire, the flight deck was on the upswing of its pitch as I crossed the round down and in consequence the hook picked up No 1 wire and I came to a halt with astonishingly mild deceleration.' Lt-Cdr Brown had successfully accomplished the first deck landing of a jet aircraft, and the ship's log recorded the event thus: '11.27 - De H Vampire landed on'.

The Vampire trials continued each day, with Lt-Cdr Brown making a number of landings and take-offs, which he describes as follows: 'The aircraft was held on the brakes until the full 10,200 rpm were reached on run-up, and then released and the stick held central until 60 mph registered on the ASI when the stick was eased back until the tail booms were estimated to be one foot off the deck and I passed the island superstructure at bridge level.' During the afternoon of Thursday 6 December, with the Vampire trials having been completed, Lt-Cdr Brown took off from *Ocean's* flight deck and flew ashore. *Ocean* continued with further flying exercises with the Fireflies of 1792 Squadron before she anchored at Greenock on 12 December to embark squadron stores and the personnel of 892 (Hellcat) Squadron. Three days later, during the forenoon of 15 December, she left home waters and set course for Gibraltar. The passage south took the carrier into the Atlantic Ocean, west of Ireland, and during the forenoon of 18 December, with Force 9 gales blowing and heavy seas, A/PO Lyle was lost overboard. With the ship rolling at up to 25 degrees to both port and starboard, a search was made for the missing man, but with no success. Four days later *Ocean* secured alongside Gibraltar's south mole, where Christmas Day was celebrated. Two days later *Ocean* was at sea again and carrying out flying operations in the exercise areas of the Western Mediterranean. At 10.00 on 27 December, just an hour after the ship left harbour, Lt (E) Parker was seriously injured by the rotating propeller of one of the aircraft, and he was taken to the military hospital in Gibraltar. *Ocean* returned to harbour for two days, but at 11.06 on New Year's Eve, escorted by the destroyer *Maywell,* she left Gibraltar to head east for Malta. Four days later, on 4 January 1946, the carrier arrived in Grand Harbour, but this initial visit was limited to just the weekend.

When *Ocean* sailed on 7 January, she would spend each weekday at sea carrying out flying practice, including the first night landings on board, then on 18 January, after flying off ten Fireflies and 12 Hellcats to Hal Far, she secured alongside Parlatorio Wharf to undergo her first dockyard-assisted maintenance period. During the 18 days she spent alongside, the establishments of Strait Street, better known as 'The Gut', were well frequented, but by 5 February *Ocean* was at sea again and, escorted by *Cheviot* and *Childers,* carrying out flying training and torpedo exercises with the two destroyers. Later in the month there were night encounter exercises with *Meywell, Sirius, Peacock* and *Wigtown Bay,* but on 22 February the carrier returned to Grand Harbour. The break was short-lived, however, and on 25 February, together with *Meywell,* she left Grand Harbour and set course for Alexandria. At the end of the Second World War Egypt, which was ostensibly an independent country, had become a gigantic staging centre for British military forces in the Middle East, and the presence of so many British troops in the country was, in the words of the Egyptian Prime Minister, 'wounding to the national dignity'. On 21 February 1946 the Egyptian people gave an alarming display of their feelings with

At anchor in the Firth of Clyde soon after leaving the builder's yard. *(UCS3/16/13/6 University of Glasgow Archive)*

violent rioting and attacks on British service clubs and other property in Cairo. The Kasr-el-Nil barracks came under heavy siege and in relieving it the Egyptian police inflicted 140 casualties. Although the British Government opened negotiations for a complete withdrawal of British forces in Egypt, it was to be a protracted departure and, with her escort, *Ocean* was dispatched to protect British interests in Alexandria. The two ships arrived in Alexandria on the last day of February, and four days later further rioting broke out in the port city. During the disturbances two British military policemen were killed by a mob, but fortunately the riots were soon suppressed by the Egyptian police.

On 6 March, with order having been restored to the streets of Cairo and Alexandria, *Ocean* and *Meywell* left for the waters off Cyprus where, with *Chaplet, Charity, Chequers, Chevron* and *Childers* they took part in night encounter exercises. On 8 March *Ocean* had to anchor off Limassol for maintenence work on a sick starboard main engine, but five days later she left for exercises in Souda Bay. By 15 March *Ocean* had returned to Grand Harbour and for the remainder of the month she operated in the exercise areas off Malta, carrying out night flying exercises which, on 26 March, included an all-night flying exercise from 21.27 until 04.40 the following morning. Next afternoon, after completing gunnery exercises *Ocean* returned to Grand Harbour. On 2 April the carrier left Malta to land on her aircraft and to set course for Gibraltar on the first stage of her return passage home. During the afternoon of 8 April, having embarked a number of passengers, *Ocean* and *Meywell* left Gibraltar and two days later the aircraft were flown off. In Plymouth Sound on 13 April Customs clearance was given and three days later, on 16 April, *Ocean* arrived at Rosyth. Soon after her arrival the first long leave party left the ship, and on 26 April the carrier was secured in Rosyth's No 2 dry dock.

By 1 May, as *Ocean* lay in dry dock, a large number of ship's company members who were due for demobilization had left the ship, and it was on 10 June that the carrier moved to an anchorage in mid-river. On Monday 17 June *Ocean* put to sea again and sailing by way of the Pentland Firth and Irish Sea, she steamed south for the Channel where, next afternoon, she anchored at Spithead. For the rest of the month *Ocean* operated from Spithead, carrying out deck landing practice with Seafires of 805 Squadron and the Fireflies of 816 Squadron, during which time she was visited by Rear-Admiral Sir Thomas Troubridge, and it was not until Saturday 29 June that she finally entered Portsmouth Harbour and secured to Middle Slip Jetty. The first week of July was spent operating from Spithead and on 7 July, as she steamed north to Glasgow, she called at Bangor Bay where shore leave was given and the ship was opened to visitors. At Glasgow's King George V Dock stores were embarked, and on 10 July *Ocean,* escorted by the destroyers *Fencer* and *Raider,* set course for the Mediterranean. At Gibraltar on 16 July she met her sister *Colossus,* which was returning from the Far East to be handed over to the French Navy. *Ocean* remained at Gibraltar until 1 August when she left for Malta where, three days later she met her sister *Vengeance* which, like *Colossus,* was on her way home from the Far East. For three weeks after her arrival in Maltese waters *Ocean* operated from Marsaxlokk Bay, with only one weekend being spent in harbour. On Monday 26 August, having spent the weekend in Malta, *Ocean* steamed south to carry out flying operations off the coast of Libya and on 30 August she spent three days at anchor in Tripoli's outer harbour. During the first three weeks of September *Ocean* operated from Marsaxlokk Bay, carrying out a number of exercises with other units of the Mediterranean Fleet, including an 'E-boat attack', during which the carrier was screened by the cruisers *Leander, Liverpool, Mauritius* and *Phoebe,* as well as destroyers. There was also a convoy escort exercise with the hospital ship *Maine* and the C-in-C's dispatch vessel, *Surprise,* acting as merchantmen. The end of the exercises came on Saturday 21 September, when the fleet anchored in the Gulf of Argolikos, off the town of Nauplia (Nauplion), where the fleet regatta took place. *Ocean* followed this with a four-day visit to Rhodes and a nine-day visit to Famagusta, where she anchored in the outer harbour.

After leaving Famagusta on 14 October, the carrier exercised with a number of escorts, including *Volage, Stevenstone* and *Enard Bay,* as they made their way to the Greek port of Yithian, where *Volage* and the other escorts detached and set course for Corfu. At 18.05 on Monday 21 October *Ocean* weighed anchor to steam through the Ionian Sea bound for Corfu, where she would again join other units of the fleet for joint exercises. At 08.00 on 22 October *Ocean* was in a position Lat 37° - 58'N/Long 19° - 53'E, and during the forenoon and afternoon watches flying operations took place, including reconnaissance missions over the channel separating the Greek island of Corfu and the mainland of Albania which was under the Communist regime of Enver Hoxha. Earlier that year artillery fire had been directed from Albania at the cruisers *Superb* and *Orion,* which were negotiating the narrow Corfu Channel, a recognized international waterway. Since coming to power in December 1945, Hoxha had declared his intention of, 'defending Albania's borders by land and sea,' so, in view of the shellfire, it was decided to keep a careful watch on the Albanian side of the channel. At 14.30 on 22 October, 'Action Stations' was exercised on board *Ocean* and the ship was still closed up at 14.53 when the destroyer *Saumarez,* which was negotiating the Corfu Channel, hit a mine. It exploded with devastating force and severely damaged the destroyer's starboard side, killing 29 men outright and critically injuring seven more. As the destroyer *Volage* went to the assistance of the crippled *Saumarez,* which was drifting helplessly towards the

Lt-Cdr E. M. Brown RN, the Royal Navy's Chief Test Pilot, circles *Ocean* as he prepares to make the first pure jet aircraft carrier landing.
(Fleet Air Arm Museum, Cars O/53)

Albanian shore, a signal with brief details was received in *Ocean,* but the full horror of the incident had yet to be played out, and at 15.35 the carrier's ship's company stood down from 'Action Stations'. Just over half an hour later, at 16.10, *Ocean* was ordered to proceed 'with all dispatch' to the assistance of *Saumarez.* Back at Corfu, meanwhile, *Volage* was towing the destroyer to the safety of an anchorage when, at 16.15, she too hit a mine, the force of which virtually blew off her bows, killing an officer and six men instantly. It was quite clear that the mines had been deliberately, and only recently, laid.

Meanwhile, out at sea *Ocean* was steaming hard for Corfu when news of the second explosion was received. It was not until 19.55 that she reached the northern part of the Corfu Channel in the vicinity of the two damaged destroyers. In view of the ever-present threat from mines it was decided that the carrier would not anchor immediately, and the main engines were used to maintain the ship's position. At 20.00 she stopped and ten minutes later the first two motor boats were slipped in order to collect injured men from the destroyers and return them to the sickbay, which had been prepared for the casualties. At 20.50 the third motor boat with fire-fighting parties and apparatus, led by Lt-Cdr W. P. T. Croome, *Ocean's* Air Engineer Officer, left the carrier for *Saumarez* which was still ablaze. They would have an extremely difficult task ahead of them, and meanwhile *Ocean's* sickbay quickly filled up with badly injured men. Despite the medical assistance two ratings from *Saumarez,* AB G. H. Hales and Ldg Stoker W. H. Sayers, died of their injuries on board the carrier. At 03.45 on 23 October it was decided that *Ocean* could manoeuvre to an anchorage nearby and by 04.15 she had anchored off Corfu. That morning fresh fire-fighting parties went across to *Saumarez* and by the forenoon the fires had been extinguished, but there remained the distressing task of searching for and identifying bodies, which were taken to a mortuary ashore. During the afternoon of 24 October the funerals of the victims from both damaged destroyers took place at Corfu Cemetery, and investigations began into the incident. In the event it was ascertained that Yugoslav minelayers had laid the mines for the Albanians, but both countries had hostile Communist governments, and Albania has consistently refused to acknowledge the findings of the International Court which adjudged that country as being guilty of deliberately laying the mines in the Corfu Channel.

At 18.40 on Friday 25 October, with her relief work over, *Ocean* weighed anchor and set course for Argostoli, where she arrived the following forenoon to meet other units of the Mediterranean Fleet, including the cruisers *Leander, Liverpool* and *Mauritius* and the escorts *Cardigan Bay* and *Childers.* On 5 November *Ocean* put to sea to carry out armed reconnaissance missions over the Corfu Channel and the Albanian coast whilst minesweeping operations were under way, and these continued until 14 November when the carrier returned to her anchorage at Malta's Marsaxlokk Bay. Next day, after flying off her aircraft, the carrier steamed in to Grand Harbour to secure alongside Parlatorio Wharf, where she would begin a three-week maintenance period.

At 09.00 on Saturday 16 November, Captain A. W. Clarke CBE DSO RN joined the ship, and three hours later he took command when Captain John left for the UK. Captain Clarke had served as a midshipman and sub lieutenant during the First World War, during which he took part in the Battle of Jutland. During the Second World War he commanded the cruiser *Sheffield* at the Battle of the Barents Sea, and *Ocean* was to be his last command before retirement. On 20 November the carrier entered No 4 dry dock in French Creek, Grand Harbour, but 14 days later she was back alongside Parlatorio Wharf and at 09.00 on 27 December she was at sea again carrying out flying operations off Malta. New Year's Eve was spent at anchor in Marsaxlokk Bay, but at 13.00 on 1 January 1947 *Ocean* weighed anchor for four hours of flying practice, but it was 4 January before she returned to Grand Harbour. Three days later flying operations began again and they continued on a daily basis until the afternoon of 23 January when the carrier returned to Marsaxlokk. Shortly after anchoring, Vice-Admiral Sir Cecil Harcourt, Flag Officer (Air) and FO2 Mediterranean Fleet, hoisted his flag in *Ocean* and next forenoon the carrier returned to Grand Harbour for a four-day break, before sailing to Port Said where she arrived on the last day of January. During the carrier's six-day visit shore leave was granted until midnight each day, and during the forenoon of 6 February *Ocean* slipped her moorings and steamed into the Suez Canal as far as Ismailia where she turned round and escorted the Italian battleship *Vittorio Veneto* and the destroyer *Velite* for the return passage to Port Said. The battleship, which had been damaged during the Battle of Matapan, had surrendered with the rest of the Italian Fleet in 1943, and she had been returned to the Italian Navy. However, she had been subsequently awarded to Britain as part of Italy's war reparations and the British Government had ordered that she be scrapped. *Velite* had been ordered to be handed over to the French Navy, where she served as *Duchafflault* until 1954. When *Ocean* left Port Said that same evening the two Italian warships followed her to sea and for two days the carrier's aircraft flew reconnaissance missions over them as they headed for Sicily. *Ocean,* however, returned to Malta, from where she operated for the next eight days, before leaving on 17 February for visits to Toulon, Leghorn (Livorno) and Rapollo, spending six days in each port and leaving for the return passage to Malta on 11 March. During the afternoon of 5 March, just outside Rapollo Harbour, one of the hazards left over from

A stern view of *Ocean* in August 1946 as she leaves Grand Harbour. *(Fleet Air Arm Museum, Cars O/20)*

the war, a floating mine, was spotted just off the carrier's port bow, but it was quickly dealt with by the escort destroyer *Raider.* During the remainder of March *Ocean* operated out of Malta with other units of the Mediterranean Fleet, including the cruisers *Leander, Liverpool* and *Mauritius* and, on occasions, her sister *Triumph,* which had arrived in the Mediterranean in February. On the last day of March, however, *Ocean* secured alongside Boiler Wharf in Grand Harbour's French Creek for a two-month refit, during which time she would spend three weeks in No 4 dry dock.

After leaving the dry dock on 23 May, *Ocean* was towed to nearby Boat House Wharf to complete the refit and by Thursday 5 June she was back at sea and landing on the squadrons. The rest of the month was spent operating out of Malta, with a two-day stopover at Tripoli during the weekend of 14 June, then on 9 July she returned to Grand Harbour for an eight-day break. When *Ocean* left Malta again during the forenoon of Thursday 17 July she was in company with a powerful force, which included *Liverpool* (flag C-in-C Mediterranean), *Leander,* her sister ship *Triumph* and the destroyers *Chaplet, Chequers, Chevron* and *Raider,* setting course for an official seven-day visit to Istanbul. During the morning of 21 July the force reached the Dardanelles where they were met by the Turkish Navy's flagship, the battleship *Yavuz,* which was built in 1911 as the Imperial German Navy's *Goeben.* Later that day, in glorious sunshine, the warships made their entrance into the Bosporus from the Sea of Marmara in perfect formation, while thousands of people on the hills and housetops of Pera, Scutari and Istanbul gave them a rousing welcome. Overall, the seven days at anchor off the city were a great success, for the VIPs on their official round of visits as well as the ordinary sailors on the streets of Istanbul. During the evening of 25 July, the C-in-C, Admiral Sir Algernon Willis, whose wife had launched *Ocean,* held an official function on board the carrier, which was attended by Istanbul's civic dignitaries. The force left Istanbul at 08.30 on Saturday 26 July, and after weighing anchor *Ocean* took station on *Triumph* for the passage through the Sea of Marmara and the Dardanelles. Shortly after leaving Turkish waters *Ocean* anchored off the island of Rhodes, and on the last day of July she was opened to visitors. On 1 August *Ocean* left Rhodes to make the passage to Nauplia, where she joined other units of the fleet for two days of sailing, evolutions and some limited shore leave. After leaving Nauplia on 4 August *Ocean* rejoined her sister *Triumph* and other units of the fleet to take part in manoeuvres off Cyprus, which included a towing exercise with *Mauritius* and a 'mass air attack' on the fleet by

Ocean at Grand Harbour in early 1947. *(Maritime Photo Library)*

aircraft from *Ocean, Triumph* and from RAF bases on the island. On 22 August, however, *Ocean* was back in Maltese waters and four days later she secured to a buoy in Grand Harbour's Bighi Bay.

The whole of September and the first three weeks of October were spent operating from Malta which, on 20 and 21 September, included searching for and rescuing the three-man crew of a disabled yacht. On 5 October, whilst at anchor in Aranci Bay, the C-in-C Mediterranean inspected Divisions on the flight deck and 17 days later, in Grand Harbour, FO (Air) Med inspected the mess decks. Next day, at 08.30 on 23 October, in company with *Verulam, Ocean* left Malta to set course for the coast of Palestine and her first patrol in the Navy's blockade designed to intercept illegal immigrant ships. In 1922 the League of Nations allocated the Mandate for the administration of Palestine, which had formerly been part of the Ottoman Empire. Although the terms of the Mandate stated that the Mandatory should be responsible for putting into effect the declaration originally made by the British Government in favour of establishing a national home for Jewish people (the 'Balfour Declaration' of November 1917), it also clearly stated that, 'Nothing shall be done which might prejudice the civil and religious rights of the existing non-Jewish communities in Palestine,' a reference to the Palestinian Arabs who had lived peacefully in the country for over a thousand years. Unfortunately, without consulting the Palestinians, between 1922 and 1946, the Mandatory administration had allowed almost a million, mainly European Jews, most of whom were fleeing Nazi persecution, into Palestine. By 1947 several Zionist terrorist groups, including the moderate Haganah and the more fanatical Irgun Svai Leumi (led by Menachem Begin), and the Stern Group, were well advanced with plans to seize the country and establish their own Jewish state, free of Arabs. They were also conducting a vicious terrorist campaign against British troops in Palestine, and doing their best to increase the number of Jewish settlers by smuggling illegal immigrants into the country. In 1946 the British Government, aware of the dangers that the mass Jewish immigration was causing, started the naval blockade to intercept the immigrants who, when detained, were put into special camps on the island of Cyprus. In July 1947 the Stern Group had blown up the British Military HQ in Jerusalem, the former King David Hotel, killing over 90 people, mainly British servicemen. Two months later the terrorist campaign had the desired effect when the British Government announced that, regardless of whether there was any agreement between the Palestinians and Jews, Britain would relinquish the Mandate in May 1948, but in the meantime the illegal immigrant blockade would continue.

As far as *Ocean* was concerned, she arrived with *Verulam* off the coast of Palestine and the port of Haifa on 27 October, and for the remainder of the month, accompanied by either *Verulam* or *Childers,* she made daily patrols off the coast with her aircraft carrying out reconnaissance missions in an attempt to detect the ships long before they were within range of the Palestinian coast. Each evening the carrier would anchor off Haifa, and with Zionist terrorists active in the city, strict security measures were put into force, with armed sentries being posted and the ship's divers making regular searches of the underwater hull. Any stores embarked had to be thoroughly searched for explosives and even the eagerly awaited post was carefully examined. On 1 November there was a break from the tension when *Ocean* left Palestinian shores to make a two-day visit to Beirut which, at that time, was still at peace. On 4 November the President of Beirut visited the ship, and the ship's company enjoyed an expensive run ashore in what was one of the Middle East's most fascinating cities. On 5 November, however, *Ocean* was back off the coast of Palestine, and although the ship anchored close to the Haifa breakwater each evening, there was no question of shore leave being granted. On 8 November the carrier left the coast of Palestine and with *Cheviot* set course for Malta. During the passage the two ships carried out an unusual exercise, with *Ocean* representing an illegal Jewish immigrant ship while *Cheviot* was charged with the difficult task of stopping the carrier as she steered an erratic course in an attempt to avoid arrest. In the event it took most of the afternoon for the destroyer to accomplish the task and to take *Ocean* in tow, which was an indication of the dangerous and difficult task which a genuine interception entailed. By 12 November, however, *Ocean* was back in Marsaxlokk bay, and after carrying out manoeuvres in local waters, on 20 November she entered Grand Harbour to begin a six-week refit.

Ocean spent both Christmas and the New Year of 1948 in No 4 dry dock, but by 5 January 1948 she was back at her buoy in Bighi Bay and nine days later she sailed to land on the squadrons. For the remainder of January the carrier operated from Grand Harbour and Marsaxlokk Bay and by the last week of the month a newly repaired and refitted HMS *Volage* was acting as her planeguard. At 13.34 on 22 January Firefly 202 crashed into the sea on take-off, with the pilot being rescued by *Volage* and then rushed into Bighi Hospital. Next day, however, Lt (A) B. B. Smith lost his life when his aircraft crashed into the sea. During the last week of January and the first week of February *Ocean* operated from Marsaxlokk Bay with her sister *Triumph* and the destroyer *Chivalrous.* On 3 February the C-in-C Mediterranean spent the day on board *Ocean* to watch flying operations, and next day the carrier returned to Grand Harbour for a 12-day break. When *Ocean* sailed again on 16 February she rendezvoused with *Triumph* and the escorts *Cardigan Bay, Bigbury Bay, Widemouth Bay, Magpie, Pelican, Troubridge, Statesman, Solent, Templar* and *Verulam,* for night encounter exercises en route to French Mediterranean ports with *Ocean's* first port of call being Algiers for a six-day visit. With *Triumph* visiting Toulon and the escorts putting into Cannes, St Raphael, Golfe Juan and Merton, on 2 March *Ocean, Solent, Statesman* and *Templar* arrived at St Tropez for an expensive, but enjoyable, five-day run ashore. From the French coast *Ocean* made the 24-hour passage to Genoa, where she spent five days, and this was followed by flying exercises off Malta in company with *Triumph,* after which both carriers returned to Grand Harbour on 18 March. For *Ocean* the whole of April was spent operating out of Marsaxlokk Bay, then on 29 April she returned to Grand Harbour again. At 08.45 on Thursday 6 May Captain W. R. C. Leggatt DSO RN joined the ship and at 12.00 he took command of *Ocean.* That afternoon, after addressing the ship's company, Captain Clarke left for the UK. Next day, at 08.00, FO (Air) Med, Vice-Admiral Sir Thomas Troubridge, transferred from *Triumph* and hoisted his flag in *Ocean.* An hour later, in company with *Cheviot, Childers* and *Euryalus, Ocean* left Malta to set course for Palestine, where she was to assist with the ending of the 26-year British Mandate and the withdrawal of British forces. She arrived off the coast on 10 May and once again she was stationed off Haifa, as this was where the final British perimeter had been established and from where the withdrawal would be

Refuelling at sea during October 1947.
(Maritime Photo Library)

made. Throughout the following days, amid tight security, a steady stream of senior British Army officers came and went from *Ocean* as plans for the withdrawal were finalized. On 13 May the carrier steamed close to the town of Jaffa to 'show the flag', but it was all in vain for as soon as British troops had evacuated Tiberius, Jaffa and Beison, the Zionist terrorist organizations moved in and deported the Arab populations. The intimidation of the Arab population had actually begun on 9 April when Menachem Begin's Irgun Svai Leumi terrorist group had massacred 300 Arab men, women and children at the village of Deir Yassin, after which panic had quickly spread throughout the country. Any thoughts that power would be shared between the majority Arabs and the minority Jewish population as required by the United Nations were being quickly dispelled.

At 17.45 on 13 May *Ocean* weighed anchor to leave Haifa Roads and to fly off 24 aircraft for a fly-past as the High Commissioner, General Sir Alan Cunningham, handed over Haifa to a Jewish Mayor and an Arab Deputy Mayor, and left the harbour for the cruiser *Euryalus.* As he made his way to the cruiser the aircraft roared overhead and *Euryalus* fired a gun salute. Later in the day *Ocean* and *Euryalus* anchored in Haifa Roads and senior Army officers, including the GOC Palestine, the GOC 1st Infantry Division and the GOC 6th Airborne Division, embarked in *Ocean.* At 20.20 General Cunningham arrived on board the carrier for a meeting which lasted for two and a half hours before he returned to *Euryalus.* At 23.30 *Ocean, Euryalus, Cheviot, Childers, Pelican, Widemouth Bay* and *Volage* weighed anchor and steamed out to the three-mile limit where they formed into line ahead. At 23.59 *Ocean's* island superstructure was floodlit and the destroyers switched on their searchlights as all units steamed past *Euryalus* and the ships' companies cheered ship. It was the end of the British Mandate, and the start of an appalling and catastrophic political situation which, over fifty years later, still reverberates around the world.

Although the official withdrawal was over it did not bring to an end *Ocean's* role in the area, for British troops still remained in certain areas of the country, and on conclusion of the ceremonial steam-past the carrier continued her course south down the coast to Gaza where, at 01.00 on Saturday 15 May, the GOC Palestine was disembarked. For the rest of that day *Ocean* remained off the coast and during the morning of Sunday 16 May she anchored in Haifa Roads once again where some British troops, their equipment and their transport were embarked, as well as the Senior Naval Officer Palestine. Finally, at 15.10 that day *Ocean* weighed anchor and set

'Sunbathing Stations' off Haifa Harbour, shortly before the end of Britain's 26-year Mandate of Palestine.

(Geoffrey Broxup)

Flying operations in the Mediterranean, 1948. *(Geoffrey Broxup)*

course for Malta, where she arrived on 19 May. As soon as all her cargo and the Air Group had been disembarked into lighters, *Ocean* was moved to Parlatorio Wharf to begin a four-week maintenance period, which included ten days in No 4 dry dock. Her commission was at last coming to an end, however, and on Friday 18 June she left Malta and set course for home. After leaving Gibraltar on 23 June she steamed north and in the early hours of Monday 28 June she passed the battleship *Queen Elizabeth,* which was being towed to the scrapyard. Just over four hours later she anchored off Greenock and by 19.30 that day she was secured alongside Glasgow's King George V Dock, where both squadron personnel and aircraft were disembarked. On 29 June she left Glasgow, and after completing trials over the Arran measured mile she set course for Devonport, arriving with full ceremony at 13.30 on Thursday 1 July. Having completed three years' service in the Mediterranean the commission was over.

Chapter Nine

HMS *Ocean* July 1948 –November 1952

Following her arrival in Devonport on 1 July large numbers of the ship's company were drafted from *Ocean,* and their places were taken by new ratings, most of whom were from Chatham. By the end of July the carrier had been shifted to No 5 basin, where the dockyard carried out essential maintenance work, but this did not stop her from being part of the Navy Days attractions during the weekend of 31 July to 2 August. In the event over 12,000 visitors toured the ship, and just over a week later she was ready for sea again. *Ocean* left Devonport during the forenoon of 12 August to set course for Portsmouth, where she spent a weekend moored to a buoy in the harbour before, on Monday 16 August, she sailed for Bangor Bay. Two days later, whilst at anchor off the Northern Irish town, she embarked the advance parties of her new Air Group, which was to comprise the Fireflies of 812 Squadron and the Seafires of 804 Squadron. Once everyone was on board *Ocean* weighed anchor and set course for the waters south of the Isle of Man, where three aircraft from each of the squadrons practised deck landing. These trials continued during 20 August, but four days later after leaving her anchorage in Bangor Bay, *Ocean* steamed up Belfast Lough to secure alongside Belfast's Sydenham Wharf, where the remainder of the Air Group and their stores were embarked. At 16.15 on 24 August, just four hours after her arrival, the carrier left Belfast to return to Portsmouth where her engineers raided the Majestic-class aircraft carrier *Leviathan* for spare parts for *Ocean's* main circulating pumps in the engine rooms. On 30 August *Ocean* left Portsmouth to steam north for Glasgow where, on the first two days of September, she loaded more squadron stores before sailing for Malta on Friday 3 September.

The passage to the Eastern Mediterranean was broken by a 24-hour stop at Gibraltar, and after a day at anchor in Marsaxlokk Bay, and flying off the squadrons, at 16.00 on Tuesday 14 September *Ocean* entered Grand Harbour and rejoined the Mediterranean Fleet. Before carrying out any flying operations, however, the carrier had to have her underwater hull scraped and painted and the spares from *Leviathan* fitted to her engine room cooling water systems, for which she was manoeuvred into AFD 35 on 21 September. The floating dock had been towed from Bombay to Malta in two sections, arriving in Grand Harbour in May 1947, and after it had been reassembled *Ocean* was the first vessel to use the dock. Six days later, with the work completed, the carrier was refloated and by midday she was at sea and ready to begin flying operations. For the last three days of September and for the whole of October and November *Ocean* operated from Malta, carrying out intensive flying training, anchoring in Marsaxlokk Bay most evenings and with weekends being spent in Grand Harbour. During these flying operations the carrier was escorted by a number of destroyers, including her old friends *Childers, Troubridge* and *Volage.* In October her aircraft made mock attacks on the battleship *Vanguard,* which was serving with the Mediterranean Fleet, and by the end of November her work-up had been completed successfully. On the last day of November *Ocean* left Malta for a short visit to Naples where, on 2 December, she secured to a buoy in the harbour, but by 8 December she had returned to the exercise areas off Malta. After further flying practice in local waters, *Ocean* entered Grand Harbour at 15.00 on 10 December, to secure at No 8 buoy. It would be over 15 weeks before she put to sea again. During the refit in Malta the carrier spent eight weeks in AFD 35 and in No 4 dry dock, and it was on Monday 28 March 1949 that she was shifted back to her buoy close to Customs House Steps. Finally, at 08.30 on Tuesday 12 April *Ocean* sailed to land on her Air Group and to carry out three days of flying operations before returning to Grand Harbour. On 19 April the carrier put to sea again, this time to carry out six days of flying operations in local waters. At 13.20 on 21 April one of the Seafires was lost over the side on landing, but fortunately the pilot was recovered safely by the ship's seaboat. Four days later Vice-Admiral Sir Douglas Tennant, FO (Air) Med, hoisted his flag in *Ocean* and on 26 April the carrier exercised with the battleship *Vanguard* before both ships, and the destroyer *Virago,* set course for Venice, where they arrived three days later. This was followed by a four-day visit to Trieste and 24 hours at Ancona, where shore leave was very limited, before the carrier returned to Malta.

On 18 May *Ocean* left Grand Harbour to carry out flying exercises in local waters and next day, at 10.50, whilst the ship's Sea Otter was landing on, its starboard wing tip hit the island superstructure and the aircraft crashed over the starboard side into the sea. The ship was stopped immediately, the seaboat was lowered and at the same time the destroyer *Chevron* raced to the scene from her position astern of the carrier. Although the destroyer

A busy flight deck as *Ocean* returns to the Mediterranean in the summer of 1948. *(Fleet Air Arm Museum, Cars O/55)*

was able to rescue the passenger, CPO Simpson, and recover a great deal of wreckage, there was no trace of the pilot, Lt (A) Hall. Next day *Ocean* took part in joint exercises with the US Sixth Fleet, before returning to Grand Harbour where she remained until the third week of June. It was 09.15 on Monday 13 June when, with full ceremony, *Ocean* followed *Vanguard* out of Grand Harbour to rendezvous with units of the 1st Cruiser Squadron, frigates, minesweepers and submarines of the fleet, to steam past HMS *Surprise,* which was carrying the Governor of Malta, Sir Francis Douglas, who had completed his term of office. The fleet then formed up in two columns, led by *Vanguard* and *Ocean,* after which *Surprise* then passed through the columns as *Ocean's* aircraft roared overhead in salute. On completion of the farewell ceremony *Surprise* returned to Grand Harbour to disembark the Governor, whilst *Ocean, Vanguard* and *Mauritius* carried out a day of manoeuvres, which ended at 17.45 when *Ocean's* Air Group carried out an 'air strike' on the battleship and cruiser. The exercises off Malta continued until the afternoon of 15 June, when the carrier returned to Grand Harbour. With *Triumph* having arrived in Malta a few weeks earlier, and having completed a refit, she was ready to take over from *Ocean* which had been earmarked for trooping and cargo voyages to the Far East.

On Tuesday 21 June, having left all her aircraft and squadron personnel ashore, *Ocean* sailed from Malta and four days later, after a fast passage home, she arrived in Devonport where squadron stores were unloaded. On 9 July she sailed north to Glasgow, where she arrived during the afternoon of 11 July, and the next three days were spent loading RAF aircraft, personnel and stores. In the event a mixture of Seafires, Tempests and Typhoons were embarked, all minus their wings so that they could be easily stowed in the hangars and on the flight deck. As well as the RAF personnel, the Secretary of State for Air, Arthur Henderson, also joined the ship to give a pep-talk to the RAF servicemen. *Ocean* left King George V Dock at 13.45 on 14 July, and after dropping the Government minister at Greenock, she set course for Aden. On 17 July she passed through the Strait of Gibraltar and two days later she was approaching Malta. At 12.30 on 19 July, when the carrier was passing through the Sicilian Channel, four Fireflies of 812 Squadron, which had been left behind at Hal Far the previous month, flew overhead and made several low passes over the ship. Unfortunately, one of them crashed into the sea half a mile astern of *Ocean,* killing both the pilot, Lt (A) Haggerty and the observer, Lt Riggins. After searching the area thoroughly, at 13.00 the carrier had to resume her voyage to Port Said. At 11.35 on 22 July *Ocean* entered the Suez Canal and three hours later she was secured alongside the bank in the Ballah by-pass, in order to allow a northbound convoy through. At 17.00 the last ship of the convoy, the frigate HMS *Mermaid,* had passed by and *Ocean's* southbound convoy was able to get under way. However, at 18.10 when her mooring ropes were slipped, it was found that the carrier was firmly aground and it was 02.45 on 23 July before tugs were able to free her so that she could continue her passage through the canal, which she did at eight knots. That afternoon she cleared Port Suez and set course for Aden where a scheduled stop of eight hours was prolonged to 40 hours, so that the engineers could deal with contaminated boiler feed water. *Ocean* arrived in Singapore Naval Base on 7 August, where some of the aircraft and personnel were disembarked and three days later she was ploughing through heavy seas for Hong Kong, where she arrived on 13 August. During her ten days in the colony the embarked squadron of Spitfires and the remaining RAF personnel were disembarked, and on 23 August she began her homeward passage, via Singapore, Colombo, Aden, Suez, Malta and Gibraltar. On 24 September, at Gibraltar, some unusual passengers in the form of three Barbary Apes, two of which were bound for Bristol Zoo and one for Edinburgh Zoo, were embarked for the passage to Portsmouth. She arrived alongside North Corner Jetty on 27 September and next day, after the Barbary Apes had been landed, *Ocean* left Portsmouth and made an overnight passage to Devonport, where it was rumoured she was to be placed in reserve. Indeed, on 7 October Captain Leggatt relinquished his command and soon afterwards the carrier was towed into No 3 basin, where her complement was reduced to little more than a care and maintenance party. The period of inactivity did not last for long, however, and on 11 November drafts of men from Portsmouth and Chatham joined the ship and ten days later, at 09.00 on Monday 21 November, Captain R. F. Elkins OBE RN, took command.

Four days later *Ocean* left Devonport to carry out three days of trials, which enabled her new ship's company to familiarize themselves with the ship, and on the last day of November she sailed on her second trooping and cargo voyage. This time she was carrying naval drafts for the Far East and among the personnel on board were new ships' companies for HM Ships *Jamaica, Hart, Concord* and *Constance,* all of whom were bound for Hong Kong. Once again she sailed via the Mediterranean and the Suez Canal, and on 22 December, when she was some 280 miles west of Colombo, she came across a small merchantman, SS *Roboba,* which was without any power and drifting helplessly. After a boarding party of one officer and ten ratings had gone across to *Roboba,* she was taken in tow to Colombo where, two days later she was handed over to harbour tugs. Next day *Ocean* arrived in Trincomalee where some passengers were disembarked and Christmas was celebrated, and from there she steamed on to Singapore and Hong Kong. Once again the return journey was made by the same route and she arrived back in Portsmouth on 28 February 1950. On 7 March *Ocean* made the short passage down Channel to Devonport where, for the remainder of the month, deammunitioning took place. On Sunday 2 April Captain B. E. W. Logan RN joined the ship and at 09.00 next day, with Captain Elkins having left the previous evening, he assumed command of *Ocean.* By the forenoon of Friday 14 April the carrier was ready for sea once again, and at 10.15 she sailed to carry out engine trials before anchoring in Plymouth Sound later in the afternoon. Next morning Mr James Callaghan MP*, the Parliamentary Secretary for Transport, was embarked and *Ocean* weighed anchor to set course for Glasgow, from where her third trooping voyage would begin. Next day, at 16.30, Mr Callaghan was disembarked off Helensburgh before *Ocean* continued her passage up the Clyde to King George V Dock. After embarking drafts of men, aircraft spares and stores, the carrier left Glasgow on 18 April to set course for the Far East once again, although this time her voyage would take her to Kure in Japan. *Ocean* arrived in Singapore on 17 May, and in Hong Kong seven days later. On 30 May she reached Kure, which was the base for the Commonwealth Occupation Force in Japan. In harbour was her sister *Triumph,* and the cruiser *Belfast* (flag FO2 FES), which were on courtesy visits to Japanese ports from the naval base at Singapore. Although Kure would become very familiar to *Ocean* in the future, with the sudden and unexpected outbreak of the Korean War barely a month later, the port was still something of a backwater for the Far East Fleet. After disembarking a draft of officers and men for the destroyer *Consort,* receiving a coat of paint and embarking the homeward-bound draft, on 8 June *Ocean* left Kure for the passage home. At Hong Kong 900 men of the 3rd Commando Brigade, Royal Marines, together with their band, were embarked and in Singapore a 1905 Rolls Royce motor car, which an officer had bought for the equivalent of £25, was loaded on board.

On 27 June when, without any prior declaration, the North Korean forces launched their devastating attack on South Korea, *Ocean* was in the Indian Ocean, five days into her passage between Singapore and Aden. Although nobody knew it at the time, the war would ensure that her operational career lasted well into the 1950s, as all rumours of the reserve fleet were dispelled. During the forenoon of Wednesday 19 July, with the Royal Marines manning the flight deck and their band playing 'Any Old Iron' (a reference to several damaged aircraft and the old Rolls Royce being carried in the hangar), *Ocean* secured alongside Portsmouth's Pitch House Jetty. Two days later she steamed down Channel to Devonport, where she was secured in No 10 dry dock for routine maintenance.

On Monday 31 July there was another change of command when Captain R. C. V. Ross DSO RN took over from Captain Logan, who left the ship that evening. It was on 23 August that *Ocean* was moved back to the sea wall, and nine days later she began embarking naval drafts and cargo, which included a number of assault craft, for this time she was reinforcing a fleet which was at war. *Ocean* left Devonport on 6 September, to make her fourth voyage to the Far East, via Suez. At Aden there was a 24-hour delay when the carrier's turbo-generators broke down, but by the end of the month she had arrived in Singapore. On Monday 9 October *Ocean* arrived in Hong Kong, where Army, RAF and naval personnel, as well as embarked aircraft, were disembarked. On 19 October she arrived in the Japanese port of Sasebo, which had been hurriedly set up as the forward operating base for units of the Far East Fleet involved in the Korean war. On board *Ocean* was a draft for HMS *Ladybird,* a converted merchantman which Admiral Andrewes was using as his headquarters ship, and the destroyer *Charity.* For the passage home she embarked men from the cruiser *Ceylon.* The carrier left Sasebo on 18 October and steamed home by way of Hong Kong, Singapore, Trincomalee and Aden. She passed through Port Said on 29 November and after embarking 119 more ratings at Malta, she anchored in Plymouth Sound at 21.45 on Sunday 10 December. Next day, after clearing Customs, she

December 1948, Christmas celebrations on a mess deck. *(Geoffrey Broxup)*

*Leonard James Callaghan, former Royal Navy Petty Officer, became Prime Minister 1976-79. Now Lord Callaghan of Cardiff.

secured alongside 5 & 6 wharves of Devonport Dockyard. Her days as a troop transport and cargo carrier were over.

The outbreak of war in Korea had come as a complete surprise to the meagre US forces stationed in that country, and the initial North Korean assault had almost overwhelmed the Americans who were pushed back to a small perimeter round the port of Pusan. However, they soon recovered from this initial setback and the British Government quickly pledged its support for America. As far as the Royal Navy was concerned, the main British and Commonwealth effort would be in the form of air support for the Army units ashore, with *Triumph, Theseus, Glory* and *Ocean* all being involved in operations off the Korean coast. Although it meant a return to an operational role for *Ocean,* the immediate future saw the carrier undergoing a long refit before joining the Mediterranean Fleet. *Ocean* left Devonport on Monday 15 January 1951, to sail by way of the Strait of Dover for Rosyth where she arrived two days later. By 19 January she had been shifted into the main dockyard basin, and six days later, when she was taken over by the dockyard, Captain Ross relinquished his command. By the end of the month *Ocean* had been moved to No 3 dry dock, which is where she remained until mid-June when she was secured in the main basin once again. During the morning of Monday 18 June *Ocean's* new commanding officer, Captain C. L. G. Evans DSO DSC RN, joined the ship, and on Wednesday 27 June the carrier was recommissioned. Captain Evans was a distinguished Fleet Air Arm Officer who had entered the Royal Navy in 1922. By February 1940 he was commanding 806 Squadron and he led attacks against oil installations and shipping during the Norwegian campaign, for which he was awarded the DSC. Later the squadron embarked in the fleet carrier *Illustrious* for service in the Mediterranean where it provided fighter patrols for convoys and for operations over Greece. It also provided cover for the crippling Fleet Air Arm attack on the Italian naval base at Taranto, and for these operations Evans was awarded the DSO. Meanwhile, ashore at RNAS Arbroath (HMS *Condor*), the three squadrons which would make up her Air Group, the Sea Furies of 807 and 890 Squadrons and the Fireflies of 810 Squadron, were undergoing intensive training. It would not be long before *Ocean* was once again an operational aircraft carrier.

At 07.45 on Wednesday 18 July *Ocean* left her buoy in the Firth of Forth and put to sea for trials of her main propulsion machinery, before returning to her buoy that evening. Two days later there was another day of trials and during the afternoon of 24 July she successfully landed on her Air Group. Two days later she left Rosyth to set course down the North Sea, arriving at Portland on 28 July. Her stay in harbour was limited to just three hours and by 15.30, in company with the destroyer *Saintes,* she was at sea and heading for Malta. She arrived in Marsaxlokk Bay during the forenoon of 3 August, and later that day she entered Grand Harbour. During the rest of August and for most of September *Ocean* operated in the Malta exercise areas, and in late August she carried out joint flying training with the Canadian aircraft carrier *Magnificent.* On 28 August, at the end of the day's flying, the two carriers anchored in Marsaxlokk Bay and six hours later, at 20.40, a signal from the C-in-C at Malta ordered both ships to be quarantined. On 26 August seven men in *Magnificent* and three in *Ocean* had been admitted to Bighi Hospital with suspected poliomyelitis, and both carriers had to remain under strict quarantine regulations which could only be lifted on 12 September at the earliest, which would be 16 clear days following the last outbreak. During this period the two ships were able to operate from Marsaxlokk Bay, and on some afternoons some very limited banyan leave was granted.

At 09.18 on 10 September, while operating just off Malta's south coast, a Sea Fury made a faulty landing and the aircraft crashed over the starboard side into the sea. Unfortunately, the plane sank quickly with the loss of its pilot, Lt (A) R. E. Dubber. Later that day, at 13.20, Ldg Pilot's Mate N. Fisher was killed by an aircraft propeller as the engine was started up. Two days later, with no further cases of poliomyelitis having been reported, both carriers returned to Grand Harbour and at 15.30 the quarantine regulations were lifted. After a five-day break the two carriers resumed their joint flying operations, with a change of scenery on 26 September when they called at La Spezia in the Gulf of Genoa for six days. After leaving the port they anchored off San Raphael, but no shore leave was granted and next day there were joint exercises with British, Canadian and French units, including the cruisers *George Leygues, Gloire* and *Liverpool,* the destroyers *Marceau* (ex German Z31), *Micmac* and *Cheviot* and the torpedo boat *L'Alsacien.* During the manoeuvres *Ocean* operated French Avengers and the whole exercise concluded in the early hours of 12 October at Golfe Juan, where shore leave was granted. Three days later *Ocean* and *Cheviot* had a bumpy 48-hour passage to Malta, where the carrier secured to No 7 buoy in Grand Harbour.

Meanwhile, whilst *Ocean* had been operating in the Western Mediterranean, Prime Minister Nahas Pasha of Egypt had abrogated the 1936 Anglo-Egyptian Treaty, following which 'celebrations' were held in the form of anti-British riots in various towns and cities, the worst being at Ismailia and Port Said. In response to the civil unrest, which at one stage seriously threatened the safety of British service families in the Suez Canal Zone, the British Government moved troops to Cyprus in readiness for a possible move to Egypt. At Malta, on 15 November, *Ocean* and *Liverpool,* the destroyers *Aisne* and *Jutland* and the frigate *Mermaid* were all ordered to sea, where they were directed to the North African coast. In the event they

Ocean high and dry in Malta's floating dry dock (AFD 35) during September 1948. She was the first vessel to use the dock, which had been towed to Malta from Bombay. *(Geoffrey Broxup)*

anchored in Tobruk's outer harbour. On 26 November, with the situation in Egypt having quietened, *Ocean* returned to Grand Harbour. During the first two weeks of December, escorted by *Chieftain* or *Gravelines, Ocean* operated out of Marsaxlokk Bay, but on Friday 14 December she returned to Grand Harbour, where she would remain until early January 1952. On Sunday 16 December, the C-in-C Mediterranean, Admiral Sir John Edelstone, inspected Divisions on the flight deck and took the salute at the march past. Christmas and New Year were celebrated at Malta and it was not until Wednesday 2 January 1952 that *Ocean* put to sea again, with *Glasgow, Cleopatra* and *Cheviot,* to carry out flying exercises in local waters. On 19 January further rioting and civil unrest broke out, directed at the British military bases in the Suez Canal Zone, and by 25 January a state of emergency had been declared in Cairo, with the newspaper headline, 'Three-hour Battle in Ismailia' summing up the situation in the Canal Zone. In Malta, meanwhile, at 15.15 that day, *Ocean,* the cruisers *Cleopatra, Euryalus, Glasgow* and *Liverpool,* the destroyers *Aisne, Agincourt, Armada, Corunna, Jutland* and *Saintes,* together with the fast minelayer *Manxman,* were ordered to proceed to the coast of Cyprus in case they were required to reinforce the Canal Zone, which was fast becoming a strategic liability rather than an asset to the British Military Forces stationed there. In the event the naval force remained off Cyprus and in London the War Office began to work on plans to move the British Military Headquarters from Egypt to Cyprus, which at that time was still the 'gem' it had been in 1878 when Turkey ceded the island to Benjamin Disraeli at the Congress of Berlin. At 06.15 on Thursday 7 February, when *Ocean* was at anchor in Kyrenia Bay, her Sea Otter crashed over the port side. Although the wreckage of the seaplane was recovered, there was no sign of the pilot, Lt (A) G. Main, who was posted as 'missing presumed dead'. Next day *Ocean* and the rest of the force left Cyprus to return to Malta and at 11.25 on 11 February, after rendezvousing with her sister *Theseus,* which had arrived in the Mediterranean in early February, all the aircraft of 807, 810 and 890 Squadrons were flown from *Ocean* to *Theseus.* That afternoon *Ocean* arrived in Grand Harbour where the personnel from all three squadrons transferred to *Theseus,* which had also entered harbour. A week later, when *Ocean* put to sea again, she landed on 802 (Sea Fury) and 825 (Firefly) Squadrons, which had come from *Theseus* and that afternoon, in Marsaxlokk Bay, she embarked the ground crews. During the remainder of February and the first few days of March, the two squadrons carried out intensive flying training and on 21 February *Ocean's* first commanding officer, Rear-Admiral Caspar John, who was now the Flag Officer 3rd Aircraft Carrier Squadron, hoisted his flag on board his old ship to watch flying operations, leaving the next day. Finally, at the end of flying on 10 March, *Ocean* returned to Grand Harbour where she secured to Parlatorio Wharf to begin a refit and to prepare for service off Korea.

Ocean's refit included 14 days in AFD 35, but by 26 March she was back alongside the wharf and seven days later she moved out to No 7 buoy. After putting to sea for two hours on 4 April to land on the squadrons, at 09.50 the next day she left Grand Harbour and, with the frigate *St Kitts,* she set course for Port Said. After starting her Suez Canal transit in the early hours of 8 April, by 17.45 that day she was heading south for Aden. There was a halt of eight hours at Aden for refuelling, and at 07.00 on 17 April she rendezvoused with the destroyer *Comus* just off Dondra Head, Ceylon, and the destroyer took over the escort. That afternoon *Comus* was called upon to rescue the crew members of a Firefly which had suffered an engine failure and crashed into the sea a quarter of a mile from the ship. On 21 April, the last flying day before arrival in Singapore, a dummy air strike by Sea Furies was made on Singapore Island from a range of 260 miles. It had been arranged by Army HQ, Malaya, and was intended to simulate a high-level bombing attack on the island, with targets in the city and the naval base coming under 'attack'. On 23 April *Ocean* arrived in Singapore Naval Base and three days later she sailed for Hong Kong. Before leaving the vicinity an air strike was made on an area in Malaya's Johore State, known to be occupied by Communist terrorists. At 13.26 on 26 April five Fireflies and 13 Sea Furies, all armed with 60lb rockets, attacked both pin-point and area targets which, according to Army sources was, 'very accurate and effective'. Four days later, on the last day of April, *Ocean* arrived in Hong Kong. During the afternoon of 3 May, her sister *Glory* arrived in Hong Kong from Sasebo and the handover of aircraft and stores began. *Glory* had borne the brunt of operations off Korea since April 1951, and to give her squadrons and ship's company some relief she and *Ocean* would exchange places for some five months, with *Glory* going to the Mediterranean Fleet. The handover between the two carriers took two days, with aircraft, helicopters, aircrew, air maintenance ratings, Chinese stewards and a mass of briefing material being transferred, after which *Ocean* took over the duties of the Far East Station's operational aircraft carrier. At 08.45 on 6 May *Ocean* sailed, and before setting course for Sasebo she carried out air defence exercises over the colony. During the early afternoon a Sea Fury reported that its engine was cutting and surging and requested an emergency landing. Unfortunately the plane lost power too quickly and the pilot was forced to ditch alongside the ship, but the manoeuvre was well executed and he was quickly recovered by helicopter. Three days later *Ocean* arrived in Sasebo ready to undertake her first patrol off Korea's west coast.

At 06.30 on Saturday 10 May, less than 24 hours after her arrival, *Ocean* sailed in company with the destroyer *Consort,* for the first of ten patrols which would set the scene for her five months in the operational area. Flying operations began at 05.00 on 11 May and during this first patrol there was a remarkably high sortie rate, with 87 being flown on the first day. The aircraft were mainly employed attacking railway bridges, tunnels, gun positions, troop concentrations, transport convoys and storage dumps. The targets were attacked with rockets, 500lb and 1,000lb bombs and cannon fire. Although the enemy camouflage was good, being very similar to that employed by the Japanese during the Second World War, there was no lack of targets. Occasionally the aircraft would carry out bombardment spotting for HM Ships and close air support duties for troops of the Commonwealth Division ashore. During this first patrol, which represented an effective flying period of seven and a half days, 569 sorties were flown, including 120 strike, 220 armed reconnaissance, 106 tactical air reconnaissance and combat air patrols (TARCAP), four bombardment spotting sorties and 116 combat air patrols (CAP). Unfortunately, the enemy anti-aircraft fire was also good and during the first patrol five aircraft were lost to enemy flak, with the loss of two pilots and one aircrewman. The first casualty came on 14 May when, during the forenoon, Lt (E) K. McDonald was shot down and killed. Five days later there were three more fatalities, the first being at 11.21 when aircraft handler, NA R. F. Herbert, was severely injured and blown overboard by the premature ignition of rocket-assisted-take-off-gear (RATOG). *Ocean's* helicopters were unserviceable through lack of spares at the time, and although the planeguard destroyer, USS *Marsh,* was quickly on the scene and lowered its boat without delay, the unfortunate rating sank when the seaboat was only 20 yards away from him. A subsequent search, during which a member of the boat's crew dived into the sea, failed to find him. That same day, at 17.15, a Firefly was shot down with the loss of its crew, Lt-Cdr T. J. C. Williamson-Napier, the squadron's senior pilot, and his observer, AC1 L. M. E. Edwards. To their credit, on 17 May the Air Department and aircrew set a new daily record for light fleet carriers of 123 sorties, 76 by 802 Squadron and 47 by 825 Squadron, with serviceability being excellently maintained. At 17.30 on Tuesday 20 May the patrol ended at Sasebo, when *Ocean* secured to No 18 buoy.

Ocean's second patrol began at 06.45 on Wednesday 28

At Venice in April 1949. *(Maritime Photo Library)*

On 14 July 1949, *Ocean* left Glasgow for her first trooping voyage to the Far East. Here she is seen passing through the Suez Canal where during her transit she grounded for eight hours. There are RAF Tempest aircraft stowed forward. *(Geoffrey Broxup)*

Leaving Aden on 27 July 1949, bound for Hong Kong. Stowed at the after end of the flight deck are RAF Spitfires and Tempests. *(Geoffrey Broxup)*

Ocean and HMCS *Magnificent* at Grand Harbour during August 1951. *(Fleet Air Arm Museum, Cars O/37)*

May when, with HMAS *Bataan* and USS *Carpenter,* she left Sasebo for the operational area, and flying operations began the next day. Although there were no fatalities due to enemy action, two pilots received serious burns after their aircraft were hit by flak, and on board *Ocean,* at 02.15 on 4 June, SBA A. Findlay fell into a coma and died. That afternoon Sea Fury 110 was shot down and it crashed into the sea, but the pilot, Sub-Lt D. L. G. Swanson, managed to bale out and he was rescued by helicopter. A few hours later a damaged Sea Fury was forced to ditch astern of the ship, with the pilot being rescued by helicopter. With bad weather having disrupted several days of flying operations, at 08.30 on Sunday 8 June, *Ocean* secured alongside the pontoon at Kure for a five-day break. The third patrol began at 16.30 on Friday 13 June, and after steaming through the Simonoseki Strait and anchoring off Saki Point for the night, *Ocean* anchored at Inchon during the forenoon of 15 June. Later that day, at 15.10, the Minister of Defence, Field Marshal Viscount Alexander of Tunis, boarded the carrier to inspect the ship's company at Divisions and give a brief address, before leaving after spending only ten minutes aboard. At 18.00, wearing the flag of FO2 FES, Rear-Admiral Scott-Moncrieff, and in company with *Belfast, Ceylon, Amethyst* and *Consort, Ocean* left for the operational area. During the early days of the patrol low cloud and fog hampered flying, but during the second half, with better weather, the number of sorties was increased. In addition to strikes on the usual targets, close air support missions were flown for the Commonwealth Division, as well as air strikes on electrical transformers. No aircraft were lost through enemy action, although a Sea Fury was forced to ditch alongside after suffering a power failure, but the pilot, Sub-Lt B. Ellis, was rescued by helicopter. At 18.30 on Wednesday 25 June, the patrol ended at Sasebo.

On 3 July, after a 13-day break, *Ocean* and the repair ship *Unicorn,* which was to carry out deck landing practice for newly joined pilots, HMAS *Bataan* and HMCS *Nootka,* left Sasebo for the operational area. During the morning of 4 July sorties were flown against enemy supply junks, coastal guns and railway tunnels, but at 17.16 that day, Firefly VT 398 ditched alongside the ship shortly after take-off. Although the observer, Lt J. Taylor, was rescued by the helicopter, an extensive search failed to find any trace of the pilot, Lt R. C. Hunter. During the eight good flying days of the patrol some 596 sorties were flown, with 13 bridges, 12 coastal defence guns, 38 buildings housing troops, and 45 supply junks being destroyed, as well as hundreds of enemy troops being killed. By the end of the patrol, at 18.30 on 13 July at Sasebo, 1,150 consecutive accident-free landings had been made. After a break of eight days, at 06.20 on Monday 21 July, *Ocean,* escorted by

Manoeuvring alongside Grand Harbour's Parlatorio Wharf with the assistance of 'Operation Pinwheel'.
(Fleet Air Arm Museum, Sea Fury/42)

Concord, left Sasebo for her fifth patrol. A heavy swell hampered flying operations during the first two days, by making the recovery of aircraft somewhat protracted. During the afternoon of Thursday 24 July, Lt-Cdr R. A. Dick DSC, the commanding officer of 802 Squadron, was killed when his Sea Fury failed to recover from a low strafing attack on a sampan. Captain Evans described his loss as, 'a sad blow to the ship and to the service'. Three days later, three Fireflies, which were escorting a badly damaged fourth aircraft to the coastline where it could ditch, were attacked by four MiG 15 jet fighters. The MiGs dived out of the sun to carry out a stern 'no deflection' attack and they were supported by eight other MiGs above them. Although one Firefly suffered damage to its tailplane and another some superficial damage to its wing tip, by quickly adopting the correct defensive tactics, they were able to break off the action by entering cloud cover. Fortunately, the damaged aircraft was able to ditch safely and its crew were subsequently rescued. Later in the day a division of Sea Furies was attacked by four MiGs, and on this occasion they were able to outmanoeuvre the jets. As the leading MiG 'overshot', one of the Furies was able to fire two bursts at him, but as the Furies wisely broke off the action by entering cloud cover, they did not see the results. However, the pilots concluded that the 37mm cannon fitted in the enemy jets would undoubtedly be very effective against heavy bombers, but its rate of fire was too slow when used against fighters. At 07.05 on 29 July RE(A) K. P. Jordan was critically injured when he was struck by the propeller of a Sea Fury, and just over two hours later he died in the sickbay. His funeral service was held on the quarterdeck that evening. On 30 July poor weather prevented flying and next day *Ocean* anchored off Mitsuhama, entering Kure during the forenoon of 1 August.

It was at 17.00 on 7 August that *Ocean* left Kure for her sixth patrol, the opening days of which were enlivened by the presence of enemy MiG jet fighters in the area. The engagements with these aircraft on 9 August are described by Captain Evans: 'Lt P. Carmichael, leading four Furies, was attacked by about eight MiGs north-east of Chinnampo. There can be no doubt that in this encounter the MiGs took a beating. No Furies were damaged yet they were able to get in repeated attacks on the MiGs, hits on the MiGs being seen. One MiG was seen to dive into the ground and explode on impact and there is no doubt that others were damaged before they broke off the engagement.' Lt Carmichael was the first British pilot to shoot down a MiG jet fighter, and in a piston-engined aircraft at that. Other engagements that morning are described by Captain Evans: 'Lt H. M. McEnery was leading four Sea Furies with three new pilots when, at 07.55, they were attacked out of the sun by about four MiGs. One of the new pilots was hit and one of his deep tanks was set on fire. He was obliged to break away from the formation, which turned towards the MiGs in an effort to cover him whilst he either baled out or ditched. In a spirited action lasting about seven minutes, Lt McEnery was able to get in a long burst at one MiG whilst closing from 600 to 300 yards. The MiG was seen to break away emitting black smoke and flames, and the other MiGs broke off the action.' The stricken MiG was last seen flying northwards in an erratic manner, not fully under control and emitting puffs of black smoke. Fortunately, the pilot of the damaged Sea Fury managed to jettison his burning tank and he eventually landed safely on the carrier's flight deck. For the new pilot it had been a rugged debut to operations over Korea. At 08.40 that morning two more Sea Furies were attacked by MiGs, but on this occasion the enemy jets showed far more tactical ability, confining themselves to diving attacks followed immediately by a climb. Although one of the Sea Furies was badly damaged the pilot, Lt R. H. Hallam, was able to make a wheels-up landing and he was rescued by helicopter. Next day, at 11.40 on 10 August whilst over Chaenyong, Lt Carmichael's flight was again attacked by eight MiGs and they were able to get in good attacks on three of the jets, one of which was set on fire and broke away. The enemy aircraft subsequently broke off the engagement and were last seen flying north. Next day two Fireflies sighted enemy MiGs over Haeju, which dived to attack them, but they were able to take evasive action and leave the area. Whilst on balance the encounters with the MiG jets had been favourable, it was appreciated that this was because the enemy pilots had sacrificed height and had 'mixed it' with the Sea Furies. Captain Evans was concerned that, if as seemed probable, they were to adopt the tactics of diving to attack and using their superior performance to climb away for the next attack, then the balance would immediately shift in favour of the enemy jets. During the evening of 17 August, on completion of flying operations, *Ocean* steered a south-westerly course towards the China coast in order to avoid typhoon 'Karen', which was heading towards the Yellow Sea, and by 18.00 on 19 August she had arrived at Kure.

After six days alongside, at 17.30 on 25 August, *Ocean* left for her seventh patrol, which was disrupted by typhoon 'Mary'. Having been joined by *Unicorn* on 1 September, the wind speeds of 80 knots and heavy seas prevented the maintenance ship from turning and she was obliged to heave-to for a time. When the patrol ended at Sasebo on 5 September 583 sorties had been flown. The weather for *Ocean's* eighth patrol, which began on 13 September, was much better which enabled a high rate of sorties to be maintained. During the nine days of flying, an average of 83 a day was flown, with the main targets being rail

A full flight deck for *Ocean's* first tour of operations off Korea. *(Fleet Air Arm Museum, Cars O/23)*

communications. Although a number of aircraft were hit by flak and two were badly damaged, none were lost. Finally, after a full-power trial during the afternoon, at 22.30 on 24 September *Ocean* anchored off Kure and entered harbour next morning. The ninth patrol began at 13.30 on 2 October and in the nine days of flying a total of 767 sorties was flown. It was satisfying to see from reconnaissance photographs that the bombing of the railway installations was taking its toll on the enemy, with no effort having been made to repair the 41 railway bridges which had been destroyed on the previous two patrols and by the end of the ninth patrol on 14 October no railway bridges in the area were left useable. On 14 October the First Sea Lord, Admiral Sir Rhoderick McGrigor, transferred by jackstay from the cruiser *Birmingham,* and spent the forenoon aboard *Ocean,* before returning to the cruiser by helicopter. Next day, at 17.30, *Ocean* returned to Sasebo. The last patrol for *Ocean* began at 06.40 on 23 October, and during the six flying days of what was a short patrol, 493 sorties were flown. On 27 October Sea Fury

118 was lost to enemy flak, but happily the pilot made a 'wheels-up' landing, although it was well inland and north of the bomb line in an area which was swarming with enemy troops. It was the prompt action of a US helicopter, escorted by ten aircraft from *Ocean* and two from the US Marine Corps, which ensured that the pilot was rescued. Flying operations ended at 17.26 on Thursday 30 October and ten minutes later a memorial service was held on the flight deck for those who had lost their lives since the start of the first patrol on 10 May. Next day, at 17.30, *Ocean* secured to No 10 buoy in Sasebo Harbour. It was almost time for *Glory* to resume her duties as the Navy's operational aircraft carrier off Korea.

On Saturday 1 November Rear-Admiral E. G. A. Clifford, FO2 FES, visited the ship for three hours and it is worth quoting his assessment of *Ocean's* performance during her five months in the Korean theatre of war: '*Ocean's* record in Korean operations is outstanding and is an example of what can be achieved by bold leadership and good teamwork. The spirit, courage and skill of her well-led squadrons have resulted in much damage to the enemy and have been backed up by the consistently high standard of the conduct and tempo of her maintenance and deck operations. ...She has shown that a high sortie rate can be maintained by a light fleet carrier without great difficulty. Despite her strenuous tour of duty, the smartness and appearance of the ship, which was of a high order on her arrival, was not allowed to fall off. I am sure that our Allies, amongst whom the commanding officer and his officers have many admirers, will miss this fine ship - as indeed shall I.'

At just after 15.00 on 1 November *Ocean* left Sasebo and set course for Hong Kong. At just after 04.00 on 4 November she rendezvoused with *Glory* in the South China Sea outside Hong Kong and the two carriers exercised together. During the day five Sea Furies, three Fireflies and two Dragonfly helicopters were transferred to *Glory*, and that afternoon both carriers entered harbour. Two days later *Glory* left for Sasebo and on Saturday 8 November *Ocean* left to make a fast passage to Singapore, where she arrived three days later. After 48 hours in Singapore the carrier left the Far East Station, and after a seven-hour refuelling stop at Aden, during the forenoon of 26 November she completed her northbound passage of the Suez Canal. Two days later, at 15.55 on Friday 28 November she made a ceremonial entry into Malta's Grand Harbour, where she secured to No 8 buoy. On the last day of November she received a visit from HRH the Duke of Edinburgh, who came on board for an hour during the forenoon and inspected Divisions on the flight deck. *Ocean* was back with the Mediterranean Fleet.

Sea Furies ranged for operations off Korea. *(Fleet Air Arm Museum, Sea Fury/60)*

Chapter Ten

HMS *Ocean*
December 1952 – December 1957

During the afternoon of Monday 1 December 1952, three days after *Ocean's* return to the Mediterranean, her sister *Theseus,* which had filled the gap as the fleet's operational aircraft carrier during the two months that both *Glory* and *Ocean* were east of Suez, left Malta for Portsmouth. On board for the passage home were the officers and men and some aircraft from 802 and 825 Squadrons, and three days later there was a change of command for *Ocean.* Her new commanding officer was Captain B. E. W. Logan RN, who had already commanded the carrier for eight months in 1952 and he rejoined his old ship at 09.00 on Thursday 4 December. Just over two hours later Captain Evans relinquished his command and went ashore to await a passage to the UK. During the days which followed, the personnel of 807 and 810 Squadrons rejoined the ship; the former included men of 898 Squadron who had been incorporated when their own squadron was disbanded. On Tuesday 9 December *Ocean* sailed to land on the aircraft and to begin their work-up, operating out of Marsaxlokk Bay. There was an 11-day break for Christmas, but flying operations began again on 29 December and did not finish until the afternoon of 31 December, when the carrier returned to Grand Harbour in time for the New Year celebrations in Valletta. The respite was only brief, however, and at 10.00 on Thursday 1 January 1953, with hangovers still very much in evidence, *Ocean* was at sea again and bound for Crete, where she continued her work-up.

Between 3 and 16 January *Ocean* operated from Soudha Bay while the squadrons worked in co-operation with a small detachment from 42 Commando, Royal Marines, who provided the pilots with camouflaged targets to detect in what was very difficult terrain. At 12.58 on Wednesday 14 January there was a crash on deck which resulted in the death of Lt B. Hicks who, at 11.30 the next day, was committed to the deep in the Ionian Sea. By 17 January

Ocean enters Grand Harbour in December 1952 during her Mediterranean break from Korea. *(Michael Cassar)*

A busy flight deck as aircraft are ranged for flying operations off Korea. *(Fleet Air Arm Museum, Cars O/29)*

Ocean had returned to Grand Harbour and five days later she was high and dry in AFD 35, with some very noisy windy-hammers disrupting life on board. It was 19 March before the carrier was moved to Parlatorio Wharf and eight days later she was back under her own steam at No 3 buoy, close to French Creek and a long dghajsa ride to Customs House Steps. On the last day of March she put to sea to land on the squadrons, returning to Grand Harbour on 2 April. During the afternoon of Saturday 4 April there was a children's party in the hangar and five days later, with the frigate *Magpie,* she left harbour to continue her flying training. Finally, at 10.00 on Thursday 16 April, escorted by the frigate *St Kitts,* she left Malta and set course for Sasebo. As soon as she was clear of the harbour all the aircraft were launched for a fly-past over Valletta, and outside Port Said *St Kitts* returned to Malta. *Ocean* entered the Suez Canal at 01.35 on 19 April and apart from the routine 'Hands to Bathe' in the Great Bitter Lake and an exchange of compliments with a contingent of the King's Dragoon Guards at El Shaalufa, the passage through the canal was without incident. As she steamed through the Red Sea she passed HMAS *Sydney* and HMNZS *Black Prince,* both on their way to Spithead for the Coronation Review, and Aden was reached on 22 April. Between Aden and Trincomalee flying was carried out each day, with the ship's helicopter acting as planeguard, and reconnaissance missions were flown over British Somaliland (Somalia). On 25 April there was some more photographic reconnaissance practice when the Russian vessel *Marshal Govorov* was sighted towing a floating dock, which appeared to be destined for Vladivostok. On 27 April a night encounter exercise was staged with the Indian and Pakistani destroyers *Rana* (ex-HMS *Raider*) and *Tippu Sultan* (ex-HMS *Onslow*), which then provided *Ocean's* screen. Later that day exercises were held with the cruisers *Ceylon* and *Newfoundland,* and on 28 April the carrier entered Trincomalee harbour. Between Ceylon and Singapore flying exercises were carried out each day, with *Tippu Sultan* acting as planeguard. After flying all the aircraft off to RNAS Sembawang, *Ocean* secured alongside the Singapore Naval Base, where she was visited by the C-in-C FES, Admiral Sir Charles Lambe, and a large storing and ammunitioning programme was undertaken. On 7 May the carrier sailed for Hong Kong, but an anti-terrorist strike over Malaya, which Captain Logan had hoped to carry out, was vetoed by the RAF. However, during the passage to Hong Kong an intensive flying programme was undertaken. During the early morning of 11 May NA(1) J. Millar walked into the rotating propeller of a Sea Fury and died of his injuries shortly afterwards. At 14.00 that afternoon his body was buried at sea, and two hours later *Ocean* secured to a buoy in Hong Kong Harbour. During the three-day stay 30 aircrew members were taken on a guided tour of the New Territories, and on 13 May the merchantman SS *Philippine Trader* suffered a steering gear breakdown and almost collided with the carrier. In the event the cargo vessel let go her starboard anchor and laid her cable across *Ocean's* bridle. Eventually both the bridle and the merchantman's cable had to be cut in order to clear the two ships. At 09.00 on 14 May *Ocean* left Hong Kong to set course for Sasebo and during the three-day passage flying programmes were carried out to simulate Korean operating conditions. Despite the fact that most of *Ocean's* work-up had been carried out during her passage east, Captain Logan was able to report, 'I feel reasonably confident that HMS *Ocean* will be able to maintain the effort made by her predecessors.'

During the morning watch of 17 May, on *Ocean's* arrival outside Sasebo, a rendezvous was made with *Glory,* which had just completed her final Korean patrol, and the two carriers steamed into harbour to secure at their respective

Flying operations during the Korean War. *(Fleet Air Arm Museum, Cars O/52)*

Ocean alongside HMAS *Bataan* for a jackstay transfer. *(Fleet Air Arm Museum, Cars O/15)*

buoys. Once again *Ocean* took over the duties of the operational aircraft carrier for the Far East Fleet, and during the forenoon of 19 May *Glory* left for home. She would keep the record as the Navy's longest serving aircraft carrier of the Korean War, having undertaken three six-month tours of duty. *Ocean's* first patrol began at 06.10 on 21 May when, with *Cockade,* she sailed for the operating area off Korea's west coast. Due to low cloud, rain and fog, flying was cancelled on 22 May, and the first sorties were flown during the morning of 23 May. Operations were directed mainly against enemy communications, stores, troops, guns and buildings; close air support was provided for the Commonwealth Division, and bombardment spotting missions were carried out for the battleship USS *New Jersey* and HMS *Newcastle,* with the latter coming under accurate fire from enemy shore batteries. An additional event of four Sea Furies and two Fireflies was launched to meet this unexpected opposition. On Saturday 30 May FO2 FES, Rear-Admiral Clifford, transferred to *Ocean* from USS *Taylor* and on completion of flying that day the carrier sailed for Sasebo, where she arrived on the last day of the month. The second patrol began at 06.42 on 8 June, when *Ocean* left Sasebo for the operational area. The pattern of operations on this patrol was changed, with most sorties being employed on close air support for the troops in the front line. Flying was completed at midday on 17 June when, after handing over to USS *Bairoko, Ocean* returned to anchor off Matsuyama during the evening of 18 June and entered Kure the next day.

Ocean's third patrol began during the afternoon of 25 June, with a foggy passage to the patrol area, and once again the main effort was directed towards air support over the front line. On 5 July, during the return passage to Sasebo, a diversion was made round the Muckeau Islands in order to avoid typhoon 'Kit', and the carrier arrived at Sasebo on 6 July. *Ocean's* fourth, and final, operational war patrol began at 06.20 on 14 July, and flying operations commenced the next day. During the afternoon the catapult broke down and as the aircraft were supporting the front-line troops, it was important that flying operations continued. In the absence of the catapult RATOG was used for the next event, which consisted of four Fireflies and four Sea Furies. At 14.35, the pilot of the second Sea Fury fired his rockets too early and his aircraft crashed into the sea ahead of the ship. Fortunately the pilot was rescued by the ship's helicopter. Fifteen minutes later, as the first of the Fireflies was launched, some of the rockets failed to fire and it too crashed into the sea ahead of the ship. This time, however, the results were tragic with the observer, Lt (O) K. M. Thomas, being lost with the aircraft when it sank. The pilot, Lt (A) A. J. D. Evans, was quickly picked up, unconscious, by USS *Southerland,* but despite being given artificial respiration he did not regain consciousness. On completion of flying that day his body was transferred to *Ocean* and at 20.45, with the escorts USS *Buck,* HMS *Cockade* and USS *Southerland* on station abeam and astern, a combined burial and memorial service was held. About the escorts, in his report Captain Logan noted, 'We all appreciated their courtesy and sympathy deeply'. On Saturday 25 July, after *Ocean* had handed over to *Bairoko,* she returned to Kure. Two days later, with an armistice having been signed, fighting in the Korean War came to an end.

Although the fighting was over, the Allied air patrols over the front line continued, and at 16.30 on 31 July, in company with the repair ship *Unicorn, Ocean* slipped her moorings and left Kure for the west coast of Korea. The patrol got off to a bad start however, when, at 05.41 on Saturday 1 August, with the carrier off Yamasokono-Hana Light, she grounded on an uncharted shoal. Fortunately, there was no serious damage and 20 minutes later *Ocean* was refloated. However, with the starboard main engine overheating she was forced to anchor and it was found that the cooling water inlets for the condenser were choked with mud, sand and debris, some of which was found to be coal. For ten hours the engineers and ship's divers worked to clear the system, and by 15.30 the carrier was able to resume her passage to the patrol area. With the ceasefire in operation, conditions on board were far more relaxed and at night the ships were no longer darkened, with scuttles remaining open, which, in the days before air-conditioning, greatly helped ventilation on board. Air operations consisted of patrols from the Chinnampo Estuary to a position Long 126°, but no unfriendly movements of shipping were detected and, happily, there was no anti-aircraft fire to avoid. The remainder of the flying programmes consisted of a variety of exercises to keep the aircrews at immediate readiness to resume operations should hostilities recommence. At 11.40 on 10 August a Sea Fury which had suffered an engine failure ditched close to the ship, with the pilot being rescued by the helicopter. During the patrol *Unicorn* operated six of *Ocean's* Sea Furies, and at 09.20 on 11 August, while landing on *Unicorn,* one of them bounced badly and its hook engaged in the top of No 2 barrier. The aircraft struck and severely damaged another Sea Fury in the deck park before going over the side into the sea, from which the pilot was quickly recovered. The second aircraft, the engine of which had been running, ran into the mobile crane and caught fire. Although this was quickly extinguished the pilot, Lt D. G. Halliday, suffered serious head injuries and was transferred to USS *Duncan,* which rushed him to the Danish hospital ship *Jutlandia.* Happily, he made a full recovery.

On completion of flying on 11 August, *Ocean, Unicorn* and the escort USS *Dortch* sailed for Sasebo where they arrived the following day. Although *Ocean* carried out four more patrols off Korea's west coast, they were relaxed affairs and the carrier often anchored off Paengyong-do in the evenings. On 19 September, at the end of her seventh patrol, she paid a nine-day visit to Yokohama and during her eighth patrol, between 3 and 5 October, she assisted with the transfer of Indian troops who were to man the front line at the Demilitarized Zone. She also embarked Lt Derek Mather, who had been released after having been shot down and taken prisoner in January 1953, when flying from *Glory. Ocean's* final patrol ended at Kure on Saturday 24 October, and five days later she moved to Sasebo. On the last day of October she sailed for Hong Kong on the first stage of her passage home to Devonport. After leaving Hong Kong on 11 November *Ocean* called at Singapore, where she received a visit from the C-in-C FES, and there was a brief stop in Aden's outer harbour. She made her northbound transit of the Suez Canal on 4 December and three days later she arrived in Malta's Grand Harbour. On 13 December she anchored in Gibraltar Bay for 17 hours and at 07.00 on Thursday 17 December she passed Eddystone Light, to anchor in Plymouth Sound an hour later. After clearing Customs during the forenoon, at 13.45 she weighed anchor and, with the ship's company manning the flight deck, she steamed up harbour to secure alongside 6 & 7 wharves at 14.40. She had completed her last commission as an operational fixed-wing aircraft carrier.

It had been decided that *Ocean* would relieve *Indefatigable* in the Home Fleet Training Squadron based at Portland, while her sister *Theseus* would relieve *Implacable,* the two fleet carriers being far more costly to keep in commission. Soon after her arrival at Devonport *Ocean* was taken over by the dockyard and Captain Logan relinquished his command. In February 1954 the carrier was shifted into No 10 dry dock and her much reduced ship's company was accommodated in less than ideal conditions in the old tank landing ship *Zeebrugge,* although later in the year the men were transferred to *Orion.* During her refit classrooms and a library were constructed in the main hangar, and mess decks were adapted for use by the various categories of Men under Training, who would range from cadets and Upper Yardmen to Boy Seamen and National Servicemen. She would be, in effect, a floating school for the squadron, training about 650 officers and 4,500 ratings each year. The flight deck would become a ready-made parade ground, and as well as housing the classrooms, the main hangar would double up as a gymnasium, as well as a wet weather 'drill shed'. In January 1954, whilst the ship was still alongside the sea wall, a number of acts of sabotage were found to have been committed in the main machinery spaces, including damage to pressure and temperature gauges, the engine room revolution indicator and telegraphs, sight glasses and even electric light bulbs. Fortunately the damage was not serious and a stoker mechanic was subsequently convicted and sentenced to a period of detention.

In May 1954 *Ocean's* new commanding officer, Captain H. C. Browne CBE DSO RN, was appointed, but as he was still in command of *Indefatigable* it would be some months before he arrived on board and in the meantime Commander G. Kilmartin RN, who had been appointed in January, remained in command. In June 1954 the new ship's company began to be drafted to *Ocean* and by 25 June, when the ship was shifted back to the sea wall, they were living on board. Finally, at 13.15 on Thursday 1 July *Ocean* left Devonport to carry out trials in the Channel, but that evening she returned to Devonport Dockyard. Three and a half weeks later, at 09.00 on 27 July, *Ocean* sailed from Devonport once again, but this time when her trials were completed, she steamed into Portland Harbour to join her sister *Theseus* which had arrived earlier that day. During the afternoon of Monday 9 August Captain Browne came across from *Indefatigable* to take command of *Ocean* and Commander Kilmartin left the ship. Eight days later, on the afternoon of 17 August, the advance party of Men under Training and instructors, consisting of three CPOs, two POs and 51 trainees, joined from *Indefatigable.* This was the start of the transfer of personnel and equipment, including kit lockers and one aircraft for training aircraft handlers, and stores from *Indefatigable,* which was completed on 30 August. Next day Captain Browne returned to his old ship *Indefatigable,* to take temporary command and sail her up to Rosyth, where she arrived on 2 September. Three days later he returned to *Ocean* and on 13 September she put to sea for trials on the degaussing range and, on 17 September, for exercises with *Theseus,* which took the two training ships to Torbay. By 21 September, however, they were back at Portland. In October both *Ocean* and *Theseus* joined other units of the Home Fleet, including *Jamaica, Tyne, Aisne, Reward, Barrosa, Crossbow* and *Scorpion,* for a convoy escort exercise which took the force to Gibraltar and which saw the two former strike carriers acting as humble merchantmen. After arriving in Gibraltar on Tuesday 26 October, *Ocean* remained alongside until late November when, with *Theseus,* she made a four-day visit to Tangier, but by 7 December she was back in Portland Harbour and swinging to the tides round A5 buoy.

In late January 1955, with *Theseus* (flagship HF Training Squadron), *Ocean* visited Brest and on the last day of February she took part in anti-submarine exercises with five frigates of the Home Fleet. In March, following faithfully in the wake of the flagship *Theseus,* she steamed south to Gibraltar where, in the exercise areas of the Western Mediterranean, she took part in fleet air defence exercises, during which aircraft from *Karel Doorman* (ex-*Venerable*) 'attacked' her. By 1 April, however, she was back at Portland. At 09.55 on Monday 4 April Captain E. G. Roper DSO DSC RN, joined the ship and an hour and a half later he assumed command from Captain Browne. Later that month *Ocean* steamed to Devonport to undergo routine maintenance, and she returned to Portland on 27

Ocean as part of the Home Fleet Training Squadron passing Drake's Island as she leaves Devonport.
(Maritime Photo Library)

Ark Royal leads *Albion* and *Ocean* in 'Operation Steadfast', the Royal Review of the Home Fleet at Invergordon in March 1957, shortly before the post-Suez defence cuts began to take effect.
(Imperial War Museum)

Flying the Union Flag at her masthead, *Ocean* leaves Portsmouth for Oslo and the funeral of King Haakon VII.
(Wright & Logan)

May. June was a busy month for the Training Squadron and on 6 June, following behind *Theseus, Ocean* sailed for the River Mersey, where she was secured in Bootle's Gladstone Dock. From Liverpool the two carriers steamed north and whilst *Ocean* remained in the Firth of Clyde for two days, *Theseus* continued through the Pentland Firth to Invergordon. On 21 June *Ocean* anchored in Loch Eriboll, where the Men under Training had the opportunity to join outward bound parties. From there the ship steamed to Hamburg where, on 28 June she secured alongside the Überseebrücke. During the two days she was opened to the public over 10,000 people flocked to visit her, many of whom queued for hours to get on board, and one of the VIP guests was the head of the new Federal German Navy, Vice-Admiral B. Rogge. With three weeks' pay to spend everyone had a wonderful time, although it was said that the establishments of the Reeperbahn benefited the most. After leaving the city on 4 July *Ocean* rejoined *Theseus* and the two ships took part in the NATO exercise 'Long Swell' where, once again, they represented merchantmen and were subjected to 'attacks' by Seahawk jets. At the end of the exercise *Ocean* took part in Rosyth's Navy Days and, in foul weather, paid a six-day visit to Margate, where she anchored off the town's pier. On 21 July she returned to A5 buoy at Portland in time for summer leave to be taken.

On Friday 2 September *Ocean* left Portland to anchor off Penzance for a one-week visit, during which she was to act as guardship for the West of England Redwing Dinghy Sailing Championships. The people of Penzance had arranged a programme of festivities for the ship's company and the Men under Training, but the political situation on the island of Cyprus was about to change the carrier's itinerary. In April 1955 the EOKA terrorist organization, led by Colonel George Grivas and an ambitious young priest, Archbishop Mikhail Makarios, had opened a nationalist campaign against Britain's 77-year rule of the island. By early September, with terrorist shootings and bombings and serious rioting in Nicosia, it was clear that the days of contented, complacent colonial rule were gone for ever, and Army reinforcements were urgently required on the island. During the night of 6 September *Ocean* was ordered to return immediately to Devonport, and after a frantic recall of liberty men, she weighed anchor at 02.15 on 7 September and seven hours later she was alongside No 8 wharf at Devonport, with stores and military transport being loaded. She also embarked 30 officers and 600 men of 45 Commando, Royal Marines, commanded by Lt-Col N. H. Tailyour RM, and on 10 September she left for a fast passage to Malta. In Grand Harbour there was a further 'lift' of stores and equipment and at 08.00 on 17 September she anchored in the outer harbour at Famagusta, where the troops and their equipment were disembarked. Next day she left the coast of Cyprus and steamed south for Port Said where, on 19 September, she loaded artillery and military stores as part of the phased withdrawal of troops from the Suez Canal Zone, which was due to be completed in the summer of 1956. The ship's company got a run ashore until 19.30, and that evening red fez hats were very much in evidence on all the mess decks. Next day, at 06.00, *Ocean* left for the passage home. The return to Portsmouth was far more relaxed than the outward voyage had been, and after a short stop in Gibraltar Bay, *Ocean* arrived in Portsmouth Dockyard on 3 October. After a postponement due to bad weather she returned to Portland on 11 October, but two weeks later she was back in Devonport preparing for a second trooping run to Cyprus, this time in company with *Theseus. Ocean* left Devonport on 27 October and she arrived in Malta on the last day of the month, leaving *Theseus* to steam on to Famagusta. After leaving Malta with additional stores *Ocean* arrived at Famagusta on 4 November and after unloading her stores and equipment into lighters, she rejoined *Theseus* for the passage west to Gibraltar where they arrived on 11 November. Before heading back to the UK they made a short visit to Tangier, which was to have formed part of their cancelled autumn cruise, after which they returned to Portland on 1 December.

After the Christmas and New Year celebrations *Ocean* and *Theseus* left Portland on Friday 20 January 1956, to take part in manoeuvres with units of the Home Fleet, including the cruiser *Glasgow* and the destroyers *Diamond* and *Duchess.* These ended five days later and *Ocean* steamed into Vigo Bay to anchor off the town's Transatlantic Passenger Terminal for a six-day visit. After leaving Vigo on the last day of January, *Ocean* returned to Devonport to begin a four-month refit, during which the ship's company and the Men under Training moved to *Zeebrugge.* During the refit *Ocean* was adapted so that, as well as carrying her trainees, she could also operate a limited number of Sycamore and Whirlwind helicopters.

On the afternoon of Monday 4 June 1956, when *Ocean* put to sea again, she passed her sister *Glory* in the harbour and both ships exchanged salutes for the last time. That afternoon she returned to Portland, and seven days later she sailed for Invergordon, meeting *Theseus* en route. For ten days during June *Ocean* and *Theseus* underwent extensive flying trials with eight Whirlwind helicopters of 845 Squadron, four being allocated to each carrier. For *Ocean* the trials ended on 25 June with a very popular seven-day visit to Hamburg, where the helicopters put on some flying displays from the flight deck. After leaving Hamburg and joining up with *Theseus* once again, *Ocean* took part in 'Exercise Fairwind II' in the North Sea, which included the cruiser *Glasgow,* the destroyers *Battleaxe* and *Defender* and, of course, the helicopters of 845 Squadron, which were quite a novelty in the fleet. The exercise ended at Rosyth on 6 July and ten days later *Ocean* and *Theseus* left for their passage back to Portland, with the former calling at

Hartlepool for six days, where she anchored well offshore. On 24 July *Ocean* arrived back in Portland where she secured to No 1 buoy.

Two days later in Egypt, President Nasser, in melodramatic style, nationalized the Suez Canal Company in retaliation for the abrupt withdrawal of the offer of a loan by the American and British Governments, which had been earmarked for the building of a dam at Aswan on the River Nile. In fact the nationalization was no more than British Governments had imposed on their own industries, and Nasser had promised compensation for shareholders, but colonial attitudes in the Middle East were still strong and, as had been the case since 1882 when Prime Minister Gladstone had first ordered British troops to occupy Egypt, the strength of nationalist feeling in Egypt had been underestimated. On 13 June 1956, in accordance with the agreement of July 1954 between Britain and Egypt, the last British troops had left the Suez Canal Zone, following which the military installations were being maintained by several hundred British civilians. Following the 1954 agreement Britain's political relationship with Egypt continued to deteriorate, mainly because of Nasser's opposition to the British-sponsored Baghdad Pact. The day after the Egyptian takeover of the Suez Canal Company, in London the Prime Minister, Sir Anthony Eden, summoned the Chiefs of Staff to Downing Street and told them to prepare plans for the reoccupation of the Suez Canal Zone. Surprisingly, only six weeks after the final evacuation, no such plans existed but it was clear that the invasion of a country the size of Egypt would be a major military undertaking. Over the weeks which followed, the French Government was invited to co-operate and, unknown to the public, both the British and the French Governments entered into a secret agreement with Israel.

Meanwhile, at Portland on 30 July, *Ocean* sailed for Devonport where, on 5 August, she began embarking Army ammunition, and stores destined for Cyprus which was the new Army HQ in the Middle East, and which would be the forward operating base for any military operation in Egypt. By 7 August, with all the transport, weapons, stores and 1,334 officers and men of the Royal Artillery's 21st and 50th Medium Regiments having been embarked, *Ocean* left Devonport for a non-stop passage to Limassol where, during the afternoon of 13 August, she anchored in the outer harbour. Next day she moved round to Famagusta, where she joined *Theseus,* which was also employed on a similar trooping voyage, and disembarkation of all the troops and equipment began. It was nearly midnight of 15 August before the unloading of stores was completed, but by 08.00 on 16 August she had embarked 864 officers and men, 150 vehicles and 150 tons of stores of 40 Commando, Royal Marines, and she was on her way to Malta. Two days later she had disembarked her passengers and all their equipment at Parlatorio Wharf and for the return passage to Devonport *Ocean's* men had the luxury of their own company. She arrived at Devonport during the evening of 23 August and over the following weeks a number of 'top-level' meetings were held on board, at one of which the use of *Ocean, Theseus* and the newly commissioned *Warrior* as helicopter carriers for any military invasion of Egypt was discussed. At 07.40 on Thursday 13 September 1956, Captain I. W. T. Beloe DSC RN joined the ship and four hours later he assumed command from Captain Roper. For the rest of the month *Ocean* remained at Devonport, as one member of the ship's company described it, 'waiting for something to turn up', and at the end of the month it did, in the form of four Whirlwind helicopters of 845 Squadron.

On Wednesday 3 October *Ocean* left Plymouth Sound to steam up Channel for Spithead where, next day, she met *Theseus,* and the two carriers began ten days of intensive flying exercises with the helicopters, during which time there was very little shore leave. In fact the exercises were rehearsals for the forthcoming landings at Port Said, and they ended on 13 October when *Ocean* steamed into Portsmouth Harbour to secure alongside South Railway Jetty. Five days later she made the return passage to Devonport, where she secured to a buoy in the Hamoaze. Mick Dunne, who was a Telegraphist on board, remembers those days: 'The Government had mobilized "Z Reservists", who were all ex-naval men, and they also delayed the discharge of time-expired men. The latter became very disgruntled and on board *Ocean* we exchanged trainees for these reservists, who occupied the forward seamen's mess decks. We spent some time off the Isle of Wight carrying out what we considered to be unusual exercises with helicopters, but we later realized that they were rehearsals for the Suez landings. During this training a number of the time-expired men became even more disgruntled and they locked themselves into their mess deck. All sorts of rumours flew round the ship, and after we had returned to Devonport some even took over an MFV and, after loading it with their kit, they headed for the nearest jetty. Before they reached their destination, however, they were intercepted and returned to *Ocean*.'

On 23 October *Ocean* was shifted to No 8 Coaling Wharf, and next day the 145 personnel of the Joint Helicopter Unit, their 36 vehicles and 12 Whirlwind and Sycamore helicopters were embarked. At 10.00 on Saturday 27 October, when *Ocean* sailed from Devonport, most members of the ship's company thought the ship was destined for exercises in the Western Mediterranean, but as Mick Dunne remembers: 'Our destination was secret and our mail was censored, needless to say rumours were rife. When we were off the North African coast we rendezvoused with other ships.' In fact *Ocean* passed through the Strait of Gibraltar on 29 October, and during the evening of 31 October she arrived in Grand Harbour where half the troops of 45 Commando, Royal Marines, and men of the RAF's 215 Wing, together with various other units, boarded the ship. In all she embarked 612 officers and men, most of whom were Royal Marines. Amongst the huge fleet which had assembled in Grand Harbour was *Ocean's* sister *Theseus,* which had on board ten Whirlwind helicopters of 845 Squadron, together with the other half of 45 Commando. On Saturday 3 November the invasion fleet sailed, bound for Port Said. *Theseus* left harbour during the forenoon, and she was followed at 17.00 by *Ocean.*

On 29 October 1956, as *Ocean* was passing through the Strait of Gibraltar, the Israeli forces launched an invasion of Egypt across the Sinai Desert, towards the Suez Canal. The British and French Governments called on both the Israelis and Egyptians to cease fire, and to withdraw from an area on both sides of the canal. They also announced that if the combatants did not comply then British and French forces would invade and occupy the area around the Suez Canal, in order to safeguard the waterway. What was not known at the time was that the British, French and Israelis had colluded in the invasion and that Egypt was going to be invaded regardless of what action she took to defend herself against the aggressive Israeli action. In the short term it appears that Britain wished to topple Nasser from power, but what the long-term aims were is less clear for the reoccupation of the bases in the Suez Canal Zone would have been as untenable as it had been between 1951 and 1956, under different Egyptian regimes. Even more ominous for the British and French was the opinion of the rest of the world, including usually friendly Commonwealth countries and the all-important Americans, all of whom were vehemently opposed to a military invasion. At home the situation was far from happy as public opinion was polarized, which in itself did not augur well for the forthcoming operations.

Meanwhile, after leaving Grand Harbour *Ocean* formed up with the fast convoy which was following the slower convoy carrying the assault troops. During the two-day passage the helicopters on board *Ocean* and *Theseus* cross-operated as the two Colossus-class carriers took on the role of the Navy's first commando ships, while a third aircraft carrier of the class, the old *Colossus* herself, was part of the French fleet, now renamed FS *Arromanches.* During the passage there were numerous briefings and rehearsals of loading and manning drills, when the ship was darkened and the troops filed from their mess decks led by guides to the forward hangar, where they assembled in helicopter 'sticks'. In those days the idea of landing troops by helicopter was new and with the aircraft having been

Ocean laid up in the River Tamar in 1961. She became a familiar sight to those travelling by rail over Brunel's Royal Albert Bridge. In the following year she would be sold for scrap. *(Fleet Air Arm Museum, Cars O/48)*

stripped of all equipment the troops had to sit on the floor, hanging onto anything which they could reach. The Sycamore was very limited in its troop-carrying capacity, having room for only three men and their weapons. The first phase of the assault started in the early hours of Thursday 1 November, when aircraft from the carriers *Eagle, Albion, Bulwark* and *Arromanches* bombed Egyptian airfields. The main Allied seaborne landing was made during the early morning of Tuesday 6 November and at 01.30 that morning *Ocean* and *Theseus* were on station with the main assault convoy. At 05.56 *Ocean* anchored in Port Said Roads, about eight and a half miles offshore, and at 08.10 the first six Whirlwinds carrying Royal Marines of 45 Commando were launched to their landing sight in Port Said, close to the De-Lesseps statue. They were followed 15 minutes later by six Sycamores and thereafter the helicopters shuttled back and forth between the ship and shore, landing the Marines and transporting the men of 215 Wing, RAF, to Gamil airfield, west of Port Said, where they were to prepare to land heavy transport aircraft. By mid-morning the 'lift' of 45 Commando was complete and by 13.45 three Whirlwind helicopters were providing a shuttle service carrying casualties back to *Ocean.* Altogether the carrier took on board 40 wounded men, including four Egyptians, and at 15.52 she was ordered to move into Port Said Harbour. By 18.15 she had secured to No 7a buoy, just off the town itself and close to where *Theseus* had secured just a few minutes earlier. During the afternoon the helicopters continued to land the transport, ammunition and stores, but that evening as the advancing troops regrouped in preparation for a move on Ismailia, political events came to dominate the campaign and, in response to repeated ceasefire demands by the United Nations Secretary-General and heavy political pressure from the USA, the British Government announced that, pending confirmation that hostilities had ceased between Egyptian and Israeli forces (in fact the Government knew exactly what the Israeli Army was doing) and that a United Nations force would be sent into the combat area, British forces in Egypt would cease fire with effect from midnight. The ill-advised Suez campaign was over, but in the days that followed *Ocean* would be required as a troop transport while British military forces finally, and this time under humiliating circum-stances, left Egypt after a 'temporary' occupation which had lasted some 74 years.

During the forenoon of 8 December, 573 men of the Parachute Regiment embarked in *Ocean* and at midday the carrier left Port Said and set course for Famagusta, where she arrived at 08.00 the next day. Within two hours of her arrival the troops were disembarked and *Ocean* left for Malta, arriving 48 hours later in Grand Harbour where her casualties were taken ashore to RNH Bighi. Any thoughts of a run ashore were soon dispelled, however, when 843 officers and men of the 1st Battalion, Somerset Light Infantry, together with 146 vehicles, were embarked and at just after 20.00 *Ocean* left Parlatorio Wharf to set course for Limassol, where she anchored after a passage of two days. At 16.00 on 14 November, after the last Army vehicles and personnel had left the ship, *Ocean* weighed anchor and set course for Port Said. Soon after leaving came a landmark in the carrier's career when three Army Austers landed safely on board. *Ocean* then continued her passage towards Port Said, and at 07.00 on Thursday 15 November, when she was some 36 miles off the Egyptian port, the Austers were flown off to Gamil airfield. They were the last fixed-wing aircraft to land on and take off from *Ocean's* flight deck and as soon as they were safely away the ship set course for Malta.

That afternoon she offered assistance to a Russian cargo ship which had 'not under control' balls hoisted, but the offer was refused and at 11.06 on 17 November she secured to a buoy in Grand Harbour. It was rumoured on board that *Ocean* would be undergoing a maintenance period in Malta and, indeed, there was some chipping and painting carried out, but on Sunday 25 November the ship was ordered to sea to an 'unknown destination' which, two days later, turned out to be Port Said. Once secured to a buoy in the harbour she commenced the embarkation of 591 officers and men of 42 Commando, Royal Marines, together with their 92 vehicles and 117 motor cycles. Finally, at 15.23 on Tuesday 27 November, some six hours after her arrival, *Ocean* left Port Said for the last time and returned to Malta, where she arrived during the afternoon of 29 November. There then followed a 48-hour period of indecision before, during the forenoon of 1 December, having embarked a further 200 men of the Royal Artillery and a few RAF personnel, *Ocean* left Malta for Devonport. Once at sea five Sycamore helicopters of the JHU landed on and the ship steamed west. During the evening of Thursday 6 December she passed Ushant, and next morning, at 06.30, she anchored in Plymouth Sound. That forenoon, while Customs officials were on board, the C-in-C Plymouth, Admiral Sir Mark Pizey, and the Commandant-General, Royal Marines came on board to address the ship's company and troops, and at 13.30 *Ocean* weighed anchor to steam up harbour, securing alongside the Coaling Wharf in Devonport Dockyard an hour later. Once alongside the disembarkation of troops began and next day the JHU helicopters flew off, with the ship's company's first long leave party leaving at just before midday. It was the end of an eventful period in the ship's career.

Ocean remained at Devonport until Thursday 17 January 1957, when she returned to Portland, but this time she was not joined by *Theseus* as she had been decommissioned and laid up at Portsmouth. *Ocean* now became the new flagship of the Training Squadron and hoisted the flag of Vice-Admiral G. B. Sayer. In February she sailed north, calling at Milford Haven where, having anchored off South Hook Point some two miles from the harbour, inclement weather and a heavy swell prevented liberty men from getting ashore. However, it did not stop a party of 30 Wrens from visiting and they toured the ship from compass platform to engine rooms. From the coast of Wales *Ocean* steamed north to Rothesay, where the ship's company found plenty of pubs within a few minutes walk of the landing jetty. At 10.00 on Tuesday 12 February, *Ocean* secured alongside Glasgow's King George V Dock from where, almost 12 years before, she had first set sail. With Glasgow's city centre being, in the words of one member of the ship's company, 'a good 40 minutes away by Glasgow tram, or a quick 15 minutes' walk', it was not as popular as Rothesay. After leaving Glasgow on 19 February *Ocean* spent 12 days at sea carrying out oceanography trials, for much of which she operated east of the Faeroes. On Friday 1 March, with the trials over, *Ocean* set course for Rosyth and that night, when the ship was some 50 miles north of the Firth of Forth, Lt-Cdr M. W. Barker was lost overboard. A few hours later, at 08.25, as the ship was preparing to secure to a buoy at Rosyth, the attendant tug took the strain of a towing wire before it had been secured and four men were injured, two of them requiring hospital treatment.

After leaving Rosyth on 13 March *Ocean* steamed south to Antwerp where, after negotiating the River Scheldt, she secured alongside No 22 berth, close to the city centre. The eight days alongside were described as 'fantastic' and the carrier proved very popular with the local people, 10,000 of whom came to visit the ship. *Ocean* left Antwerp at 16.15 on 23 March, and although she touched ground as she left the river, there was only minor damage to the hull, and at 12.50 on 25 March she arrived at Devonport. Most of April was spent in dry dock where the damage to the underwater hull was repaired and the hangar was converted for use as the 'Home Fleet Dining Room' for a banquet which was to be attended by the Queen. It was on Monday 13 May that *Ocean* put to sea again and steamed up Channel for the North Sea and Invergordon, calling at Rosyth on the way and arriving at Invergordon on 21 May, where she joined other units of the Home Fleet, including *Ark Royal, Albion, Apollo, Superb, Gambia* and numerous escorts. With other units *Ocean* was to take part in 'Operation Steadfast', a Royal Review of the Home Fleet at Invergordon. During the days leading up to the Review the fleet rehearsed for the Royal steam-past and on 24 May a full rehearsal was carried out with *Maidstone* (flag C-in-C Home Fleet) playing the part of the royal yacht. The Review itself took place on Monday 27 May, with the steam-past taking place during the forenoon, when *Ocean,* her decks fully manned, passed close by *Britannia's* starboard side. At 19.45 that evening, with the fleet floodlit and at anchor off Invergordon, on board *Ocean* the alert was sounded and the Royal Barge came alongside the starboard after gangway, where the Queen and Duke of Edinburgh were received by Admiral Sir John Eccles, the C-in-C Home Fleet, and FOST, who was flying his flag in *Ocean.* After being introduced to Captain Beloe and his Heads of Department, the royal visitors were escorted to the quarterdeck and then to the hangar by way of the after lift well. The after end of the hangar and the lift well had been decorated with bunting and diffused lighting, with ponds and small stone grottoes. After the dinner the guests were entertained on the quarterdeck and at 23.20 the royal visitors left in the Royal Barge. Next day, between 15.00 and 15.30 the Queen briefly inspected Divisions on the flight deck, and at 09.00 on 29 May, the ship's company cheered ship as *Britannia,* escorted by *Agincourt, Alamein* and *Corunna,* put to sea. *Ocean* herself remained at Invergordon for another six days and during the forenoon of Saturday 1 June there was a final change of command, when Captain J. Smallwood RN relieved Captain Beloe, who left for an appointment with the Pakistan Navy.

During the afternoon of 4 June *Ocean* steamed south for Rosyth, where she renewed her acquaintance with two helicopters of the JHU, which were to use the flight deck for the rest of the month. On 6 June *Ocean* left Rosyth and two days later anchored off Reykjavik which one member of the ship's company described as looking, at first sight, like, 'a Klondike settlement, with grim and forbidding snow-tipped volcanic mountains.' However, once ashore the very expensive beer, the hot springs and coach trips, plus hospitable entertainment at an American base 35 miles from the anchorage, all proved to be very popular. There was even a visit to *Ocean* by the President of Iceland. On leaving Reykjavik on 14 June, *Ocean* steamed to Trondheim via the Arctic Circle, thus qualifying for 'Bluenose' certificates. In an unusual ceremony 'Queen Aurora Borealis' (looking like a cross between Nell Gwynn and a witch) came on board, escorted by an itinerant band of musicians. On 17 June *Ocean* arrived alongside Pier 2 at Trondheim where, once again, the beer was expensive. The highlight of the cruise was the visit to Hamburg, where *Ocean* arrived on 24 June, and for which pay day came just in time. The city and the Reeperbahn stood up well to *Ocean's* third visit, and the hospitality shown by the people of Hamburg was even greater than that on the previous occasions, with coach trips, harbour tours, brewery visits and free cinema tickets. After leaving Hamburg on 1 July *Ocean* steamed north to take a minor role in the Home Fleet exercise, 'Fairwind II', which included visits to Rosyth and Invergordon and then Penzance before, on 22 July, she returned to Devonport. In the first week of August she took part in Plymouth's Navy Days, during which time over 28,000 people visited her. On 30 August, after summer leave had been taken, most of the trainees were put ashore to make room for three fixed-wing aircraft and two helicopters. *Ocean* then left harbour to rendezvous with *Maidstone* (flag Admiral Sir John Eccles) before setting course for Helsinki, for an official visit which coincided with the British Trade Fair in the city. In the Baltic Sea, even though they hardly posed a threat to the Soviet Union, they were shadowed by six Soviet warships, including a Riga-class destroyer which passed dangerously close to *Ocean.* With a Wyvern parked at the forward end of the flight deck, and a Venom and a Seahawk parked further aft, it is possible they took her for an operational aircraft carrier equipped with the latest jet aircraft, but when Captain Smallwood signalled 'Good Morning', he received only a curt acknowledgement.

Although the weather in Helsinki was wet and overcast, *Ocean* received visits from some 20 foreign ambassadors, from all over the world including the Chinese and Brazilian, although Miss Great Britain and ten British models who were in the city for a fashion show proved to be more popular. For the ship's company there was the novelty of steam saunas, complete with birch twig treatment, and even more expensive beer. After leaving Helsinki on 12 September *Ocean* returned to Portsmouth for 24 hours, before taking part in NATO's 'Exercise Standfirm' in the Western Approaches and the Channel. At just after midnight on 21 September she left Plymouth Sound in her usual role of a merchantman plodding up Channel at some four knots then, during the forenoon watch, a signal was received ordering her to return to Portsmouth 'with all dispatch', and adding that she was to take no further part in the exercise. Rumours had been circulating round the ship for some days that King Haakon VII of Norway was critically ill and that should he die *Ocean* would be required to represent the Royal Navy at the funeral. When she arrived at Portsmouth that same afternoon the rumours were confirmed and it was announced that she would carry a number of contingents to Oslo. The first of these was the Portsmouth Group Band of the Royal Marines, the second was a party of three officers and 18 other ranks of the Green Howards (King Haakon had been an honorary Colonel-in-Chief of the regiment), and the third was a large contingent of sailors from *Victory* and *Excellent,* who were to combine with men from *Ocean* to form a Royal Guard. It was also announced that a VIP would be taking passage, and on 27 September the embarkation of passengers took place with the VIP passenger, Admiral of the Fleet Lord Fraser of the North Cape, joining the ship at midday when the Union Flag was broken at the masthead. At 15.00 that day *Ocean* sailed for Oslo and, to the consternation of Admiral Fraser, members of the guard and musicians fell victim to an outbreak of influenza, which spread rapidly round the ship. Happily, by the time she reached Oslo it was under control. During the passage to Norway, *Ocean's* long-term future became known when the Admiralty announced that she was to be paid off into reserve at the end of the year, the reason being that with dwindling numbers of National Servicemen, she was no longer required. During the forenoon of Monday 30 September *Ocean* secured to a buoy in Oslo Harbour, where she joined units from the USA, France, Sweden and Denmark, each of which provided a ceremonial guard. The funeral took place next day, and with muffled drums the Royal Marines Band led the British contingents through Oslo's cobbled streets to the Akershus, the royal fortress which would be the King's last resting place. With the funeral over *Ocean* left Oslo during the forenoon of 2 October and two days later Admiral Fraser was disembarked at Spithead before the carrier left for Plymouth Sound.

On Monday 7 October, after two days at anchor in Plymouth Sound, and once again in her training ship role, *Ocean* left for Gibraltar. During the passage the trainees performed various evolutions designed to put them through their paces, and on 11 October she arrived in Gibraltar to secure alongside the South Mole where, during her 18-day stay, she was joined by *Ark Royal* and *Albion.* On 29 October she left Gibraltar for Bilbao where she arrived two days later, to spend four days secured in the harbour. After leaving Spain and taking part in manoeuvres with Spanish naval units, she returned to Devonport and the Coaling Wharf for four days before, on 11 November, she left for her final cruise. After steaming up the North Sea she called at Rosyth for five days, before steaming round the Pentland Firth and, in company with the destroyers *Cavendish* and *Comet,* securing alongside Liverpool's Prince's Landing Stage for a six-day visit. After leaving the Mersey on 27 November she made a two-day passage to Spithead, before securing alongside Portsmouth's South Railway Jetty during the forenoon of 29 November.

Ocean's final voyage under her own steam began at 08.40 on Monday 2 December, when she left Portsmouth to carry out helicopter trials off the Isle of Wight, before setting course for Devonport. During the passage down Channel she carried out a final full-power trial and at 18.45 on 4 December she anchored in Cawsand Bay. Next afternoon, with her paying-off pennant flying, she steamed up harbour to secure alongside the Coaling Wharf for the last time. Four days later destoring began in earnest and on 20 December Captain Smallwood relinquished his command. By the end of the year only a handful of the ship's company remained on board and they were employed preparing the ship for paying off, an event which took place in early January 1958. Two months later *Ocean* was placed on the disposal list and it was not long before she was laid up at a buoy in the River Tamar, off Bull Point, close to Brunel's Royal Albert Bridge. In fact, over the years that she remained at this lay-up berth she became a familiar sight to rail passengers passing over the bridge. In early 1962, whilst travelling by train to Saltash, the author saw her looking desolate and forlorn and he has an abiding memory of her flight deck which had become covered in moss and weeds. In late 1958 there was a suggestion in Parliament that she, together with *Glory* and *Theseus,* be converted for use as a troop transport, but this idea was rejected by the Government. In August 1959 a company called Oceanwise Exhibits Ltd tried to buy her for use as a trade exhibition ship, but their offer to the Admiralty was described as 'insufficient', and they also made unacceptable demands as to the condition of the ship. In early 1960 there were rumours that *Ocean* had been sold for use as a fisheries factory ship, but on 6 May 1962 her true fate became apparent when she was towed out of Devonport bound for Faslane for scrapping. By the autumn of that year she had ceased to exist.

Commanding Officers:

Captain C. John RN	May 1945
Captain A. W. Clarke CBE DSO RN	16 November 1946
Captain W. R. C. Leggatt DSO RN	6 May 1948
Captain R. F. Elkins OBE RN	21 November 1949
Captain B. E. W. Logan RN	3 April 1950
Captain R. C. V. Ross DSO RN	31 July 1950
Captain C. L. G. Evans DSO DSC RN	18 June 1951
Captain B. E. W. Logan RN	4 December 1952
Captain H. C. Browne CBE DSO RN	9 August 1954
Captain E. G. Roper DSO DSC RN	4 April 1955
Captain I. W. T. Beloe DSC RN	13 September 1956
Captain J. Smallwood RN	1 June 1957

Battle Honours:

Ushant 1781
Mesopotamia 1914
Suez Canal 1915
Dardanelles 1915
Korea 1952-53

Chapter Eleven

HMS *Theseus*
January 1946 – January 1948

On 6 January 1943 the keel of what was to be the sixth aircraft carrier of the Colossus class was laid at Glasgow's Fairfield shipyard, within sight of the Linthouse yard where *Ocean* was already under construction. This new carrier would not leave the shipyard until four months after the Second World War had ended, and on Thursday 6 July 1944, she was launched by Lady Mary Somerville, the wife of Admiral Sir James Somerville who, after a long and distinguished career in the Royal Navy which dated back to the 19th century, had been recalled to the Active List to become the C-in-C of the beleaguered Eastern Fleet. At the time of the launch he was actually serving as the Head of the Admiralty Delegation in Washington. After naming her *Theseus,* Lady Somerville broke the bottle of Empire wine on her bows and sent her down into the River Clyde to be towed to her fitting-out berth near *Ocean* at King George V Dock. On 9 October 1945 her first commanding officer, Captain T. M. Brownrigg CBE DSO RN, joined the ship. *Theseus* was commissioned on 9 January 1946, and seven days later she was ready to undertake her initial trials.

At 09.30 on Wednesday 16 January *Theseus* slipped her moorings and left King George V Dock, Glasgow, to make her way slowly down the River Clyde and at just after midday she anchored off Greenock. Her initial acceptance trials were carried out between 23 and 26 January and they concluded with a full-power trial over the Arran measured mile. Four days later she left her anchorage off Campbeltown Loch to set course for Spithead, and at midnight on the last day of January she was passing Berry Head. Seven hours later she anchored at Spithead ready to carry out initial flying trials, but before they got underway there was a weekend at the anchorage, with MFVs running a shuttle service for liberty men. On Tuesday 5 February

Theseus at sea shortly after the completion of repairs resulting from her collision with HMLSD *Oceanway* in the Solent.
(Fleet Air Arm Museum, Cars T/65)

Theseus sailed early, and at 10.00 the first deck landing was successfully performed. The trials continued throughout that day and during the next day, and at the end of flying on 6 February *Theseus* anchored at Spithead to disembark her trials party. Following this there was to be a six-day break at Spithead before the carrier carried out her final acceptance trials and, again, liberty men took full advantage of the break as it was to be followed by long weeks at sea in northern waters. However, during the night of Friday 8 February, strong winds were blowing through the Solent and at 04.10 on the morning of 9 February lookouts on board *Theseus* suddenly saw the 7,930-ton Lend-Lease Landing Ship Dock, HMS *Oceanway**, which had been moored nearby, dragging her anchor and drifting towards *Theseus.* The duty emergency parties were immediately mustered and they commenced shortening in the carrier's anchor cables, whilst down below the boiler room personnel began to raise steam for the main engines. By 05.15, with *Oceanway* still drifting towards her, *Theseus* had assumed Damage Control State 1 and three minutes later the landing ship's bow crashed into the carrier's starboard quarter, tearing a hole some 20 feet by 15 feet in her hull, ripping away the starboard walkway and crushing the starboard after gun sponson. Fortunately nobody was injured on either ship but the vessels remained locked together until 06.58 when *Theseus* managed to manoeuvre herself clear, after the landing ship had once again crashed into the carrier's starboard quarter. By the time she was completely clear the carrier had three separate holes in her starboard quarter, with frames and beams broken and distorted. Once the danger had been cleared and *Oceanway* was under control, *Theseus* anchored again, and at 16.00 that afternoon, despite the collision damage, the carrier was officially accepted from Fairfield Shipbuilders. Finally, during the forenoon of Monday 11 February, instead of putting to sea as planned, the carrier weighed anchor and, with a slightly battered appearance, she steamed up harbour to secure alongside North Corner Jetty. Four days later she was moved into dry dock to undergo repairs to her damaged hull. For the ship's company this temporary setback had its rewards, for Captain Brownrigg granted ten days' leave to each watch.

During the unexpected nine weeks alongside in Portsmouth the ship was inspected by Vice-Admiral Sir Denis Boyd. A Sikorsky Hoverfly helicopter which landed on the flight deck, caused quite a stir and attracted a lot of inquisitive spectators to what was an unusual event in 1946. By early April, with the ship almost ready for sea, the opportunity was taken to ammunition ship and the ship's company learned that *Theseus* was to assume the duties of a training carrier for the Home Fleet, during which time the north-east of Scotland would become very familiar to them. After sailing on the afternoon of Tuesday 16 April *Theseus* completed her flying trials which had been so rudely interrupted, and these too were not without incident. One of the first deck landings was made by a Firefly carrying Admiral of the Fleet Sir James Somerville, whose late wife had launched *Theseus,* and before leaving he addressed the ship's company. The last day of the trials was Thursday 25 April, and after the usual pipe of 'Secure for Sea Drills', *Theseus* was once again steaming from Spithead into the Channel. The deck landings were being carried out by the Fireflies of 816 Squadron, amongst whom were a number of pilots who found landing on a heaving flight deck to be something of a novelty. Twelve aircraft were due to land and the first eight touched down without incident and were quickly struck down into the hangar, but at 11.50 the ninth was waved off as he approached the flight deck. Instead of making the usual turn to port, the aircraft banked to starboard and crashed into the sea, turning onto its back and sinking rapidly. As this was the first aircraft accident, tension on the flight deck was high, and when the pilot bobbed to the surface there was a loud cheer from both flight deck personnel and goofers. He was soon safely picked up by the planeguard escort *Fernie.* At 15.07 there was another serious mishap when a Firefly pilot failed to cut his engine while landing on and he soared over the crash barrier, smashing into the island between the mast and the funnel. The outcome was a terrific blaze as spilled aviation fuel caught fire and soon, with the aircraft wedged between the funnel and mast, the whole of the island seemed to be a blazing pyre. As the ship steamed on, a pall of black smoke hung in the air, but the pilot had been flung clear into the sea, as was a signalman who was on the flag deck at the time. Meanwhile, two officers who had been watching proceedings, one of whom was Commander (S), were badly burned. Happily the pilot and the signalman were rescued from the sea and the two officers made a full recovery from their injuries. Next day, with the flying trials over, *Theseus* and *Fernie* steamed north via the Pentland Firth for Rosyth, carrying out flying practice on the way and arriving on 2 May. During the passage there was another major accident when an aircraft crashed over the port side and into P2 pom-pom director. Fortunately it was not manned at the time and the pilot escaped unscathed.

During the first three weeks of May *Theseus* operated between Rosyth and Peterhead, anchoring each weekend in the shadow of Scotland's famous Forth Bridge. On 21 May, having flown off 816 Squadron, the carrier arrived off the Irish coast where, 20 miles north of Lough Foyle, she landed on the Fireflies of 794 Squadron. During operations

*HMLSD *Oceanway* was a Second World War version of *Fearless* and *Intrepid*, serving with the Royal Navy under Lend-Lease agreements. She was eventually returned to the US Navy in 1947.

A Firefly which bounced over the crash barrier and ended up wedged in the island superstructure, between the mast and the funnel. Fortunately no lives were lost and the fire was soon extinguished. *(Alan Gordon)*

Another crash on deck which has left the aircraft on fire in a port side gun sponson. *(Alan Gordon)*

that day a rating was lost overboard, but a search by *Fernie* failed to find him, and that evening the squadron ground crews were embarked in Lough Foyle. Next day *Theseus* was once again under way, this time bound for Bergen and her first foreign visit. Despite the language handicap, many strong friendships were formed and when the carrier was opened to the public thousands of people came out to the anchorage to look round, many of them using their own small boats. Also in Bergen at the time was USS *Houston,* which offered some scope for sports and a joint Royal Navy, Norwegian and US Navy parade. After leaving Bergen on 28 May and steaming through the fjords and into the North Sea, *Theseus* returned to Scotland where she anchored off Largs in the Firth of Clyde to commence a week of painting, polishing and training for a special 'Victory Week' parade in Glasgow. This was preceded by a parade in Rothesay, and on 6 June *Theseus* steamed up the River Clyde to secure alongside Meadowside Quay of Glasgow's King George V Dock that evening, close to where she had first put to sea some six months earlier. As well as contingents from *Theseus,* men from the Netherlands and Polish armed forces took part in the parade which marched to the saluting base in the city's St George's Square. Back on board a free gangway was in operation and, apart from the duty watch, the ship was deserted during the five-day visit. After leaving the Clyde on 11 June *Theseus* returned to Scotland's east coast where, once again, she operated from Rosyth in her training, which took her to anchorages off Arbroath, Peterhead, Lossiemouth and St Ann's Cove. During the second week of July there were strong rumours that the carrier would visit Belfast before steaming south to Portsmouth for a refit, and she had actually set out for Bangor Bay when a signal was received recalling her to Rosyth, and on 13 July she secured to No 14 buoy close to the Forth Bridge to begin a six-week refit. Ten days later she was moved into the dockyard, and by the end of the month she had been shifted into the dry dock.

With both the refit and leave periods over *Theseus* left Rosyth on 29 August, and after meeting her faithful escort *Fernie* she resumed her deck landing training. No sooner was the Isle of May astern than the first 'clockwork mice' were circling in their waiting position 1,000 feet up on the port side, and flying operations were under way again. This time *Theseus* and *Fernie* made their way round the north of Scotland to Greenock, where some old Glasgow friendships were renewed. There were brief respites from the continual roar of aircraft, the first at Bangor and the second at Aberdeen on 6 September. On Monday 9 September, however, the ship was once again trembling to the thunder of aircraft engines as she swung into the wind for the first fly-on of the week. At 13.25 that afternoon there was a tragic accident when a Firefly coming into land crashed into S4 pom-pom director and Nos 5 & 7 Bofors sponson before bursting into flames and plummeting into the sea. Unfortunately it left behind a large pool of blazing aviation spirit and although the conflagration was soon extinguished by a prompt and efficient fire-fighting crew, a midshipman and two ratings were seriously injured. The pilot of the aircraft was swiftly rescued by *Fernie,* but Midshipman O. C. Sawers, a petty officer and an able seaman were so seriously injured that during the afternoon the ship anchored off Peterhead and they were rushed to hospital. Next day *Theseus* weighed anchor and resumed

Theseus at sea off Trincomalee.

(Fleet Air Arm Museum, Cars T/40)

A mess deck laid out neatly for Captain's Rounds.
(Fleet Air Arm Museum, Cars T/60)

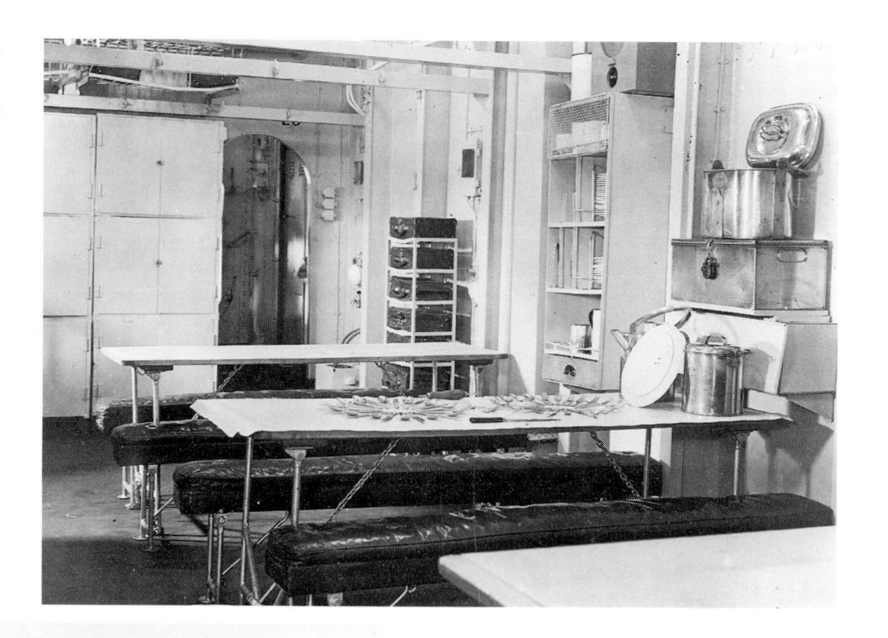

Flying operations east of Suez. An RAF Beaufighter flies in low across *Theseus'* bow.
(Fleet Air Arm Museum, Cars T/58)

her flying operations, but during the afternoon it was learned that Midshipman Sawers had died of his injuries, and after anchoring offshore his body was brought back to the ship. During the forenoon of 11 September, with the Ensign at half mast, *Theseus* entered Rosyth where, two days later, the funeral took place.

On Tuesday 24 September *Theseus* left the Firth of Forth to meet the fleet carrier *Implacable* and the destroyer *Zodiac* for a 30-hour flying programme, before returning to Rosyth. The first day of October saw *Theseus* once again passing down the Firth of Forth to pick up her Royal Marines Band at Invergordon, before steaming round to the Firth of Clyde where the ship was painted and polished in preparation for another round of ceremonial visits. After a 24-hour visit to Glasgow to load a Vampire jet and other exhibition items on board, *Theseus* left the Firth of Clyde for a visit to the Mersey for 'Sailors' Week'. At 15.10 on 8 October, as she was steaming out of the area, she met the giant Cunarder RMS *Queen Elizabeth,* which had just been completely refitted after her wartime service. The liner had never made a peacetime passenger voyage and, having been refurbished, she had on board her royal sponsor, Her Majesty Queen Elizabeth, together with the Princesses Elizabeth and Margaret who had embarked for her speed trials over the measured mile. As she passed the liner *Theseus* fired a 21-gun royal salute, and three days later,

Crossing the Line on 24 June 1947 and Neptune is welcomed on board.
(Fleet Air Arm Museum, Cars T/102)

having met the destroyers *Rapid* and *Saga,* she arrived off the Bar lightship in the Mersey Estuary. With full ceremony, her flight deck manned and a full guard and band paraded, she steamed slowly upriver to her berth. After much manoeuvring she was secured alongside Bootle's Gladstone Dock where the festivities of 'Sailors' Week' started that afternoon with the ship being opened to the public. Visitors were welcomed on board each afternoon and the few members of the ship's company who remained had to get used to a steady stream of people making their way through the mess decks as they toured the ship. One member of the ship's company was heard to comment that it was like, 'trying to "crash out" in Piccadilly Circus'. During the ten-day stay the city provided plenty of entertainment for the ship's company, including free cinema and theatre tickets, dances and free transport on Liverpool's buses. There were some official visits to the carrier, one by Vice-Admiral Sir Philip Vian, who addressed the ship's company, and Captain Brownrigg laid a wreath at the city's *Titanic* memorial, a ceremony which was attended by survivors and relatives of crew members who were lost. The visit to Liverpool ended during the morning watch of Monday 21 October when *Theseus* steamed back down the Mersey to anchor for nine hours off Douglas, Isle of Man. Although no shore leave was given the ship was opened to visitors from youth organizations, then at 22.00 the carrier set course for Glasgow where the Vampire jet and other exhibits were unloaded. On 23 October it was back to work as the ship steamed round to Scotland's east coast to continue flying training from Rosyth. These duties continued all through November, with a break of five days at Belfast, but by early December rumours of paying-off and a refit were rife and on Friday 6 December *Theseus* entered Portsmouth Harbour where she was indeed paid off and taken over by the dockyard.

On Tuesday 31 December 1946, as *Theseus* lay in No 14 dry dock at Portsmouth, there was a change of command when Captain R. K. Dickson DSO RN relieved Captain Brownrigg. The new captain was an officer of great experience, having served through both World Wars and having taken part in the Battle of the Falkland Islands in 1914, at Gallipoli the following year and at Jutland in 1916. In the Second World War he commanded the fast minelayer *Manxman* and this was followed by service with the Eastern Fleet. On Wednesday 5 February 1947, having been recommissioned with a new ship's company, *Theseus* left Portsmouth to carry out main machinery trials and two days later, in Bangor Bay, she landed on the Fireflies of 812 Squadron, followed by the Seafires of 804 Squadron. In company with the destroyer *Blencathra,* she then carried out flying practice in the Firth of Clyde before securing in Glasgow's King George V Dock on 19 February to embark stores. Two days later Rear-Admiral G. E. Creasy, FO (Air) designate, for the Far East Station, boarded the ship and an hour later *Theseus* sailed for Gibraltar. After calling at Gibraltar and Malta, *Theseus* made her transit of the Suez Canal on 4 March. Four days later she made a 48-hour call at Aden and during the early evening of 15 March, after flying off her aircraft, she entered Trincomalee Harbour where, ten days later, she was joined by *Glory.* Having replaced *Venerable* on the Far East Station, during the whole of April *Theseus* carried out joint flying exercises with *Glory* in the waters off Trincomalee, in company with *Jamaica, Consort* and *Constance.* On 22 April the two carriers met the French escort carrier *Dixmude* (Ex-HMS *Biter*), which was on her way to join the French fleet off Indo-China, where she would be involved in operations

Theseus is off the coast of New South Wales with Seafires and Fireflies ranged for take-off.

(Fleet Air Arm Museum, Cars T/57)

against the nationalist Viet Minh forces. At 12.49 on Tuesday 29 April a Seafire crashed into the sea astern of the ship, with the loss of the pilot, Lt A. P. Todd DSC. Despite a long search by the escorting units, no trace of him or the aircraft was found. Only an hour before the accident a Seafire and its pilot had been lost in *Glory*. On 1 May *Theseus* arrived in Colombo and from there she steamed back to Trincomalee, and it was 12 May before she sailed again when, with *Glory*, she headed east across the Bay of Bengal. Three days later, as *Glory* steamed on to Singapore, *Theseus* anchored off Port Blair in the Andaman Islands, before proceeding to Nancowry in the Nicobar Islands. Both sets of islands were soon to become part of independent India and *Theseus'* visit was one of the last by a Royal Navy warship whilst they remained British territories. On 20 May, the last day of the visit to Nancowry, a petty officer died of heat stroke on board and that evening, with *Theseus* on her way to Penang, his funeral service took place. Next day *Theseus* anchored off Penang's main port of George Town, for 13-day a visit, and on 4 June, as she made her way south through the Strait of Malacca, she spent 48 hours anchored off the port for the Malayan capital, Port Swettenham (Port Kelang). Finally, on 7 June, she joined *Glory* at Singapore Naval Base.

Visits to Australian ports had been arranged for both *Glory* and *Theseus* during July and August, after which *Theseus* would visit New Zealand and the Pacific, but first she would undergo a dockyard assisted maintenance period, and as she was moved into the King George VI dry dock the ship's company moved into HMS *Terror*. It was on Sunday 22 June that *Theseus* and *Glory* left Singapore to set course for the Australian coast and during the afternoon of 24 June the Crossing the Line ceremony was held on *Theseus'* flight deck. On 4 July, as *Glory* detached for Adelaide, *Theseus* set course for Hobart where she arrived on 6 July, to secure alongside Ocean Pier. During the three-day visit a substantial programme of entertainment was on offer, including sightseeing tours, visits to the races, football matches and dances. On 9 July she sailed to rendezvous with *Glory* for a joint visit to Melbourne, and the two carriers entered the port during the forenoon of 11 July, securing alongside Station Pier. Once again the hospitality was overwhelming, but they had to interrupt their nine-day visit on 15 July to put to sea for nine hours to rehearse a farewell fly-past. At the end of the visit on Sunday 20 July both carriers left during the forenoon, with *Glory* staging a flying demonstration for senior RAAF officers, and at 14.00 aircraft from both carriers took off to perform the farewell fly-past. As the aircraft formed up into formation before flying over the city, two Fireflies from *Theseus* collided in mid-air, with the loss of all four aircrew members, Lt-Cdr Hearle, Lt Sellars, Lt Walker and CPO Lovatt. Only the body of Lt-Cdr Hearle was recovered from the sea, and this was brought back on board *Theseus*. Less than an hour later, with the fly-past over, the aircraft landed back on board, but a crash on deck claimed another life, when one of the handlers, AB Timmons, was killed. Next afternoon, as *Theseus* steamed towards Sydney, the joint funeral service was held and their bodies were committed to the deep. On Thursday 24 July *Theseus* and *Glory* arrived in Sydney to secure alongside 1 and 2 berths at Woolloomooloo.

After 12 days alongside in Sydney *Theseus* and *Glory* left harbour to land on their aircraft and to set course for Brisbane, the final port of call on the Australian cruise. During 6 August, whilst flying operations were being carried out en route, three aircraft crashed on *Theseus'* flight deck whilst landing, resulting in the death of an aircraft handler, NA Daley. Although all three aircraft crashed into the sea, the aircrew members were rescued by the destroyer *Cockade.* During the afternoon of 8 August the two aircraft carriers secured alongside Brisbane's Hamilton Wharf and as always during a stay in an Australian port the ship's company were treated to lavish hospitality. On leaving Brisbane on 18 August *Glory* began the first stage of her passage home and *Theseus* set course for New Zealand. The two carriers parted company at 15.40 and *Theseus'* ship's company cleared lower deck to cheer *Glory* on her way. Five days later *Theseus* and her escort *Cockade* arrived in Wellington and from there they went on to Auckland, with the New Zealand Governor-General taking passage and flying ashore in a Firefly. During the 18-day visit to Auckland *Theseus* went to sea twice to put on flying displays for guests. She finally left New Zealand waters on 17 September, and with *Cockade* set course into the Pacific Ocean for Honaria on Guadalcanal Island. From there the two ships visited Port Moresby on the island of New Guinea, which they left on 1 October to return to Singapore, arriving in the naval base ten days later. The stay in Singapore did not last for long, however, and on 14 October, after embarking 200 Army personnel, *Theseus* left for Hong Kong where she secured to a buoy in the harbour.

During the last days of October and the first two days of November *Theseus* operated out of Hong Kong, and this culminated in an inspection of Divisions by Admiral Boyd, the C-in-C British Pacific Fleet. On 14 November she departed from Hong Kong at the start of her passage home, and five days later she left Singapore for Trincomalee and Aden. On Friday 5 December she steamed north through the Suez Canal and five days later she made a 24-hour stop at Gibraltar. Finally, after an extremely rough passage through the Bay of Biscay, *Theseus* arrived in Plymouth Sound during the forenoon of Sunday 14 December. That evening, after clearing Customs, she set course for Glasgow, arriving in King George V Dock on 18 December. Once alongside all the Seafires and Fireflies were unloaded before *Theseus* steamed south to Portsmouth where, on 20 December she secured alongside North Corner Jetty. The ship's company took Christmas and New Year leave whilst the ship was in Portsmouth, but on 21 January 1948 the carrier sailed for Rosyth where she was to undergo a refit before recommissioning. By the end of January she was in dockyard hands and the process of deammunitioning and destoring was well under way.

Chapter Twelve

HMS *Theseus* February 1948 – May 1951

Following her return from the Far East *Theseus* remained in dockyard hands until the summer of 1948, and in mid-May she took part in Navy Days at Rosyth. On one day alone, of the 8,000 visitors who entered the dockyard, nearly 7,000 of them boarded *Theseus* which was clearly the main attraction, despite the presence of the battleship *Nelson.* There were PT displays on the flight deck, exhibitions in the hangar and drill and marching displays by the Royal Marines in the hangar and on the flight deck. It was an indication that, after her long refit, life on board was getting back to normal. The new ship's company had some notable successes on the sports field, with the soccer team reaching the inter-ship finals, only to be beaten by *Nelson,* and the cricket team beating teams from *Swiftsure* and *Vengeance.* On Thursday 10 June there was a change of command when Captain J. P. Wright DSO RN took over from Captain Dickson. Seven days later *Theseus* was ready for sea.

At 10.30 on Thursday 17 June *Theseus* left Rosyth and, having shaken off the dust of the dockyard, she set course for the old wartime haunt of Scapa Flow where, for eight hours on 18 June, she carried out turning trials. Once these were completed the carrier steamed south through calm seas and under blue skies for Portsmouth, arriving at Spithead during the forenoon of 21 June. *Theseus* remained at the anchorage for the weekend, and whilst most members of the ship's company were happy with the traditional run ashore, the Royal Marines Detachment took part in an amphibious landing exercise where, for the benefit of the holidaymakers, they 'invaded' the pebbly beach at Southsea. On Tuesday 22 June, after making an early start, *Theseus* carried out catapult trials off the Isle of Wight, before returning to her anchorage at Spithead. On Monday 19 July she hoisted the flag of Rear-Admiral M. J. Mansergh, Flag Officer 3rd Aircraft Carrier Squadron, and three days later she steamed up harbour to secure alongside Middle Slip Jetty. On 26 July she received a visit from the Shah of Iran, who had already been shown round the battleship *Duke of York,* flagship of the Home Fleet, and a few days later she took part in Portsmouth's Navy Days. She also received a final visit from Admiral of the Fleet Sir James Somerville*, who had a special interest in the aircraft carrier which his late wife had launched. However, on 5 August, with the summer leave period over, *Theseus* left Portsmouth Harbour to nose her way past Fort Blockhouse and set course for the Firth of Forth, where she

On Monday 18 October 1948, *Theseus* entered Cape Town Harbour for an eight-day official visit. *(Maritime Photo Library)*

*Admiral of the Fleet Sir James Somerville died on 19 March 1949.

A Sea Fury is freed from the barrier as firefighters stand by with foam equipment while two more go in to rescue the pilot.

(Fleet Air Arm Museum, Sea Fury/66)

Theseus leaves Portsmouth Harbour during the afternoon of 14 August 1950 to land on the aircraft of the 17th Carrier Air Group.

(Fleet Air Arm Museum, Cars T/18)

was to begin her work-up. On Sunday 8 August, during a lull in proceedings when the carrier was anchored off Lamlash, the ship was opened to visitors and to everyone's surprise, instead of the expected few hundred visitors, over 2,000 people made the journey out to the carrier. From the Clyde *Theseus* continued her journey round Scotland to Rosyth and on 17 August flying operations began in earnest, with the Fireflies and Sea Furies of the 17th Carrier Air Group carrying out deck landing training. Using Rosyth and Invergordon as her base *Theseus* continued the flying practice right through to mid-September, but on Friday 17 September, having steamed south, she entered Portland Harbour to join her sister *Vengeance* and other units of the Home Fleet.

On Thursday 23 September, together with the battleship *Duke of York,* the fleet carrier *Illustrious,* her sister *Vengeance,* units of the 2nd Cruiser Squadron and an escort screen which included *Agincourt, Alamein, Corunna, Gabbard* and *Jutland, Theseus* left Portland to set course for Freetown. She and *Vengeance* had been chosen to undertake a 'flag showing' cruise to South African ports, but during the first few days they carried out exercises with the other Home Fleet units. In the vicinity of the Azores *Duke of York, Illustrious* and the cruisers detached and returned to Portland, leaving *Theseus, Vengeance* and their escort screen to continue the passage south. By 3 October the ship's company had changed into white uniforms and, when flying had finished each afternoon, a makeshift canvas swimming pool was rigged on the flight deck. During the forenoon of Tuesday 5 October the force anchored in Freetown Harbour. That evening the band of the Sierra Leone and Gambia Regiment gave a display of Beating Retreat on the flight deck, followed by a 45-minute programme of light music, which even the Royal Marines described as 'magnificent'. Two days later the two carriers and their escorts weighed anchor to continue their passage south and 24 hours after leaving harbour 'Crossing the Line' was celebrated with the usual ceremonies. King Neptune and his companions having made their appearance, many duckings were given before the ships settled down to ten interrupted days at sea as they steamed further south. Flying practice was undertaken on most days with *Theseus* and *Vengeance* providing spare decks for each other and one or more of the escorts acting as planeguard. During the morning of Monday 18 October all the aircraft were flown off to Brooklyn airfield close to Cape Town and three and a half hours later, at 10.00, *Theseus* secured alongside Duncan Dock. During the eight days at Cape Town the ship's company enjoyed lavish hospitality and over four successive afternoons the two aircraft carriers were opened to the public, both of them attracting about 4,000 people each day. The visit came to an end during the forenoon of 26 October when the whole force put to sea, with *Theseus* and *Vengeance* giving a flying display before they set course for Port Elizabeth where they anchored on 28 October. Unfortunately, as is often the case off that part of South Africa's coast, the heavy swell prevented the liberty boats from getting alongside and consequently shore leave was very restricted. Durban was the furthest point of the cruise, and upon their arrival during the morning of 2 November they were welcomed by the 'Lady in White', Mrs Perla Gibson who, from the breakwater, sang many songs as the two aircraft carriers and their escorts entered harbour. One unusual entertainment on board *Theseus* was an Impi of Zulu warriors who performed one of their war dances on the flight deck, which literally shuddered from the stamping of hundreds of bare feet. The visit ended on 8 November, when the carriers made their way back to Cape Town where, during the second visit, the highlight was a civic dance for the ships' companies, which Admiral Mansergh also attended. During the passage north the two aircraft carriers put on an impressive fly-past over St Helena, while the ships themselves steamed in close to the coast, and there was a 24-hour stop at Freetown, during which hundreds of coconuts, still an unheard of luxury at home, were taken on board. On 30 November *Theseus* suffered her only flying accident of the cruise when a Firefly ditched in the sea, but the aircrew were safely rescued by *Alamein.* As the force approached the English Channel they were met by *Duke of York* and *Illustrious* and a convoy escort exercise was carried out, with the battleship and *Theseus, Sirius, Agincourt, Barrosa* and *Cadiz* representing the merchant ships. The exercise ended off the Isle of Wight during the forenoon of Sunday 12 December, after which *Theseus* flew her Air Group off to Lee-on-the-Solent and anchored at Spithead. Next day she steamed up harbour to secure alongside North Corner Jetty for Christmas and New Year leave to be taken.

On 17 January 1949 *Theseus* sailed to carry out ten days of flying exercises in the Channel before she entered Portland where the Home Fleet was assembling for its spring cruise to the Mediterranean. The fleet, led by *Duke of York* and *Theseus,* left Portland in the cold mist of Monday 31 January to carry out a short anti-submarine exercise with the submarine *Tantalus* before setting course for Gibraltar. Next day, when the exercise was over, *Tantalus* surfaced to give a snorkel demonstration but, at 11.47, as *Theseus* and *Duke of York* stopped to watch, the carrier collided with the battleship's stern. Fortunately, with only dents and scrapes to paintwork, there were no injuries or serious damage to either ship and the fleet continued their passage. After further exercises en route, the fleet arrived in Gibraltar on 4 February and three days later they were on their way to Malta, where *Theseus* operated from Marsaxlokk Bay, with weekends spent in Grand Harbour. On 1 March *Theseus* left Malta to make her way west again and as she steamed into the teeth of severe gales, life on board became distinctly uncomfortable and flying was curtailed.

In the second week of March, operating out of Gibraltar, *Theseus* exercised with *Duke of York,* the fleet carrier *Implacable* and the cruiser *Superb* then, after a brief respite at Gibraltar, she sailed for the island of Madeira. Four days were spent at anchor off the picturesque town of Funchal and, after a mixture of sub-tropical rain and warm sunshine, she set course, with the destroyer *St James,* for a rendezvous with the fleet before heading for home. At 10.15 on Monday 21 March, during an air defence exercise with *Implacable's* Sea Hornets, one of *Theseus'* aircraft crashed on landing, which resulted in the death of NA P. R. Fallows. Next day his body was committed to the deep. The final phase of the exercise involved nuclear fallout precautions, and on Saturday 26 March, after a brief pause at Portland, *Theseus* arrived in Portsmouth where seasonal leave was taken. During April the ship took part in Navy Days, but on 2 May she was back at sea and operating her aircraft in the Channel and Western Approaches. There were breaks at Torbay, Falmouth and Devonport, which provided brief respites from flying operations, but on 22 May *Theseus* set course for Invergordon. With Admiral's mess deck rounds due to be carried out everyone was kept busy en route with kit musters, cleaning and polishing. For ten days *Theseus* operated from Invergordon and in addition to the usual fixed-wing flying, on two occasions Sikorsky Hoverfly helicopters landed on board carrying VIP visitors. On Friday 3 June *Theseus* anchored at Invergordon for a five-day break from her flying operations. Monday 6 June in the Cromarty Firth dawned bright and warm, with seven-knot southerly winds, and boat services were running as usual between the ship and shore. Later that day, at about 16.30, one of the ship's motor cutters, manned by a midshipman and four ratings, left the ship for the pier at Invergordon. However, no sooner was it on its way than strong south-westerly winds, with speeds of up to 45 knots, blew up and the boat was soon in difficulties as it shipped large amounts of water. The cutter was last seen at 16.45, but a quarter of an hour later when it did not arrive at its destination, a search was started. Unfortunately, the weather conditions hampered

On 18 August 1950, after carrying out four days of flying practice, *Theseus* leaves Spithead for the Far East. *(Fleet Air Arm Museum, Cars T/17)*

the search, and when one survivor was rescued off Balintraide, it became clear that the boat and four of its crew members had been lost. In the event Midshipman O. H. Mills RN, LS T. J. Owen, AB L. A. Ronnan and Stoker M. M. Popple lost their lives in the accident.

During the evening of 8 June *Theseus* weighed anchor to steam round to the Firth of Clyde, where she took part in a convoy escort exercise, before operating out of Greenock for seven days of intensive flying operations. By 1 July, however, the carrier was anchored off Penzance, which provided a pleasant weekend break before she took part in 'Exercise Verity', an air-defence exercise in the Western Approaches, with *Implacable* and *Arromanches.* Flying exercises continued throughout July, with breaks at Bournemouth, Torbay and St Peter Port, Guernsey. Finally, however, on Thursday 21 July, *Theseus* secured alongside Portsmouth's North Corner Jetty, in time for Navy Days and for leave to be taken. After putting to sea again on 5 September *Theseus* began another very busy programme of flying with the Seafires of 767 Squadron, and with the destroyer *Wizard* acting as planeguard. Once again there were only short weekend breaks, at Penzance and Milford Haven, but on 30 September, after two days of 'Shop Window' exercises for the benefit of senior Army and RAF officers, *Theseus* secured in Portsmouth Dockyard to begin a four-month refit. As *Theseus* was moved into No 14 dry dock, many members of the ship's company were of the opinion that the hull would not require scraping and painting, as with all the sea time over the past months there had been few opportunities for barnacles to secure themselves to the hull.

On Monday 18 October there was a change of command when Captain A. S. Bolt DSC* RN, a distinguished naval aviator, relieved Captain Wright. However, on 26 January 1950, he went temporarily to *Implacable* for three weeks, but by 17 February he was back on board *Theseus* and four days later she left Portsmouth to begin barrier trials with Sea Vampire jet fighters. The trials were carried out in the Channel, with the destroyers *Rapid* and *Ulster* acting as planeguard. By 2 March *Theseus* was in the Firth of Clyde where the trials were concluded and after disembarking her trials party and calling at Mevagissy in Cornwall she arrived back in Portsmouth on 13 March. Later that month, as she lay in No 3 basin, it was announced that *Theseus* would leave for the Far East in August, to relieve *Triumph* on the Far East Station before handing over in turn to *Glory* in May 1951. At the time of the announcement nobody thought that all three carriers would be participating in a major war in South-East Asia. It was on 18 April that *Theseus* put to sea again, but this time she operated her own Air Group in the Channel. By mid-May, however, she was operating a squadron of RNVR aircraft, with short weekend breaks at Torbay, Penzance and St Mary's in the Scilly Islands. In early June she operated her own Sea Furies of 807 Squadron, and on 16 June, after they had flown off to RNAS Ford, *Theseus* put into Portsmouth for a weekend break. At 15.15 on Monday 19 June, when she steamed out into the Channel again she was to begin more trials with the Sea Vampires, which would be landmarks for the Fleet Air Arm, and at 18.25 two of the jets landed on the flight deck. Three and a half hours later, at just after 22.00, the two Vampires took off and during the next hour they made a number of launchings and landings in what were the first night operations on an aircraft carrier by jet aircraft. For the remainder of the month *Theseus* continued to operate in the Channel, with breaks at Folkestone, Boulogne and Bournemouth and during this period of operations, on 25 June, Communist forces from North Korea invaded the Republic of South Korea. The United Nations' response, led by the USA, committed British troops and the Royal Navy to the war, which would become a major commitment for them. However, at the start of the war, it was not thought that hostilities would last for long and the last day of June saw *Theseus* returning to Portsmouth for maintenance, and for foreign service leave to be taken before she left for the Far East.

On Monday 14 August *Theseus* left Portsmouth to land on the 17th Carrier Air Group, which consisted of the Sea Furies of 807 Squadron and the Fireflies of 813 Squadron. Four days later, having carried out some flying practice, she left Spithead with the destroyer *Ulster* and set course for the Mediterranean. There was a short stop at Malta, and on Thursday 31 August *Theseus* completed her 17-hour transit of the Suez Canal. In the Red Sea *Cheviot* took over the escort, and on 4 September there was a 48-hour stop at Aden. During the non-stop passage between Aden and Singapore the aircraft were put through their paces before, on 15 September, they were flown off to Sembawang. Next day *Theseus* entered Singapore Naval Base where she secured to flagship buoy in the Johore Strait for four days. *Theseus* arrived in Hong Kong on Sunday 24 September, and five days later she was joined by *Triumph,* which had been in Far Eastern waters when the Korean War broke out and she was the first British aircraft carrier to become involved. Over the next three days stores and other material were transferred to *Theseus,* and at 11.30 on Monday 2 October she sailed for Sasebo, encountering some severe gales and heavy seas en route as she skirted the edge of a typhoon. She arrived in Sasebo, which was the Royal Navy's forward base for operations off Korea, on 5 October, to join Task Element 95.11. Flying the flag of Rear-Admiral W. G. Andrewes, Flag Officer, Second in Command Far East Station, her first patrol began at 09.50 on 8 October when she left Sasebo for the Yellow Sea, off Korea's west coast. During this first patrol she was accompanied by the cruiser *Kenya,* the destroyer *Charity* and the Canadian destroyers *Cayuga* and *Sioux.* Flying

Theseus at sea in the Korean war zone.
(Fleet Air Arm Museum, Cars T/8)

A snowbound flight deck during winter flying operations off Korea.
(Fleet Air Arm Museum, Sea Fury/158)

On 20 April 1951, having carried out her final flying operations in the Korean war zone and with the ship's company spelling out *Theseus*, the carrier enters Sasebo for the last time before sailing for home.
(Fleet Air Arm Museum, Cars T/62)

operations began that day with reconnaissance missions being flown and thereafter, as well as carrying out mine-spotting sweeps, air strikes were directed against enemy defences and communications.

On Tuesday 10 October, one of the missions flown was against enemy transport, and as four Sea Furies fired their rockets, one of the aircraft, flown by Lt S. Leonard, was hit by flak and forced down in a nearby paddy field. Lt Leonard, who had suffered a broken spine, was trapped in the wreckage and whilst his aircraft was covered by other Sea Furies, a USAF helicopter with a doctor on board flew to his rescue. The helicopter arrived on the scene to find enemy troops being driven off by the covering aircraft, and under fire from enemy troops the US pilot and doctor gave Leonard a blood transfusion and morphia injections, before literally dragging him to the helicopter. At one stage the helicopter pilot had to open fire on the enemy soldiers with his sub-machine gun, but they successfully accomplished the rescue and got the seriously wounded officer to hospital. Both the American pilot and the doctor were awarded the Military Cross for their actions, receiving them from the British Ambassador to Washington. Of Lt Leonard, his commanding officer wrote: 'I wish to record the courage and endurance shown over the period of two hours while he was trapped in his aircraft, seriously wounded, 70 miles behind enemy lines. His conduct during the rescue when he helped the doctor free him, was very highly praised by the American helicopter crew.' Lt Leonard, despite a severe physical handicap, went on to fly again and in the 1970s, as Captain, he commanded RNAS Culdrose.

On 11 October, with the weather having deteriorated, *Theseus* anchored close to Inchon and next day, with *Charity,* she resumed her air attacks on railways and gun emplacements. On 14 October the carrier withdrew in order to replenish, but operations resumed the following day and continued until Sunday 22 October, when she returned to Sasebo. During her five-day break between patrols a US Navy Sikorsky S51 helicopter joined the ship to assist with mine-spotting duties, and it would soon prove its worth carrying out a host of other functions. The second patrol began during the afternoon of Friday 27 October, but flying operations were hampered by the failure of the catapult, which meant that the Sea Furies were unable to be launched with offensive loads, other than gun armament, and when *Theseus* returned to Sasebo on 7 November it was decided that she would go to Hong Kong for repairs.

Theseus arrived in Hong Kong on 11 November which proved an unexpected bonus for the ship's company, but with the reeving of new catapult wires having been carried out by the ship's engineers prior to her arrival, by the end of November she was ready to return to Korea. Having embarked Rear-Admiral Andrewes and his staff, during the afternoon of Friday 1 December *Theseus* left Hong Kong to return to Sasebo where she arrived three days later to disembark the Admiral, leaving directly afterwards for the operational area. During the time that *Theseus* had been in and around Hong Kong, the military situation in Korea had been stabilized as far as the United Nations forces were concerned and Allied troops had reoccupied the country up to the 38th Parallel. It was thought that the main campaign was over and that in future the military effort could be directed at securing the border against further attacks from the north. However, by late November the North Koreans, reinforced by Chinese troops, were again advancing south and the UN forces were in retreat which meant that once again air support from *Theseus* was required urgently. During her third patrol, as well as the usual offensive air strikes, *Theseus* provided support for Allied coastal operations and on 14 December, as she was on her way back to Sasebo, she received a report of a suspicious convoy, possibly a Chinese invasion force, which she was required to investigate. Fortunately, it proved to be a false alarm and at 16.30 on 15 December *Theseus* arrived at Sasebo. Her stay in the port, however, was limited to just 15 hours and at 07.30 the next day, having refuelled and replenished stores and ammunition, she was back at sea and bound for the operational area. By this time the Korean winter had set in and for the first two days of the patrol gale force winds, sleet, snow and driving rain prevented any flying; when the aircraft were eventually launched they were attacking enemy transport on snowbound roads. On Christmas Day targets around the town of Sariwon, including the power station, were hit and the patrol ended on 27 December, when *Theseus* returned to Sasebo. That night fuel, ammunition and stores were embarked and at 08.30 on 28 December the carrier sailed for Kure, where she secured alongside the following day. On Sunday 31 December, with Christmas Day having been spent in the operational area, a belated celebration was held, which merged into the New Year festivities. There was still time for Divisions, however, and during the forenoon of New Year's Eve, the C-in-C FES, Admiral Sir Patrick Brind, inspected the ship's company.

Throughout December *Theseus* had carried out long periods of intensive flying and Admiral Andrewes reported of her efforts: 'Since arriving in the operational area on 5 December HMS *Theseus'* aircraft have flown 630 accident-free sorties in 18 days. This averages more than one sortie per flying day for each pilot and aircraft, a fine and enviable achievement, brought about by a combination of skill and stamina on the part of the aircrews and of hard work and keenness on the part of the Air Group's maintenance personnel.' For its efforts the 17th Carrier Air Group was awarded the Boyd Trophy for 1950.

Despite the fact that *Theseus* had spent most of December in the operational area, with the enemy still advancing there could be no let-up in operations, and on 5

Sea Furies and Fireflies ranged on the flight deck during *Theseus'* operations in the Korean War.

(Fleet Air Arm Museum, Cars T/38)

January 1951 *Theseus* began her fifth patrol. Flying began two days later and the main task for the Air Group was to carry out reconnaissance missions along the front line, and to prevent any enemy landings from the sea. They also provided close air support for the US 25th Division in the front line and patrolled enemy-held coastline. Once again gales and severe weather disrupted flying and on 17 January, when she returned to Sasebo, some 301 sorties had been flown. This time, however, with USS *Bataan* having arrived in the operational area, *Theseus* would have a break of eight days. During her stay in Sasebo the carrier's Sea Otter, which needed a new engine, was replaced by a loaned US Navy Sikorsky S51 helicopter, and on Thursday 25 January *Theseus* sailed for her sixth patrol. The period of operations started with several days of fine weather, which made for much improved working conditions on the flight deck, and during her eight operational days 408 sorties were flown, over 300 of which were offensive operations. However, there were casualties and on Friday 26 January Lt A. C. Beavan was killed when his Sea Fury crashed into the sea about ten miles away from the fleet. Although *Comus* arrived on the scene within 15 minutes, only small pieces of wreckage were found. Next day two Sea Furies were forced down after being hit by enemy flak. The first, flown by Lt P. L. Keighly-Peach, was shot down over enemy-held territory, but fortunately, being only slightly injured, he was able to hide in a ditch until he was rescued by a US Army helicopter. The second, piloted by Lt-Cdr M. P. Gordon-Smith, the Air Group Commander, ditched alongside the ship, from where he was quickly rescued by HMCS *Nootka,* which was acting as 'bird-dog'. On 3 February *Theseus* set a new record for herself when 66 operational sorties were flown, to the great credit of the maintenance personnel, as 807 Squadron had lost four of its aircraft. During the afternoon of 3 February, Lt J. M. Pinsent, whose Sea Fury had been damaged by anti-aircraft fire, was forced to ditch in the sea close to USS *St Paul,* but he was picked up safely by a US Navy helicopter. During the forenoon of 5 February the patrol ended at Kure.

Theseus' seventh patrol began on Monday 12 February, and once again bad weather disrupted flying, which had to be abandoned altogether on three of the nine flying days. On two occasions it was because of gale force winds and on the third because of low cloud and poor visibility. At 17.30 on 14 February, as three Fireflies were landing on, and as one of them was arrested, its 20mm cannon accidentally fired and killed an aircraft handler, PO J. F. Wigley, who was working on the forward deck park. Next day his body was buried at sea. During the patrol some 380 sorties were flown, and on Saturday 24 February the carrier returned to Sasebo. On 4 March *Theseus* left Sasebo for her eighth patrol, and once again her air effort was directed at bridges, tunnels and road and rail transport. The Sea Furies also carried out spotting duties for the cruiser *Kenya* and on one occasion a journalist was taken over the front line to take movie film of an attack on railway bridges. During the afternoon of 13 March, the last day of the patrol, while carrying out an air strike on targets in the Hongchon region, a Firefly crashed near Sariwon killing both its crew members, Lt G. H. Cooles RN and Flt-Lt D. W. Guy RAF. That same afternoon the C-in-C FES, Vice-Admiral Sir Guy Russell, transferred by jackstay from *Cockade* to watch flying operations. Next day, at 18.15, the patrol ended at Sasebo. During the forenoon of 18 March the outgoing FO2, Vice-Admiral Sir W. G. Andrewes, inspected Divisions and a memorial service was held for Lt Cooles and Flt-Lt Guy. At 07.00 on Thursday 22 March, in company with *Consort* and the Canadian destroyers *Nootka* and *Huron, Theseus* sailed to the operational area. Soon afterwards they were joined by HMCS *Athabaskan,* and flying operations followed the familiar pattern. During this patrol a marked increase in anti-aircraft fire was noted and a number of aircraft were damaged. On 24 March a Sea Fury being flown by Lt-Cdr M. P. Gordon-Smith DSC, was hit in its main petrol tank, and although he was able to land safely in friendly territory, he was almost overcome by the escaping fumes. During the patrol 385 sorties were flown and since leaving Spithead on 18 August, 4,204 deck landings had been made. The patrol ended at Sasebo on Monday 2 April.

The tenth, and final, Korean War patrol for *Theseus* began on Sunday 8 April when with *Consort,* HMAS *Bataan* and the Canadian destroyers *Athabaskan* and *Huron,* she left Sasebo, this time bound for the east coast of Korea. Once at sea they met USS *Bataan, English* and *Sperry,* and with *Theseus* working with USS *Bataan* it had been decided that, as they were operating similar types of aircraft, and because of the disparity in their speeds (*Bataan's* had an operating speed nine knots faster than *Theseus*), all sorties would be launched by catapult, with the two carriers turning into the wind together. Flying operations were conducted by the two vessels from 9 to 15 April and, apart from some disruption caused by bad weather on 11 April, air operations took place every day. No difficulties were experienced in operating together, and once USS *Bataan* became accustomed to the slow acceleration of *Theseus,* station keeping was found to be quite easy. The flying operations included reconnaissance of the Choppeki area, and strikes on road and rail bridges, supply dumps and warehouses. The introduction of competition between the two carriers resulted in the speeding up of flying operations and *Theseus,* with her one catapult, was usually able to launch quicker than *Bataan* with her two catapults. The catapulting interval for Sea Furies was brought down to 40-42 seconds and the US Marine Reserve Air Group in *Bataan* could not quite compete with the landing rate of the experienced pilots of the 17th Carrier Air Group. The casualty rate to *Theseus'* aircraft through enemy action was the highest experienced, and on 10 April a Sea Fury being flown by Pilot 3 R. H. Johnson was shot down and although it was thought that he had been killed, in fact he had been taken prisoner. Also that day a shore-based US Corsair attacked a Sea Fury which, despite severe damage, made a successful forced landing. Shortly afterwards a Sea Fury was damaged by enemy fire but, despite the fact that one aileron control was shot away, the pilot made a successful emergency landing in friendly territory. During this period the US Navy helicopter which had been lent to *Theseus* carried out some valuable rescue work by picking up the pilot of a Firefly which had been shot down, with the observer being rescued by *Bataan's* helicopter. On 13 and 14 April, a helicopter from USS *Manchester* rescued aircrew members from *Theseus* who had been shot down behind enemy lines. Flying operations on Korea's east coast concluded during the late afternoon of Sunday 15 April, with USS *Bataan* and her escorts returning to Sasebo, and *Theseus* steaming round to the west coast to carry out three more days of operations. Finally, however, at 11.52 on 19 April, she landed on the last of her aircraft and set course for Sasebo, arriving there the next day. Of her part in the Korean operations, FO2 FES, Rear-Admiral Scott-Moncrieff reported: 'I was particularly pleased to be able to watch the last two days' flying in this very efficient carrier.' Since her initial arrival in Korea *Theseus* had steamed 36,000 miles, flown 3,446 operational sorties in 86 flying days, dropped 1,390 bombs and expended over half a million rounds of cannon shells against enemy targets.

On Saturday 28 April *Glory* arrived in Hong Kong from Sasebo and two days later, with the handover complete, *Theseus* sailed from the Japanese port on the first stage of her homeward passage. She spent two days in Hong Kong and on 4 May, when she arrived in Singapore Naval base, one of the first to board her was the C-in-C. After a refuelling stop of 12 hours at Aden, *Theseus* passed through the Suez Canal on 18 May. She spent 24 hours in Grand Harbour and on 24 May she passed Gibraltar's Europa Point, arriving in Falmouth Bay at 18.00 on Sunday 27 May, when press representatives and HM Customs were embarked. During the afternoon of 28 May she weighed anchor to make an overnight passage up the Channel, to embark the Portsmouth pilot off the Nab next morning. She then steamed up harbour to secure alongside South Railway Jetty at 08.30, and that forenoon there was a steady stream of VIP visitors over the brow, including the First Sea Lord, Admiral of the Fleet Lord Fraser, who presented the Boyd Trophy to the Air Group. Also present at the ceremony on the flight deck were the C-in-C Portsmouth, Admiral Sir Arthur Power; the Fifth Sea Lord, Vice-Admiral M. J. Mansergh; the Flag Officer Air (Home), Vice-Admiral Sir W. G. Andrewes, under whose command *Theseus* had been during most of her service in Korean waters; Admiral Sir Reginald Portal; Admiral Sir Denis Boyd (the sponsor of the trophy) and Sir Richard Fairey. The most keenly awaited visitors, however, were the relatives and friends of the officers and men of *Theseus.* It was a fitting end to a successful commission.

Chapter Thirteen

HMS *Theseus* June 1951 – January 1957

On Friday 8 June 1951, soon after her arrival in Portsmouth from the Far East and as *Theseus* lay in dry dock, there was a change of command when Captain C. N. Lentaigne DSO RN joined the ship and took over from Captain Bolt. The refit kept *Theseus* in Portsmouth Dockyard until mid-September and after recommissioning it was during the forenoon of Thursday 13 September that she put to sea to carry out engine and flying trials. By 19 September *Theseus* was operating off the Cornish coast and carrying out flying practice with the Sea Furies of 807 Squadron and the Fireflies of 814 Squadron during which, apart from short breaks at Falmouth and Penzance, there was little opportunity for shore leave. *Theseus* had been allocated to the Home Fleet and, flying the flag of Rear-Admiral C. John, she was the flagship of the 3rd Aircraft Carrier Squadron. From Penzance she steamed north to the Firth of Clyde and on 10 October she began an important convoy defence exercise, code-named 'Assess', which took place over a wide area of Scottish waters, the Atlantic and the South Western Approaches and lasted for five days. Also taking part were the fleet carrier *Indomitable,* (flag C-in-C Home Fleet, Admiral Sir Philip Vian), *Swiftsure* and 21 destroyers and frigates. On board *Theseus,* as well as her own aircraft, were the Sea Furies from No 4 Squadron of the Royal Netherlands Navy. On 14 October the fleet set course for Gibraltar, and after operating her aircraft in the Western Mediterranean, when they cross-operated with *Indomitable's* squadrons, on 19 October *Theseus* put into Gibraltar. During the time she was alongside she operated a Hoverfly helicopter, but during the forenoon of 27 October the machine crashed in Gibraltar Bay, killing its crew member, NA Amies; his funeral was held in Gibraltar.

During the whole of November *Theseus* and the other units of the Home Fleet used Gibraltar as their base, and on 13 and 14 of the month she took part in an anti-submarine exercise with *Indomitable,* an escort screen and the submarine *Alliance.* On 2 December, with *Indomitable, Swiftsure* and escorts, *Theseus* left Gibraltar to make her way back to Portsmouth, where she arrived four days later. Whilst *Theseus* was in Portsmouth Dockyard it was announced that, in February 1952, she was to be temporarily deployed to the Mediterranean Fleet to relieve *Ocean,* which was being prepared for service in Korea where, in May, she would take over from *Glory.* Before that, however, on 16 January, *Theseus* sailed for more Home Fleet exercises in the Channel. On 22 January *Theseus* left Plymouth Sound to set course for Gibraltar and then Malta, arriving off the island on 4 February. That morning the aircraft of 802 and 825 Squadrons were flown

Theseus anchored at Spithead for the 1953 Coronation Review. Also in the picture is HMCS *Ontario* and part of HMCS *Quebec.* *(FotoFlite)*

Having completed a trooping voyage to Cyprus, in early November 1955, whilst homeward-bound, *Theseus* called at Malta. Here she is entering Grand Harbour, with her ship's company and trainees manning the flight deck.
(Michael Cassar)

ashore and during the forenoon the personnel were disembarked in Marsaxlokk Bay, before *Theseus* entered Grand Harbour in the afternoon. On 11 February *Theseus* put to sea to land on the Sea Furies of 807 Squadron and the Fireflies of 810 Squadron, which had come from *Ocean.* The last week of February saw *Theseus* at sea and taking part in fleet manoeuvres with the cruisers *Glasgow* and *Liverpool,* together with various escorts. On 6 March there was a seven-day visit to Naples and later in the month, with other units of the fleet, she took part in 'Exercise Full Toes' in the Malta exercise areas. In early April she visited Tripoli and on 19 April, having returned to Malta, she hoisted the Flag of FO2 Mediterranean, Vice-Admiral R. A. B. Edwards, for an official visit to Greek ports. During the forenoon of Monday 21 April, in company with *Glasgow* (flag C-in-C Mediterranean, Admiral Sir John Edelston), *Euryalus, Manxman, Armada, Cheviot, St James, Saintes, Solebay, Vigo,* and two RFAs, *Theseus* left Grand Harbour and set course for Piraeus. For ceremonial occasions *Theseus* was also carrying the pipe band of the Highland Light Infantry and a 70-strong detachment and guard of the RAF. During the passage an air defence exercise was carried out, in conjunction with RAF Mosquito and Vampire aircraft, and on 23 April the fleet anchored in Phaleron Bay outside Piraeus, the port for Athens. The visit was to mark the unveiling of a memorial to men of the Commonwealth Forces who had died in Greece during the Second World War, and this was performed on 25 April by King Paul of the Hellenes. Next day the King visited the fleet at anchor in the bay and for half an hour between 10.30 and 11.00 he inspected Divisions on *Theseus'* flight deck. When the carrier left Phaleron Bay on 28 April, she had on board the Greek Minister of Defence and his staff who were given a flying display before they were transferred to the Greek destroyer *Niki,* and *Theseus* set course for Malta where she arrived on the last day of the month.

During the first week of May *Theseus* operated from Grand Harbour, but on 27 May, with *Glory* having arrived in Malta from the Far East the previous day, she was able to begin her passage back to the UK, and she left for Gibraltar. On board for the journey were the personnel and aircraft of 812 and 814 Squadrons, who had completed a tour of duty in *Glory. Theseus* left Gibraltar on 1 June and she arrived at Spithead three days later, before steaming up harbour on 5 June to secure alongside South Railway Jetty. Seven days later she was towed to No 14 dry dock for a nine-week assisted maintenance period, and although she was alongside Pitch House Jetty by the end of July, in time to take part in Navy Days, it was mid-August before she put to sea again. After leaving Portsmouth on Monday 18 August and meeting the destroyer *Broadsword, Theseus* landed on the aircraft of 804 Squadron before making her way north for exercises off Scotland's west coast and then Invergordon, from where she operated until 10 September, when she secured to a buoy at Rosyth. On Monday 15 September *Theseus* joined 'Exercise Mainbrace' in northern waters, where she operated with the US Navy's aircraft carrier *Mindoro* and the Canadian carrier *Magnificent.* 'Mainbrace' was a major NATO exercise and *Theseus'* part involved convoy escort duties round the Pentland Firth. On the opposing side were the fleet carriers *Eagle* and *Illustrious,* and *Theseus'* part in the exercise was concluded on 23 September when she left Danish waters for Portsmouth, arriving during the afternoon of 25 September. Five days later *Theseus* sailed for the Mediterranean, once again to provide the necessary air cover whilst *Glory* returned to Korean waters and *Ocean* made her way back to the Mediterranean. It was on 9 October that she arrived in Grand Harbour, from where she operated the Sea Furies and Fireflies of 898 and 807 Squadrons. On the last day of October, with the destroyers

Chevron and *Chivalrous,* she left Grand Harbour for a seven-day visit to the city of Trieste which, at that time, was under joint Allied and Yugoslav control. The visit was followed by flying exercises in the Adriatic, but by 12 November *Theseus* was back at Malta. On 17 November the carrier sailed from Grand Harbour to carry out three sessions of night flying operations, but at 20.56 the next day a Firefly ditched into the sea on take-off and although the pilot was recovered by *Chevron,* there was no trace of the observer, Lt B. E. Clutterbuck. *Theseus* continued to operate from Malta and on Friday 28 November she embarked the Duke of Edinburgh and left Grand Harbour to put on a display of dive-bombing, cannon and rocket firing. Her escort *Daring* put on a gunnery display with her main 4.5-inch armament, before both ships anchored in Marsaxlokk Bay and the Duke of Edinburgh lowered his personal standard and left the carrier by launch. The display marked the end of *Theseus'* second stint in the Mediterranean Fleet, for that same day *Ocean* had arrived back in Malta and on Monday 1 December, having embarked 802 and 825 Squadrons, *Theseus* left Malta to return via Gibraltar to Portsmouth. She arrived at Spithead on Tuesday 9 December, and next day she steamed up harbour to secure alongside Pitch House Jetty. On 15 December Captain D. McI Russell RN joined the ship, and at 09.00 the following day he took command of the carrier.

Having spent Christmas and New Year at Portsmouth *Theseus* put to sea again on 20 January 1953 to operate the Sea Furies of 812 and the Fireflies of 824 Squadron, together with aircraft from the Royal Netherlands Navy's No 3 Squadron at Portland. On 26 January, however, with the cruiser *Swiftsure* and the destroyers *Barrosa* and *St James,* she set course for Gibraltar from where, during the whole of February and the first two weeks of March, she operated with *Eagle, Vanguard* and the destroyers *Broadsword, Corunna, Diamond* and *St James.* At 12.30 on Wednesday 25 February, whilst off Gibraltar, a Firefly crashed into the sea off the port side and although the pilot was rescued by *Barrosa,* the passenger, Midshipman F. F. Meeks RN, from HMS *Diamond,* was lost. On the last day of February a memorial service was held for the young sailor. The flying exercises continued during the first two weeks of March and on 12 March, as the Yugoslav warship *Galeb,* carrying Marshal Tito on his way to Britain for a State Visit, passed through the Strait of Gibraltar, *Theseus, Eagle* and *Indomitable* all steamed past and fired a 21-gun salute while their aircraft roared overhead in a joint fly-past. On Monday 16 March, having flown off her aircraft whilst steaming up Channel, *Theseus* returned to Portsmouth. For Navy Days in the first week of April an Attacker jet fighter was loaded on board and put on display on the flight deck and three weeks later *Theseus* put to sea again. On Wednesday 29 April she sailed to land on the Sea Furies of 802 Squadron and the Fireflies of 824 Squadron, for operations in the Channel until the end of May. On Monday 4 May, off the Isle of Wight, there was a catapult failure and as a result a Sea Fury ditched into the sea over the bow. Fortunately, the pilot was rescued by the planeguard destroyer *Cadiz.* In early June there was a visit to Torquay, which was followed on Monday 15 June by the Coronation Fleet Review at Spithead. *Theseus* took her place with the other capital ships in 'F-line', where she anchored between *Illustrious* and the Canadian aircraft carrier *Magnificent.* Later in the afternoon some of her aircraft took part in the Fleet Air Arm fly-past over the Solent.

After leaving Spithead with *St Kitts* on 16 June *Theseus* steamed round to Milford Haven from where, after embarking 802 and 824 Squadrons, she sailed for the Mediterranean. For this third short stint with the Mediterranean Fleet *Theseus* was to take the place of *Ocean,* which had sailed east to relieve *Glory* off Korea, whilst the latter returned home to Portsmouth. *Theseus* arrived in Malta on 26 June and 17 days later, after seven days of flying exercises off the island, she was ready to accompany the fleet on its summer cruise. At 09.15 on Monday 13 July, led by the cruiser *Glasgow* (flag C-in-C Mediterranean, Admiral Lord Mountbatten), *Theseus* joined Bermuda, HMNZS *Black Prince,* INS *Delhi* (ex-HMS *Achilles*) and an escort screen to carry out an air defence exercise as they steamed towards Neapolis, before moving on to Phaleron Bay. The main port of call was Istanbul where, after passing units of the US Sixth Fleet which had just left the Turkish capital, the Mediterranean Fleet made a majestic entry into the Bosporus, watched by thousands of people gathered on both the Asian and European shores. Altogether, including minesweepers and auxiliaries, 22 units of the fleet anchored off the city and this huge presence led to protests from the Soviet Union that the earlier US visit, followed by the Mediterranean Fleet's visit were 'tantamount to military demonstrations against the Soviet Union.' However, the Turkish Government replied that, '...the frequency of naval visits could only be interpreted as felicitous evidence of the friendly ties binding Turkey to the countries to which these fleets belong.' Whilst the ship's company enjoyed their runs ashore in Istanbul, Lord Mountbatten was involved in numerous diplomatic functions, including a reception on board *Theseus* for Turkish Government ministers, which included the ceremony of Beating Retreat by the Royal Marines. The visit ended on Monday 3 August when, accompanied by Turkish naval units, the ships of the Mediterranean Fleet left Istanbul to carry out tactical exercises in the Aegean, following which *Theseus* returned to Malta on 6 August to carry out maintenance.

On Thursday 27 August *Theseus* sailed from Grand Harbour to land on her aircraft and to carry out flying

Theseus alongside Portsmouth Dockyard's South Railway Jetty in September 1956 shortly before leaving for the Suez campaign.
(Maritime Photo Library)

practice in local waters. At 07.21 on Wednesday 9 September, with *Theseus* en route to Phaleron Bay for a visit to Athens, Firefly VT 404 crashed into the sea over the port side of the ship whilst the first detail of aircraft was being launched. Despite a thorough search of the area there was no sign of the pilot, Lt V. A. Parkes, or his observer, Sub-Lt J. F. walker, who were posted as 'missing presumed dead'. Later that day, at 16.40, *Theseus* anchored in Phaleron Bay and shore leave was granted. Next day, at 12.30, the first liberty men left the ship and thereafter at regular intervals there was a steady stream of men leaving for a trip into Piraeus. However, at just after 06.00 that morning, at the western end of the island of Cyprus, within a 20-mile radius of the town of Paphos, a severe earthquake had rocked the area killing over 40 people, injuring hundreds more and leaving at least 50,000 without any food, water or accommodation. Although British Army units on the island had joined the rescue teams, it was clear that more help was urgently needed and at 19.00 on 10 September *Theseus* was ordered to sail for Paphos as soon as possible. All shore leave was cancelled immediately and additional embarkation patrols were landed to round up liberty men. Finally, at just after midnight on 11 September, with everyone back on board and with steam having been raised, *Theseus* weighed anchor and set course for Paphos Bay. As well as the carrier other units, including the destroyers *Daring* and *Saintes,* and the tank landing ships *Reggio* and *Striker,* were also ordered to the coast of Cyprus. *Theseus* anchored in Paphos Bay during the morning of 12 September and Derek Lander, who was serving as a Naval Air Mechanic, recalls that first day: 'Volunteers were called for to help with the work ashore and I was one of those who offered my services. When we got ashore we mustered at the Limassol football ground where the Army had deposited a huge supply of tents and we were split into working parties to go up into the hills to identify areas where the tents were urgently needed. It was gruelling work and we were on the go for 16 hours every day.'

Two Dragonfly helicopters which used *Theseus* as a base for two days, flew some 136 sorties carrying food, tents and injured people, whilst the working parties from the ship did magnificent work in pitching tents and distributing food to over 4,000 villagers in the worst affected area. Finally, during the evening of 14 September, *Theseus* weighed anchor to return to Malta, arriving in Grand Harbour on 17 September. A few days later, flying the flag of Flag Officer Flotillas (Med), and accompanied by the destroyer *St Kitts, Theseus* carried out flying exercises in preparation for a major naval exercise. During this period the First Lord of the Admiralty, Mr J. L. P. Thomas, paid two visits to the ship. The exercise, code-named 'Weldfast', began on 29 September and for the squadrons it involved nine days of very intensive flying operations. On 5 October there was a break of 12 hours at Soudha Bay in Crete, where aircrew members were allowed ashore for some relaxation before the exercise resumed; it finally ended on 8 October.

On Saturday 10 October *Theseus* secured in Port Said Harbour for three days to embark stores from the Suez Canal Zone, from where a phased withdrawal of British Forces had started, but by 16 October she was back in Malta. *Theseus'* time with the Mediterranean Fleet, and her career as a fixed-wing aircraft carrier, was drawing to a close and on Tuesday 20 October she left Malta, where her place was taken by *Glory,* to return home to Portsmouth. She made a three-day stop at Gibraltar and on Thursday 29 October, she carried out her final fixed-wing flying operations when the aircraft were launched to their bases ashore. That evening she anchored at Spithead, and the following forenoon she steamed up harbour to secure alongside Pitch House Jetty. By mid-November the ship's company had been much reduced, and on 20 January 1954 she was taken into dockyard hands for a refit which would convert her for use as a training ship with the Home Fleet.

Theseus spent the first months of 1954 in No 14 dry dock, during which time classrooms were built in the main hangar, which also doubled up as a wet weather parade ground. In addition her mess decks were adapted to accommodate the various types of trainees who would go to sea for the first time in *Theseus.* In mid-May she was moved out of dry dock and on Monday 12 July *Theseus* sailed from Portsmouth to carry out trials and after returning for further adjustments, on 26 July she left for Portland where she secured to a buoy in the harbour. *Theseus* was replacing *Implacable* on the Home Fleet Training Squadron and during the weeks which followed Men under Training and stores were transferred from *Implacable.* On Tuesday 17 August, Captain H. N. S. Brown CBE RN left the fleet carrier as he too transferred to *Theseus* and officially took command of the smaller carrier. Next day the Flag Officer Training Squadron, Rear-Admiral Carlill, hoisted his flag in *Theseus,* which would remain the Squadron flagship until the end of her career. As a Home Fleet training ship *Theseus* would take all Seamen of the Navy, except boy entrants, to carry out their Part I and Part II training in the squadron which would undoubtedly be the ship's largest commitment. The course of disciplinary seamanship, basic gunnery and educational training took 17 weeks for the adult entry ordinary seamen, while junior seamen stayed for 20 weeks. During this time each class was, if possible, sent out for a two-week spell in a small ship. The course for National Service ordinary seamen was broadly similar, but lasted only ten weeks as 'school' was omitted. The other main categories of ratings were the adult entry signalmen and junior signalmen who carried out a 14-week disciplinary seamanship and technical training course, and the specially selected engineer mechanics who did a 12-week course. During the school holiday periods another important function of *Theseus* was the training of large numbers of school and university entry RNVR ratings. Their two-week course qualified them as 'passed Part I', which represented a great saving of time when they were called up for their National Service.

On 17 September, with a full complement of trainees, *Theseus* put to sea for the first time as a training ship and after manoeuvres with *Ocean,* they both put into Torquay for four days before returning to Portland. On 21 October they took part in a Home Fleet convoy escort exercise, which took them to Gibraltar in the role of merchantmen. In late November, again with *Ocean, Theseus* made a four-day visit to Tangier, before returning to Portland on 1 December. Nine days later, on Friday 10 December, there was a change of command when Captain A. C. C. Miers VC DSO* RN took over from Captain Brown. Captain Miers won his VC whilst in command of the Submarine *Torbay* and in an unprecedented Investiture at Buckingham Palace he was accompanied by his engineer officer who was awarded the DSC, two of his lieutenants who were awarded Bars to their DSCs and 24 of his ratings who were awarded DSMs.

In late January 1955 *Theseus* and *Ocean* visited Brest where the damaged harbour and fort installations still bore witness to the RAF's wartime raids on *Scharnhorst* and *Gneisenau. Theseus* also carried out anti-submarine exercises with Home Fleet units and on 7 March, leading *Ocean,* she sailed for Gibraltar. During their stay in Gibraltar the training ships took part in manoeuvres in the Western Mediterranean, during which they were 'attacked' by Avengers from *Albion.* On 1 April *Theseus* returned to Portland and later that month Rear-Admiral H. W. Biggs took over as FOTS. On 23 May *Theseus* left Portland to take part in 'Exercise New Moon', a convoy escort exercise, with units of the Home Fleet as well as Dutch and French vessels. The exercise also allowed for a short call at Plymouth but, a few days later, she was back at Portland. On 6 June, having been delayed by bad weather, *Theseus* led *Ocean* to sea again, this time to Liverpool where, two days later, whilst *Ocean* secured alongside, *Theseus* anchored in mid-river. However, the open-hearted hospitality of the city more than made up for the inconvenience and for the ship's company there were dances, including a Civic Ball given by the city authorities, and visits to factories. The officers enjoyed luncheon parties and a Civic Dinner, and generally much use was made of the 'late' liberty boats, with sleep becoming a valuable commodity. From Liverpool *Theseus* made a short stop at Portree, where 'exped' parties spent two days on Raasay Island. From Portree *Theseus* steamed round to Invergordon and from there to Bergen where, during the approach to the town she passed the picturesque fjords. During the evening of Monday 4 July, the last full day of the visit, there was a huge fire in some wooden warehouses close to the town and members of the ship's company lent a hand with the fire-fighting. Next day, as *Theseus* left Bergen, a thick pall of black smoke was still hanging over the site.

On passage from Bergen to Rosyth *Theseus* joined the Home Fleet and NATO units for a convoy exercise code-named 'Long Swell'. *Theseus* stayed at Rosyth for seven days until 14 July when, with *Ocean,* she left for Portland via an east coast resort. Whilst *Ocean* called at Margate, *Theseus* anchored off Scarborough for five days. With no easterly gales to interfere with the boat service between ship and shore, everyone enjoyed the visit with all sorts of attractions free to members of the ship's company. On 21 July *Theseus* returned to Portland for a rather quieter life, interrupted only by the visit of a French Training Squadron and Navy Days when, on 1 August, nearly 4,500 visitors toured the ship.

In mid-August *Theseus* sailed for her annual docking and maintenance period, most of which was spent in the floating dry dock in Portsmouth Harbour. By 20 September, however, she was back at Portland, but in October she was ordered to Portsmouth to prepare for a trooping voyage to Cyprus where, following an escalation of the EOKA terrorist campaign, she was required to carry troops and army transport to the island. *Theseus* arrived in Portsmouth on 25 October, and two days later after loading army trucks and stores she sailed for Famagusta. During the passage the weather took its toll on some of the more inexperienced seafarers, but on 2 November she anchored in Famagusta's outer harbour where the Men under Training helped to unload all the trucks. When the task was completed *Theseus* steamed to Malta where she met *Ocean* and on 8 November the two ships left for Gibraltar and Tangier, before returning to Portland on 1 December. Later that month, on Thursday 29 December, there was a final change of command for *Theseus* when Captain E. F. Pizey DSO RN took over from Captain Miers for the final 12 months of *Theseus'* operational career.

On 20 January 1956, Captain Pizey took *Theseus* to sea and, with *Ocean,* she took part in Home Fleet exercises, which included air attacks by Wyverns and Sea Hawk jets. On 25 January, with the exercises over, *Theseus* paid a six-day visit to the Spanish naval base at El Ferrol on Spain's northern Atlantic coast. Following this *Theseus* joined *Ocean* again and the two ships returned to the UK with *Theseus* arriving at Portsmouth on 2 February. Ahead lay a four-month refit, during which she would be adapted to operate a limited number of Whirlwind helicopters. Soon after her arrival in Portsmouth, during the afternoon of 28 February, she landed on four Whirlwinds of 845 Squadron for a brief visit and by 15.00 they had taken off again. On 4 May 1956 Rear-Admiral G. B. Sayers, having taken over as FOTS, hoisted his flag in *Theseus* and on 11 June she sailed for Invergordon. For the next ten days, together with *Ocean,* she operated the Whirlwind helicopters of 845 Squadron, with four being allocated to each ship. This was followed on 25 June by a visit to Kristiansand, and after leaving Norway on 3 July *Theseus* met *Ocean,* as well as *Glasgow, Battleaxe, Defender* and *Scorpion* for 'Exercise Fairwind'. The exercise was followed by ten days at Rosyth and, during the return passage to Portland, she paid a six-day visit to Tynemouth where she anchored off the coast. Unfortunately, strong winds disrupted the liberty boats, but when the ship was opened to visitors one afternoon she proved to be very popular. When *Theseus* weighed anchor to set course for Portland she met *Ocean,* and on 24 July the two ships arrived at their respective buoys.

Two days later, despite the fact that the lease was not due to expire until 1968, President Nasser of Egypt nationalized the Suez Canal Company, which led the British Government under Sir Anthony Eden to declare that Britain, as a majority shareholder, should intervene. However, with British troops having left Egypt only in the previous month any reoccupation was fraught with difficulty and both Britain and France publicly entered diplomatic negotiations, whilst covertly they made preparations, in collusion with Israel, to invade Egypt. *Theseus* was to be an important unit in the invasion plans, the forward bases for which were to be Malta and Cyprus, and on 30 July the ship was ordered to Portsmouth, where she arrived that evening. With all long leave having been cancelled, preparations went ahead for *Theseus* to make a trooping voyage to Cyprus and the task of embarking ammunition, stores, transport and troops of the 16th Independent Parachute Regiment began. After five days of hard work and with the embarkation complete, at 17.30 on Sunday 5 August *Theseus* sailed for Cyprus. Five days into the passage, in the warmer waters of the Mediterranean, there was some drama when a soldier fell overboard. The ship's emergency procedures were extremely well rehearsed and within minutes the sea boat was away and 14 minutes later the man was rescued. Next day, on 11 August, *Theseus* arrived at Famagusta where all the transport and troops were disembarked and men of the 4th Commando Brigade, Royal Marines, boarded the ship for the passage to Malta. Finally, on the morning of 18 August, *Theseus* left Malta for a fast passage home and during the evening of 22 August she secured alongside Portsmouth's South Railway Jetty. During the whole of September *Theseus* remained at Portsmouth whilst her ship's company took the summer leave which had been cancelled a few weeks earlier, but on Monday 1 October she left harbour for Spithead and the Channel where she carried out 12 days of intensive training with the Whirlwind helicopters of 845 Squadron. Although it was not generally known at the time, with the helicopters transporting troops between the ship and shore, this was the training for the Suez landings when both *Theseus* and *Ocean* would, for the first time, carry out an amphibious landing of Royal Marines by helicopter.

Having embarked the 12 helicopters of 845 Squadron and more troops, *Theseus* left Portsmouth on 22 October to set course for Malta where, on Friday 26 October, she secured alongside Parlatorio Wharf. Seven days later, at 09.30 on 2 November, the embarkation of half of the men and transport of 45 Commando, Royal Marines, began and by 18.00 it had been completed. That evening the Royal Marines were allowed shore leave and in the words of one member of 45 Commando they 'had a last boisterous night in Valletta, with the Maltese police quite unable to withstand the onslaught as we ravaged the "Gut".' Next day, at 11.15, *Theseus* sailed from Malta bound for Port Said and three days later, at 05.56, she anchored in Port Said Roads, some eight and a half miles offshore, where preparations to land the Royal Marines began. The campaign had actually started in the early hours of 1 November, when aircraft from *Eagle, Albion, Bulwark* and *Arromanches* bombed Egyptian airfields, with the main seaborne landings being made in the early hours of 6 November. For *Theseus* flying started at 08.00, when one helicopter carrying Lt Col Tailyour RM took off to make a reconnaissance of Port Said, which by that time had been covered by a haze of smoke. As a result of the reconnaissance it was decided that a landing in the sports stadium, as had been originally intended, would be too dangerous and it was decided instead to put 45 Commando ashore on some open ground adjacent to the De Lesseps statue. Their task, during the initial stages of the operation, was to contain enemy opposition that came from the poorer shanty quarter of Port Said. At 08.15 four helicopters carrying the first wave of the marines took off from *Theseus'* flight deck, and thereafter they continued a shuttle service between the ship and shore until 10.02, when *Theseus* was able to signal, 'Helo lift complete'. Shortly after the troop lift had been completed the helicopters began evacuating casualties, supplementing the LCAs which were also evacuating the wounded to both *Theseus* and *Ocean.* That afternoon, at 15.49, *Theseus* received orders to enter Port Said Harbour and by 18.00 she was secured to 8a buoy, close to *Ocean,* and just off the town's waterfront. Sadly, that evening at 20.15 Royal Marine M. J. Fowler of 45 Commando died on board as a result of wounds he had received in the assault. Three-quarters of an hour later, at 21.00, under intense diplomatic and economic pressure, the British Government ordered a ceasefire from midnight, and agreed to a complete withdrawal from Egypt. It had become clear that British Governments no longer had the power to carry out such invasions, and in future any such interventions would require American support, or be American-led.

For *Theseus* there still remained the task of evacuating the wounded and at 10.03 on Wednesday 7 November, with casualties embarked, she left Port Said. Just over three hours later, at 13.30, in a position Lat 31° - 53'N/Long 32° - 26'E, the funeral service was held for Marine M. J. Fowler and his body was committed to the deep. Three days later *Theseus* arrived in Malta where the casualties were disembarked and troops and transport of the Duke of Wellington's Regiment boarded. That evening the ship sailed for Cyprus where, off Famagusta, they were landed. *Theseus* then returned to Malta, arriving in Grand Harbour on 17 November, and where she would remain until the first week of December, with only two days spent at sea carrying out flying practice with 845 Squadron. During the forenoon of 5 December the helicopters were flown ashore and *Theseus* set course for Port Said where she arrived two days later. During the next 24 hours she embarked troops and their vehicles, landing them in Malta on 10 December before leaving for Port Said once again. At 16.15 on 13 December, when she was some 30 miles outside Port Said, three Army Austers made successful landings on the flight deck and they remained on board until 07.35 the next morning when they took off for Gamil airfield. Later that day, having been cruising off the coast since the previous day, *Theseus* entered Port Said Harbour to undertake her last embarkation of troops, equipment and transport. Over the 24 hours that she remained in Port Said 84 officers and 1,069 other ranks of the RAOC, RASC, REME and Royal Engineers, together with 100 3-ton lorries were embarked, and at 07.30 on Saturday 15 December she left Egypt for home. During the homeward passage *Theseus* steamed the 3,000 miles between Port Said and the Isle of Wight in six days, but during the morning of 21 December the Solent was blanketed in fog and at 08.18 she anchored at Spithead. Early that afternoon, whilst at anchor, the small Norwegian oil tanker *Geira* collided with the carrier, but neither ship suffered any serious damage and at 14.05 *Theseus* weighed anchor to make her way up harbour. Less than half an hour later she was secured alongside South Railway Jetty. She had completed her last voyage under her own steam and her career had started and ended with a collision at Spithead.

On Saturday 22 December, Captain Pizey made his farewell address to the ship's company, and two days later he relinquished his command and left the ship for a well-earned retirement. He was followed by the main body of the ship's company who left for leave and for fresh drafts. In January 1957 *Theseus* was decommissioned, and for over four years she lay in Portsmouth Harbour, much of that time at a buoy in Fareham Creek. The end finally came in late 1961 when, having been sold for scrap, on 29 November she was towed out of harbour and up to Inverkeithing where she was broken up.

Commanding Officers:

Captain T. M. Brownrigg CBE DSO RN	9 October 1945
Captain R. K. Dickson DSO RN	31 December 1946
Captain J. P. Wright DSO RN	10 June 1948
Captain A. S. Bolt DSC RN	18 October 1949
Captain C. N. Lentaigne DSO RN	8 June 1951
Captain D. McI Russell RN	16 December 1952
Captain H. N. S. Brown CBE RN	17 August 1954
Captain A. C. C. Miers VC DSO* RN	10 December 1954
Captain E. F. Pizey DSO RN	29 December 1955

Battle Honours:

Nile 1798
Acre 1799
Dardanelles 1915-16
Basque Roads 1809
Benin 1897
Korea 1950-51

Theseus and the battleship *Vanguard* laid up in Fareham Creek. The carrier was sent to the breaker's yard in late 1961. *(FotoFlite)*

Chapter Fourteen

HMS *Triumph*
April 1946 – November 1950

The last of the Colossus-class light fleet carriers to be laid down was *Triumph,* and the contract for the ship went to the Tyneside shipbuilders of R & W Hawthorn Leslie & Co Ltd of Hebburn-on-Tyne. The first keel plates for the new aircraft carrier were laid on 27 January 1943 and some 20 months later the hull was ready to take to the water. The launching ceremony took place on Monday 2 October 1944, and it was performed by Lady Edwina Mountbatten, the wife of Admiral Lord Mountbatten who, at that time, was the Supreme Allied Commander, South-East Asia, based in Ceylon. As she sent the new carrier into the waters of the River Tyne Lady Mountbatten named her *Triumph,* the eighth ship to bear the name. The first had been a 1,000-ton First Rate ship of the line which, with 42 guns, had been built in 1561 and had taken part in battles against the Armada. The seventh *Triumph,* commissioned in 1937, was a T-class submarine which was lost to an enemy mine in January 1942. In November 1944, as the eighth *Triumph* lay at her fitting-out berth on the River Tyne, the first naval personnel, under the command of Cdr (E) H. L. Matthews RN, joined the ship although, with much work still to be done on the accommodation, they had to live ashore. Eleven months later, on 9 October 1945, her first commanding officer, Captain H. W. Faulkner CBE DSO RN, was appointed. By that time, with the Second World War over, it was clear that *Triumph* would not be required by the British Pacific Fleet and, for her first commission, she was allocated to the Home Fleet.

At noon on 9 April 1946, the officers and ratings who had been standing by the ship, reinforced by a draft of 244 ratings from Chatham who had joined that forenoon, commissioned the carrier. The occasion was marked by a ceremony on the flight deck, with the Royal Marines providing a guard and the ship's company a band. Over the days which followed stores were embarked and more personnel joined until, finally, at 13.00 on Monday 15 April, *Triumph* slipped her moorings and began her passage down the River Tyne. At 14.15 she passed the Tynemouth breakwater and once out into the North Sea course was set for Rosyth, with full-power trials being carried out en route. That evening, at 21.34, she anchored in the Firth of Forth and next morning she was at sea early to carry out trials over the St Abbs Head measured mile. As she worked up to full power she passed her sister *Ocean* which was returning from the Mediterranean. *Triumph* continued her initial machinery trials, returning to the Firth of Forth each afternoon, and these were followed by catapult deadload trials. On Friday 26 April, while she lay in the Firth of Forth, the first aircraft in the form of two Seafires and two Sea Furies were embarked from lighters, which gave the aircraft handlers some practice. Two days later the C-in-C Rosyth inspected Divisions, and this was followed by a Dedication Service in the hangar which was conducted by

The Commissioning Ceremony on *Triumph's* flight deck at R & W Hawthorne Leslie & Co's shipyard. The ceremony took place at midday on 9 April 1946. *(E. C Moore)*

the Bishop of Jarrow. On Monday 29 April preparations got under way again for *Triumph's* flying trials.

On the morning of Sunday 5 May, accompanied by the destroyer *Blencathra, Triumph* left the Firth of Forth to set course south for Spithead. During the morning watch of the next day she passed the South Goodwin lightship, and by the afternoon watch the Nab Tower was sighted and soon afterwards she anchored at Spithead. Flying trials were due to begin during the forenoon of 8 May, but poor visibility caused them to be postponed and it was at 15.28 that afternoon when the first deck landing was made by a Barracuda from RNAS Ford. After this the tempo increased and flying continued into the evening with more landings and catapult launches by a number of different aircraft. Next day the trials continued, with a Sea Otter joining the ship and this machine made a number of sea landings close to the ship before being hoisted on board. By the end of May, in the absence of *Illustrious* which was undergoing a refit, *Triumph* was carrying out the duties of the Home Fleet trials and training carrier off the Isle of Wight and operating Fireflies which were being launched by RATOG.

On Monday 3 June, after an early start from her anchorage, a Vampire jet carried out landing and launching trials, and these continued for three days before, on Friday 7 June, *Triumph* steamed up Southampton Water to secure alongside 101 berth in Southampton's Western Docks, close to the city's Royal Pier. This was a berth normally reserved for the crack Union Castle Line's luxury passenger liners, but *Triumph's* visit to Southampton was to mark 'Victory Week' and she was the centre of attraction in this port city usually more closely associated with passenger shipping. The ship was opened to visitors on most days, with detachments of seamen and Royal Marines marching in the 'Victory Parade' through the city centre. After leaving Southampton on 11 June and meeting the destroyer *Cadiz, Triumph* continued her duties as trials and training carrier, with Sea Hornets, Avengers, Barracudas and Seafire F17s all landing and taking off from the flight deck. During the forenoon of 20 June one of the Seafires was involved in the ship's first flight deck accident when it suffered a collapsed undercarriage, but there were no casualties. On 28 June, during a weekend break in Portsmouth, two worn-out Mosquito aircraft were loaded on board, and when *Triumph* put to sea the old twin-engined planes were broken up in barrier trials, before being dumped overboard.

In early July there was a short break at St Helier and in the middle of the month, at the end of each day's flying, *Triumph* anchored off Torquay, quite close to the shore. For the ship's company the holiday resort made for a good run ashore, but the dulcet tones of the Quartermaster calling all hands to 'lash up and stow' at 05.30 was not appreciated by some of the guests at nearby hotels. On Thursday 18 July, after several days operating from Torbay, *Triumph* returned to Portsmouth for a weekend break, during which it was learned that, flying the flag of the C-in-C Home Fleet, Admiral Lord Fraser of North Cape, the carrier was to visit Russia to attend the celebration of 'Red Fleet Day' on 28 July. The news, in the words of one of *Triumph's* Royal Marines, made 'saluting guns appear in a twinkling and Portsmouth Division produced an extra 30 marines, kitted-up and ready. They were all volunteers and in many cases it was their first big ship experience.'

On Sunday 21 July, *Triumph* left harbour to anchor at Spithead and at 13.30, with Admiral Fraser having arrived on board, she weighed anchor to steam up Channel. That evening she passed the South Goodwin lightship, and during the evening of 23 July she anchored for the night off the coast of Denmark, to continue her passage through the Baltic Sea the next morning. During the forenoon of 25 July a Russian liaison officer was embarked and that afternoon four Russian minesweepers met *Triumph* to escort her through the Gulf of Finland. At 06.50 on Friday 26 July the old Russian battleship *Oktyabrskaya Revolutsia* was sighted and by 09.15 *Triumph* was secured to a buoy at the Russian naval base on the island of Kronstadt. Whilst Admiral Fraser left for Moscow, where the main Russian parades and celebrations were to take place, shore leave for the officers and men on board *Triumph* and her escort *Rapid* consisted of organized visits to Leningrad (St Petersburg), where they were shown round museums and other centres of culture. They had few opportunities to explore on their own, but they did discover that beer was about six shillings (30p) a bottle. Although they were pleased to have had the opportunity to visit Leningrad, there were few who would have volunteered for a transfer to the Red Fleet, particularly for a commission at Kronstadt, which was extremely bleak. Admiral Fraser returned to the ship from Moscow on 3 August and *Triumph* sailed the next day, parading a guard and a band as she left the Russian naval base. The return home was a fast passage to Sheerness where she anchored during the evening of 8 August, moving to a buoy next morning where Admiral Fraser disembarked.

Triumph remained at Sheerness until the third week of September, a period which gave the Chatham ship's company some time at home, and during one weekend the ship was opened to visitors. During the morning watch of 14 August the Thames barge *Beaumont Belle* collided with *Triumph's* starboard forward gun sponson and lost its mainmast, but apart from some scuffed paintwork the carrier was unscathed. In the second week of September it was decided that *Triumph* would steam to Portsmouth for a short refit before joining the Mediterranean Fleet as the flagship to Flag Officer (Air) and FO2 Mediterranean. On Tuesday 24 September she left Sheerness to steam round to Portsmouth where, after five days at a buoy in Fareham Creek, she was moved to No 14 dry dock, where she

A single Seafire has plenty of room in *Triumph's* hangar.
(E. C. Moore)

Triumph enters Southampton Docks to celebrate 'Victory Week'. On the flight deck are a Sea Vampire, a Mosquito, a Firefly, a Seafire and a Barracuda, all of which were involved in the trials which *Triumph* was carrying out.
(Fleet Air Arm Museum, Cars T/38)

Dressed overall for HM Queen Elizabeth's birthday in 1946. *(E. C. Moore)*

remained until 10 December. Five days later, at South Railway Jetty, *Triumph* was visited by Admiral and Lady Mountbatten who spent four hours on board, and addressed the ship's company. Finally, on 17 December, with the refit over, *Triumph* steamed round to Sheerness where, once again, she secured to No 2 buoy. On Christmas Day there was a carol service in the hangar, and in the afternoon the ship was opened to guests of the ship's company.

On 7 January 1947, Vice-Admiral Sir Cecil Harcourt, who was to be Flag Officer (Air) and FO2, Mediterranean Fleet, hoisted his flag in *Triumph* and three days later the carrier left Sheerness to anchor off the Great Nore lightship for the night before steaming to Belfast to secure alongside Sydenham Jetty in order to embark the Firefly aircraft, stores and personnel of 827 Squadron. During the afternoon of 14 January, after just 24 hours alongside, the carrier left Belfast for Gibraltar where, four days later, she anchored in the bay. During the break Admiral Harcourt left by air for *Ocean* at Malta, and until the end of the month *Triumph* operated out of Gibraltar. On the last day of January, having embarked an unusual passenger in the form of a German national who was facing war crimes charges, she left Gibraltar to steam north for Glasgow. After a short delay off Greenock because of fog, she arrived in Glasgow's King George V Dock on 5 February, and after the German prisoner had been escorted ashore by the military police, *Triumph* spent five days embarking the Seafire aircraft, the stores and personnel of 800 Squadron. In addition she also took on a deck cargo of Seafires, and on 10 February she left Glasgow to steam direct to Malta, arriving six days later. For over four weeks *Triumph* operated from Grand Harbour or Marsaxlokk Bay, carrying out intensive flying operations, with weekend breaks in Grand Harbour. At 16.05 on 7 March a Seafire and its pilot were lost off Delimara Point, and a memorial service was held over the spot. In the second week of March, with Admiral Harcourt having rejoined, she carried out day and night exercises with other units of the fleet as the squadrons worked up. In mid-April, after a two-week maintenance period at Malta, *Triumph* was chosen to steam into the Atlantic to represent the Mediterranean Fleet in the duty of escorting the Royal Family in the battleship *Vanguard,* who were travelling home from their tour of South Africa. With the destroyer *Raider,* she left Malta on 17 April, steaming at economical speed and making a short stop at Gibraltar and arriving in Freetown on the last day of April. During the two days in Sierra Leone the army trucks of the RWAFF provided transport to nearby Lumli Beach and their regimental band entertained the ship's company on the flight deck. At 10.40 on 2 May, both *Triumph* and *Raider* left harbour and at 09.47 the next day, some 250 miles south-west of Freetown, they sighted *Vanguard* and her escort cruiser *Nigeria.* At 10.00 precisely, 20 Seafires and Fireflies of the Air Group were launched and an hour later, with the flight deck fully manned and guard and band paraded, *Triumph* steamed past *Vanguard's* port side and as the ship's company cheered ship, the aircraft roared overhead in a Royal Salute. So well synchronised were the meeting of the two ships, the gun salute, the fly-past and cheer ship, that the King sent a personal signal complimenting *Triumph.*

It had been hoped that the Royal Family would visit *Triumph* that day, but the weather prevented any boat transfers, and after landing on the Air Group *Triumph* took up her station astern of *Vanguard.* On Monday 5 May, as part of an air defence exercise, *Triumph's* Air Group carried out an 'attack' on the battleship, with the aircraft flying low over *Vanguard's* quarterdeck. Next day a signal was received from the Queen to say that she and the two Princesses, Elizabeth and Margaret, would visit the carrier on the following day. At 09.25 on Wednesday 7 May, midway between the islands of Tenerife and Fuerteventura, *Vanguard* and *Triumph* stopped and, accompanied by the two Princesses, the Queen boarded the carrier. The King, being under doctor's orders, was unable to leave *Vanguard.* After arriving on board and meeting *Triumph's* officers, they inspected the ship's company at Divisions and took the salute at the march past. At 11.45 the royal visitors left the carrier to return to the battleship's motor cutter which, as it rose and fell to a considerable height alongside the lower platform of the embarkation ladder, was no mean feat. Fortunately, they returned safely to *Vanguard* after their short visit which had involved the battleship and the aircraft carrier in a little bit of naval history in that it was the first time that both the King's and Queen's personal standards had flown together at sea. At 10.00 on 8 May the Air Group was flown off and an hour later, after five days of escort duties, *Triumph* and *Raider* parted company with *Vanguard.* To mark the event the ship's company manned the flight deck and once again, as *Triumph* steamed past, the Air Group roared overhead in salute. Soon afterwards, as *Triumph* landed on her aircraft and set course for Tangier, a signal of appreciation was received from the Royal Family, which ended with the ever-popular, 'Splice the Main Brace!'

During the forenoon of 9 May *Triumph* anchored in Tangier harbour for a two-day visit, which was notable for enormous meals in the restaurants ashore, and a children's party which was held in the wardroom. By 15 May, however, *Triumph* was off Malta, where her aircraft were launched to carry out an 'air strike' on Valletta, before landing at Hal Far. Next day the carrier secured to a buoy in Grand Harbour. During June *Triumph* operated out of Malta and in early July, with her sister *Ocean,* she joined the fleet in exercises off the island. On Tuesday 8 July there was a change of command when Captain E. M. C. Abel-Smith CVO RN took over from Captain Faulkner, and five days later the new captain inspected the ship's company at

Triumph's Sea Otter lands on. *(E. C. Moore)*

Divisions on the flight deck. By mid-July *Triumph* was at sea again and exercising with the cruisers *Liverpool* (C-in-C Med), *Leander* and *Norfolk.* At 06.20 on 19 July, whilst carrying out a convoy escort exercise with *Ocean* and other units, a Seafire crashed into the sea some miles from the ship, but fortunately the pilot was rescued by *Leander.* Two days later, with *Liverpool, Leander, Ocean* and four destroyers, *Triumph* anchored in the Bosporus at Istanbul for a five-day visit to the Turkish capital, and this was followed by five days at Piraeus. Whilst at the port King Paul of the Hellenes paid a visit to the carrier and he returned during the afternoon of 1 August, shortly before *Triumph* sailed, to be given a flying display off the Greek coast. The carrier remained in Greek waters, taking part in fleet exercises, and on 7 August, whilst in Nauplia Bay, the Greek King and Queen paid another visit to the ship. On 11 August, with the destroyers *Venus* and *Verulam, Triumph* operated off the coast of Palestine for four days where the Royal Navy was involved in the thankless task of preventing illegal immigrants from reaching the country by sea. This was followed by fleet exercises off Cyprus during which, at 04.30 on 19 August, an aircraft handler, OS Deakes, was killed by a rotating propeller blade. Later that day his funeral service was held on the flight deck and on 23 August the carrier returned to Malta. During September and October *Triumph* operated mainly from Malta, but there were periods spent off Tripoli and Aranci Bay, and in November she undertook a maintenance period in Grand Harbour. After operating off North Africa and Malta in early December, Christmas and New Year were spent in Grand Harbour.

On 7 January 1948 Vice-Admiral Harcourt struck his flag and left to take up his appointment as Second Sea Lord; he was relieved by Vice-Admiral Sir Thomas Troubridge, who hoisted his flag in *Triumph.* For most of January *Triumph* operated with *Ocean* off Malta, and on 17 February, with eight escorts, the two carriers sailed for fleet exercises en route to Gibraltar. At 10.30 on Wednesday 25

During *Triumph's* visit to Kronstadt in July 1946, the C-in-C of the Soviet Navy inspects Divisions on the flight deck. He is accompanied by Admiral of the Fleet, Lord Fraser of the North Cape. *(E. C. Moore)*

February, whilst heading for Toulon and during an air defence exercise, Seafire 179 ditched into the sea ahead of the ship. Despite a thorough search by both *Triumph* and the planeguard *Chequers,* there was no trace of the aircraft or of the pilot, Lt E. C. Marshall, and on 29 February, when flying was concluded, a memorial service was held on the flight deck. On 2 March there was a break at Toulon, where *Triumph* secured alongside Milhaud Quay, and this was followed by more exercises as the fleet made its way back to Malta. At 08.00 on 17 March, whilst *Triumph* was off the south coast of Sardinia, Firefly 274 ditched into the sea some miles away from the ship. The Sea Otter was quickly launched and the destroyer *Chaplet* also raced to the scene. At 10.25 the body of the observer, CPO (A) F. A. Dean, was recovered from the sea, and two hours later the pilot, Lt McDermott, was rescued from a small island off the Sardinian coast. At 18.10 the funeral service for CPO Dean was held and next day the carrier arrived in Grand Harbour. During April *Triumph* continued her flying operations, using Malta as her base, with visits to Venice and Trieste. On 19 April, however, the Air Group was flown ashore and after entering Grand Harbour the

On 3 May 1947, *Triumph* escorted the battleship *Vanguard* which was carrying the Royal Family home from their Royal Tour of South Africa. In this view the ship's company is manning the flight deck and preparing to cheer ship as the carrier passes *Vanguard* and her Air Group flies overhead in salute. *(E. C. Moore)*

With *Vanguard* in the background, the Queen and the two Princesses inspect the Royal Marines Guard of Honour on *Triumph's* flight deck. Two Fireflies and the Sea Otter are parked aft. *(E. C. Moore)*

carrier was moved into dry dock where she remained until mid-May.

During the forenoon of Tuesday 1 June *Triumph* put to sea again, but instead of sailing to the Far East as had been announced, she remained with the Mediterranean Fleet. After two weeks of flying operations off Malta she steamed east to Cyprus where she operated off Limassol. These exercises ended on 28 June, and next day saw *Triumph* off the coast of the newly self-proclaimed state of Israel where, for a week, with the destroyers *Virago* and *Volage,* she operated her aircraft off Haifa to provide air cover during the final withdrawal of British troops from what had been Palestine. On Tuesday 6 July *Triumph* was back in Turkish waters at the city of Smyrna (Izmir), whilst her Air Group, which had been flown ashore, made a tour of Turkish towns and cities. After further flying operations off Malta, mid-September saw *Triumph* start a three-month refit in Grand Harbour, during which she spent a month in AFD 35. On 20 December *Triumph* was at sea again, with Christmas and New Year being spent at Grand Harbour. Having sailed from Malta on 3 January 1949, for fleet exercises and the start of the fleet's first cruise of the year, on 9 January *Triumph* and the cruiser *Phoebe* were recalled to Malta so that they could be ready to sail for the coast of Israel should they be required. Two days earlier the Israeli forces had shot down five RAF Spitfires, and with diplomatic tensions high, *Triumph* spent the rest of the month in and around Grand Harbour. In February and March she continued to operate in the Malta exercise areas, on occasions with her sister *Theseus* and with the battleship *Vanguard,* but on 23 March she left Malta to return home and pay off. On 30 March she arrived in Glasgow's King George V Dock to disembark the squadron personnel and stores, and to embark Captain R. M. J. Hutton DSO** RN. After leaving Glasgow *Triumph* made a slow three-day voyage to Sheerness where she arrived on 4 April to be greeted by hundreds of relatives and friends who were ferried out to the ship. Next day Captain Hutton assumed command of *Triumph,* and she was paid off.

During the 18 days which followed the change of command a new ship's company was drafted to *Triumph* and on Thursday 21 April she was recommissioned. Two days later she left Sheerness to steam round to Glasgow to re-embark the 13th Carrier Air Group of 800 (Seafire) Squadron and 827 (Firefly) Squadron. Leaving Glasgow and the River Clyde on 28 April *Triumph* set course for the Mediterranean and during the forenoon of 6 May the first flying operations of the second commission took place when the aircraft were launched to Hal Far. Later that forenoon *Triumph* entered Grand Harbour to carry out an assisted maintenance period, and it was the last day of June when she put to sea and landed on the Air Group. During

Triumph enters Istanbul in July 1947. The cruiser in the background is HMS *Leander.*
(Fleet Air Arm Museum, Cars T/67)

On 15 October 1948, *Triumph* was manoeuvred into the Admiralty Floating Dock (AFD 35) in Grand Harbour for a refit.
(Fleet Air Arm Museum, Cars T/80)

Triumph and dghajsas in Grand Harbour. These local boats provided a very efficient ferry service for liberty men returning to their ships. *(Fleet Air Arm Museum, Cars T/85)*

Triumph's second commission was spent in the Far East and in this photograph she is seen at Aden during her passage to Singapore and Hong Kong.
(Fleet Air Arm Museum, Cars T/101)

the whole of July the carrier, accompanied by the destroyer *Alamein,* carried out her work-up with weekend breaks in Grand Harbour. At 07.37 on Tuesday 12 July, during early flying operations, a Seafire which was landing on hit the round down aft, killing the pilot, Lt (P) Sugden. Although most of the wreckage fell into the sea, large portions, including the engine and wings, were stuck on the carrier's stern. In order to clear it *Triumph* stopped her engines and the destroyer *Corunna* had to manoeuvre in close to *Triumph's* stern in order to get a line round the wreckage and then steam astern, pulling it away from the carrier's round down. Meanwhile, *Corunna's* sea boat had been searching the area, but no trace of the pilot was found and only small pieces of wreckage were recovered. Later that day a memorial service for Lt Sugden was held on the flight deck. On Thursday 4 August, having spent five days in Grand Harbour, *Triumph* left Malta to steam east for a deployment with the Far East Fleet. She made her transit of the Suez Canal on 7 August, and there was a short delay before she continued her passage whilst a Seafire, which had made a successful landing on one wheel at RAF Fayid in Egypt, was recovered. On Saturday 13 August, after a 24-hour refuelling stop at Aden, *Triumph* and the destroyer *Charity* sailed for Colombo, and the two ships had a rough passage across the Arabian Sea before they reached their destination. Three days later they were at sea again and bound for Singapore, where *Triumph* met her sister *Ocean* which was employed on trooping duties. Arriving off Hong Kong on 3 September the Air Group flew a massed 'air strike' against the colony's air defences, which was 'opposed' by 24 RAF Spitfires, before landing at Kai Tak. Later that forenoon *Triumph* secured to a buoy in Hong Kong Harbour.

Triumph's operations with the Far East Fleet began on 7 September, when she sailed to carry out flying operations in the South China Sea, anchoring in Junk Bay that evening. Soon after coming to anchor for the night a report was received that a tropical depression some 150 miles east-south-east of the ship was fast becoming a typhoon with wind speeds reaching hurricane force and it was heading for the anchorage. The ship was brought to immediate notice and at 23.45 she weighed anchor, but by this time it was dark, raining hard and the winds were blowing in excess of 50 knots. Off Tathong Point, at the southern end of Tung Lung Island, where the ship cleared the lee of the land, a series of huge, steep and breaking seas met the ship head on with terrific thumps, and they literally stopped *Triumph* dead in the water. It was clear that the typhoon had struck 12 hours ahead of schedule and with rocks just a few cables from either side of the ship, she was in a dangerous predicament. With enormous seas and winds in excess of 80 knots, at ten knots and steering a course of 110 degrees the carrier could make little headway from the land. At one stage, at just after midnight on 9 September, the ship was making directly for Wang Lan Island and was only ten minutes from grounding. A drastic alteration of course was made and, risking structural damage, speed was increased to 14 knots. There then followed some very severe bumps and the ship's motion became extremely violent, with flooding causing a number of electrical fires. By 01.30 the wind speed had reached 100 knots, but as the ship was out of danger, speed was reduced to spare her from unnecessary buffeting. By 03.30, with water up to the door sill levels throughout the ship, the barometer began to rise and by dawn the centre of the typhoon was some 35 miles south-west of the ship. When daylight came *Triumph* was riding some very high, steep and confused seas, but with the worst over the damage on board could be surveyed. One whaler had disappeared altogether and the other had been smashed up by the weight of water. Bofors mountings and gun sponsons were bent and distorted, with motor boats, motor cutters and dinghies smashed up completely. Below decks water sloshed everywhere, but in the hangar all the aircraft had come through remarkably well, as had a flight deck park of four aircraft abreast of the island - apart from one which had been assaulted by the fork lift truck as it made its way over the side. In the forenoon course was altered to the north-east and during the first dog watch a rather battered and bedraggled *Triumph* was able to enter Hong Kong Harbour. Five days later, with repairs having been made, the carrier put to sea to land on her aircraft, but at 13.15, as Firefly 282 was landing on, it missed all the arrester wires and crashed into the barrier. Unfortunately, the additional fuel tank it was carrying under its belly caught fire and its port undercarriage collapsed, trapping three ratings under its blazing port wing. One of the men, Stoker Mechanic W. Martin, died of his injuries and the other two, as well as the pilot of the aircraft, were badly burned. Later that day, when *Triumph* secured alongside Hong Kong's north arm, the injured were transferred to hospital and the body of Stoker Martin was taken ashore, with the funeral being held on 14 September.

For the remainder of the month *Triumph* operated from Hong Kong, but on 29 September she left for Singapore and arrived alongside the naval base on 3 October. Whilst the ship underwent a self-maintenance period, the Air Group, which had disembarked to RNAS Sembawang, carried out air strikes against Communist terrorists in Malaya, and in all some 60 sorties were flown over the dense jungles of Johore State. On 1 November, however, *Triumph* was back at sea and, having landed on the Air Group, she carried out air defence exercises with the RAF over Malaya, before setting course for Hong Kong. For the remainder of November *Triumph* operated from the colony, and during a flying exercise on the last day of the month a Seafire pilot, who was forced to bale out, was rescued by a local junk. By 8 December *Triumph* had returned to Singapore for a dockyard assisted maintenance period, during which she would spend some time in the King George VI dry dock. On 12 December Captain A. D. Torlesse DSO RN joined the ship and three days later, shortly before the ship's company marched to the shore accommodation at HMS *Terror,* he took over from Captain Hutton. On 26 January 1950, with the ship once again at sea, the Air Group was landed on and she sailed for Hong Kong, from where she would operate until April. In early March she was in Subic Bay for combined exercises with the US Navy whose participants included the aircraft carrier USS *Boxer,* with her Panther jet aircraft. On Saturday 18 March, whilst *Triumph* was alongside Hong Kong's north arm, she was visited by her sponsor, Lady

At sea in the Far East, shortly before the outbreak of the Korean War. *(Graham Burns)*

Mountbatten, and a few days later the ship's team won the China Fleet Boxing Championships.

At 07.30 on Monday 10 April, in company with *Comus* and *Unicorn, Triumph* left Hong Kong for a summer cruise to the cooler climate of Japan, with her first stop being Iwakuni five days later. From there she steamed to Kure, where trips were organized to Hiroshima and civic receptions were held on board, as well as a children's party. From Kure *Triumph* took part in exercises off the west coast of Japan, which she reached by way of the Shumonosaki Strait, and after a brief call at Iwakuni to re-embark the Air Group, which had been based at the Australian Air Force station there, she set course for the US naval base at Yokosuka. From there members of the ship's company made trips to Tokyo and Yokohama before *Triumph* moved

Triumph dressed overall at Yokosuka, Japan. *(Graham Burns)*

on to Kobe. Next on the itinerary was a return visit to Kure, which was reached by way of Bungo Suido, and here she met *Belfast* (flag FO FES, Rear-Admiral Andrewes) and her sister *Ocean,* which was still employed in a trooping capacity. In fact some members of *Triumph's* ship's company received draft chits and travelled home in *Ocean.* On Monday 5 June, with *Belfast* and *Cossack, Triumph* left Kure for what should have been the final stage of the Japanese cruise, exercises in and around the tiny port of Ominato at the north end of Honshu Island, which lasted for two weeks. On Saturday 24 June, together with *Cossack, Triumph* left Ominato and set course for Hong Kong once again, but less than 24 hours later the outbreak of war interrupted her passage.

In the early hours of Sunday 25 June, as *Triumph* and *Cossack* steamed south-west through the Sea of Japan, towards the Tsushima Strait between Japan and Korea, about 200 miles away along the 38th Parallel which marked the border between the northern and southern zones of Korea, well-equipped Communist troops invaded the southern zone. The Communist regime of North Korea had been supplied with T34 tanks, artillery and modern fighter aircraft by the Soviet Union, and they had an army of 100,000 men. By contrast the southern zone had a small army, no tanks and very little in the way of field artillery, and this sudden and brazen act of aggression sent the South Korean Army reeling back in retreat. Fortunately, led by the USA, the United Nations Security Council acted quickly and an overwhelming majority of nations voted in favour of intervention, but the nearest troops were four divisions of the US Army in Japan, and they were at half strength. As far as *Triumph* was concerned, she continued her passage through the Tsushima Strait and at 05.00 on Tuesday 27 June, soon after she entered the East China Sea, she and *Cossack* were ordered to proceed direct to Kure. Fortunately, they were only 24 hours steaming away, and upon their arrival they were refuelled and supplied with large quantities of stores and ammunition. At 05.30 on 29 June *Triumph* left Kure and put to sea to await orders which, with Britain and the Commonwealth actively supporting the USA, would not be long in coming. That day Defence and Action Stations were exercised with a new urgency and the aircraft flew fully armed anti-submarine patrols, with *Belfast, Jamaica, Cossack* and *Consort* providing an escort screen. By that evening *Triumph* and her escorts had been ordered to the US base at Okinawa, and next morning as she steamed towards the island American signalling procedures, which had largely been abandoned at the end of the Pacific War, were dusted off and put into operation once again.

Triumph arrived at Okinawa during the morning of 1 July to find USS *Valley Forge* and *Rochester* (flag Vice-Admiral Struble USN) in harbour and she spent the day alongside the fuelling jetty. At 17.00, with *Belfast, Cossack* and *Consort* she sailed from Okinawa to meet the US Navy task force next day, whereupon the Royal Navy units became Task Group 77.5. During the passage to the west coast of Korea, from where the carriers would mount offensive operations against North Korean targets, *Triumph* maintained one Firefly on an anti-submarine patrol, and at 06.00 on Monday 3 July the first strike was ready to be launched. About 15 minutes later the first of nine Fireflies and 12 Seafires, all armed with rockets, was launched against Haeju (Kaishu) airfield, north of the 38th Parallel and about 120 miles from the ship. Although the strike found no aircraft on the airfield, buildings and secondary targets were attacked. All the aircraft returned safely, although one Seafire suffered an overheated engine caused by damage to the radiator, possibly from a rocket splinter. Another was hit in the fuselage by what was presumed to have been a small calibre bullet. At 09.00 on 4 July *Triumph* was ordered to launch a strike on a railway target, but as it was out of range a similar target in another area was designated instead. At 11.30 an armed reconnaissance force of 12 Fireflies armed with rockets and escorted by seven Seafires was launched. Although suitable targets were difficult to find, attacks were made on railway bridges, rolling stock and military transport. Once again, all aircraft returned safely and later in the day, with the force having moved southward, *Triumph* provided combat air patrols (CAP). Next day three Fireflies maintained an anti-submarine patrol.

During the first four days of operations a total of 74 sorties was flown, and one interesting fact which was reported on by Captain Torlesse was the US Navy's use of helicopters, which he noted thus: 'The use of the helicopter by USS *Rochester* and *Valley Forge* for planeguard duties was an illuminating one, and their superiority over the destroyer for close-range planeguard duty was demonstrated beyond question. A ditched pilot is usually back on the deck within three to five minutes.'

At 09.00 on 6 July *Triumph* anchored in Buckner Bay, Okinawa, to replenish and carry out maintenance. For the ship's divers this entailed some gruelling work on the stern glands which were causing problems, and the RFAs *Green Ranger* and *Fort Charlotte* provided FFO, Avgas and provisions. The ship's company was granted some limited shore leave to a beach where the US Army's canteen service provided canned beer, while the officers could use the facilities of an Army club, but with US dollars being the accepted currency, little use was made of either of them. During conferences held ashore it was decided that, for recognition purposes, the Royal Navy's aircraft would be painted with black and white stripes on both under and top surfaces of the wings and round the fuselage. At 12.00 on 16 July, in company with *Comus, Valley Forge, Rochester* and their destroyer screen, *Triumph* sailed to support American landings on the east coast of Korea, which took place two days later. *Triumph's* task was to provide CAP support and anti-submarine patrols, and at 09.50 on the forenoon of 19 July her Sea Otter rescued a downed *Valley Forge* pilot in difficult sea conditions. On 20 July typhoon 'Gracie' prevented a planned replenishment and next day, in view of the deterioration of the starboard stern gland, *Triumph* and *Comus* were ordered to detach from the main force and make for Sasebo, where they arrived at 09.30 on 22 July.

On arrival at Sasebo the engineers immediately set about repacking the faulty gland, but at 14.30 on 24 July, in response to an urgent request from the Army for air support, *Triumph* and *Comus* were ordered to prepare for sea and at midnight they sailed for the operational area. Once again *Triumph* provided CAP support and anti-submarine patrols, whilst aircraft from *Valley Forge* carried out air strikes on enemy targets. On 26 July *Triumph* and *Comus* moved to Korea's east coast and two days later, during investigative duties whilst on CAP, Commissioned Pilot D. R. White's Seafire was shot down by a USAF B29 Super Fortress. Although he was subsequently rescued by an American destroyer, he suffered first degree burns and as a result of the incident pilots were instructed not to approach within 1,000 yards while attempting to identify four-engined bombers. On 30 July, *Triumph* and *Comus* were ordered to Kure, where they arrived the next day. During their eight days in harbour *Triumph's* engineers carried out a full programme of self-maintenance, which included boiler cleaning and more work on the faulty stern gland. During this period all aircrew members were given 48 hours' leave, which most of them spent at Miya Jima, and the ship's company enjoyed the shore canteen. On 9 August *Triumph* and *Comus* sailed for Sasebo, and three days later they were heading for the operational area, this time flying the flag of Rear-Admiral Andrewes. The Royal Navy had been given the task of blockading the coast, which involved a lot of reconnaissance missions, but strikes

Triumph's ship's company pose for the traditional photograph on the way home from Korea.
(Graham Burns)

on enemy shipping were also carried out. The patrol ended at Sasebo on 16 August, but two days later she was back at sea and off Korea's west coast where, once again, she operated against enemy shipping and military targets. This time enemy anti-aircraft fire was heavy, but two coasters, railway trucks and factories were bombed before, on 22 August, *Triumph* returned to Sasebo.

Her next patrol began during the forenoon of 26 August when, flying the flag of Rear-Admiral Andrewes, and in company with *Kenya, Cockade* and the Canadian destroyers *Cayuga* and *Sioux,* she left for the patrol area off the west coast. Three days earlier *Comus* had been attacked by enemy aircraft about 85 miles west of Kunsan and as a result one man had been killed. This meant that the Seafires had to concentrate on CAP duties, leaving the armed reconnaissance missions to the Fireflies. Once again enemy shipping was attacked and destroyed but, at 10.58 on 29 August, there was a tragic accident which is described by Graham Burns who was a member of 827 Squadron at the time: 'I was a witness to the appalling accident in which the CO of 800 Squadron, Lt-Cdr Maclachlan, was killed. I was in a group of air mechanics who had taken to watching flying operations from the pom-pom sponson at the after end of the island, which offered a grandstand view. We felt that the flight deck edges were too dangerous, but we needed to be close by and found that when we were required we could get from this sponson back to the flight deck very quickly. On this occasion we watched a Firefly on its final approach and noticed that the deck hook had not been lowered, something the Batsman's teller should have spotted. The pilot made a near perfect landing and had the hook been down everything would have been fine. Instead the aircraft just trundled forward down the flight deck and into the barrier and, as usual, the propeller broke into bits and flew round the flight deck. It seemed to us that everyone had ducked the flying pieces and we laughed at what appeared to be another routine accident. Suddenly, over the tannoy came urgent requests for a doctor to attend the Air Operations Room, and we realized something was wrong. In the event, the root end of one of the propeller blades, a heavy piece of wood bound by metal strips, had broken off and flown straight through the scuttle of the Air Ops Room in the island at the same time that Lt-Cdr Maclachlan looked out to see what all the noise was about. It hit him straight in the face and killed him instantly - a terrible tragedy.' That evening at 19.30, in a position Lat 33° - 41'N/Long 126° - 07'E, the funeral service was held on the quarterdeck and his body was committed to the deep. Next day the carrier arrived at Sasebo.

Triumph's next patrol began on Sunday 3 September when, with *Cockade* and HMAS *Warramunga,* she left for more west coast blockade duties. The aircraft flew armed reconnaissance missions during the day and CAP was maintained overhead. They also flew spotting missions for bombarding warships, and railway targets were bombed and strafed. On 10 September, with weather conditions having deteriorated, *Triumph* returned to Sasebo. Her final duties off Korea would be to assist in providing air cover for US landings in the area of Inchon, close to Seoul, with the aim of liberating the South Korean capital and cutting off the retreat of enemy troops. When *Triumph* left Sasebo it was evident to the ship's company that, apart from the news of a typhoon, something big was being undertaken and this was confirmed by reconnaissance aircraft flying off to check on amphibious assault craft and supply ships which were clearly on a predetermined route. The Fireflies flew on armed reconnaissance missions over old ground at Mokpo and Kunsan, where more targets were attacked. As *Triumph* steamed north convoys of landing craft were much in evidence, and shortly afterwards it was confirmed that a large landing had taken place at Inchon. At 06.00 on 15 September US Marines landed on Walmi-do, a fortified island connected by a causeway to Inchon, and soon afterwards the UN flag was hoisted. The main assault was made early that evening during the next high tide, and whilst US carrier aircraft were bombing shore targets, *Triumph* flew off spotting aircraft for *Jamaica* and *Kenya* which were carrying out bombardments of selected targets. They also carried out missions to the north of the operating area, spotting for *Ceylon* and *Charity,* which were bombarding coastal guns near Haeju. Once the assault forces were well established and targets were too far away for the bombarding cruisers, *Triumph* was ordered to return to Sasebo, where she arrived during the afternoon of 21 September. Four days later Rear-Admiral Andrewes bade farewell to *Triumph's* officers and men, and paid tribute to the ship's achievements. That afternoon, at 16.00, *Triumph* sailed for Hong Kong, arriving there on 29 September to find *Theseus* in harbour and ready to take over from her.

On 6 October, with the handover complete, *Triumph* left Hong Kong to steam home by way of Singapore, Aden and Suez. On 28 October she cleared the Suez Canal, and after a two-day stop at Malta and seven hours in Gibraltar Bay, at 16.20 on Wednesday 8 November Eddystone Light was sighted. Next day she anchored at Spithead before, at 16.15 with her flight deck fully manned, she steamed past the crowds on Southsea seafront to secure alongside Pitch House Jetty. During her seven days at Portsmouth all the squadron personnel left the ship and on 16 November she sailed for Sheerness where, once again, she received an enthusiastic welcome. Six days later she left Sheerness and during the evening of 24 November she anchored in the Firth of Forth. Next day she steamed up harbour to secure in No 2 dry dock at Rosyth Dockyard, where she was paid off. On 28 November Captain Torlesse relinquished his command and soon afterwards *Triumph* was taken over by the dockyard. Ahead lay a long refit.

Chapter Fifteen

HMS *Triumph* December 1950 – April 1956

Triumph spent the last month of 1950 and the first three months of 1951 in dry dock at Rosyth, and during March 1951 her new ship's company began joining the ship. On 2 April her new commanding officer, Captain C. T. Jellicoe DSO DSC RN, was appointed. *Triumph* was to take on the role of trials and training carrier with the Home Fleet once again, but first she had to make a trooping voyage to the Middle East. After undertaking her post-refit trials in mid-May, by the end of the month she was in Portsmouth Dockyard and on 1 June she began loading the stores, equipment and military baggage of the 16th Independent Parachute Brigade. Two days later she embarked 300 officers and men of the regiment, plus their transport, and during the afternoon of 5 June, in company with *Warrior,* which was carrying the other half of the Parachute Brigade, *Triumph* left Portsmouth and set course for Cyprus. Whilst off Malta aircraft of 827 Squadron used the two aircraft carriers as targets to practise torpedo attacks, and 48 hours later they anchored in Famagusta Bay. Using lighters it took two days to disembark the Army units together with all their stores and transport, and on 14 June *Triumph* and *Warrior* sailed for Malta. After two days at Grand Harbour and two days at Gibraltar, *Triumph* arrived back in Portsmouth Harbour on 23 June and three days later she was ready to resume her role as an operational aircraft carrier.

It had been decided that *Triumph* would take on the role of deck landing training ship, with the training unit for Deck Landing Control Officers, or Batsmen as they were popularly known. She left Portsmouth on 26 June and, with the destroyer *Ulysses,* she began flying operations in the Channel. During the first two weeks of July the Sea Furies of 737 Squadron carried out deck landing training on board the carrier. On Friday 13 July there was a crash on deck which resulted in the death of CPO (A) G. D. White DSM and the serious injury of a junior rating. Two hours later, at 16.40, the carrier anchored in Bangor Bay and the body of CPO White was landed for burial. Five days later, in Falmouth Bay, No 18 Fighter Course was embarked, and for the rest of the month their Sea Furies carried out catapult training. On 30 July, however, *Triumph* returned to Portsmouth Harbour for seasonal leave to be taken. On 1 August there was a change of command when Captain U. H. R. James CBE RN took over from Captain Jellicoe. On 16 August the officers of the 16th Independent Parachute Brigade presented a silver salver to Captain James, as a mark of their appreciation for

In June 1951 *Triumph* carried the troops and transport of the 16th Independent Parachute Brigade to Cyprus.
(Fleet Air Arm Museum, Cars T/13)

the courtesy shown to them by *Triumph's* officers and men during their voyage from Portsmouth to Cyprus. On Monday 24 September *Triumph* was at sea again, this time accompanied by the destroyer *Grenville,* which was operating in the role of an air training target ship. On 28 September the two units anchored off St Peter Port, Guernsey, for a weekend break and at 09.00 on Monday 1 October they weighed anchor and set course for Bigbury Bay. During the forenoon and for most of the afternoon *Triumph* carried out flying operations, and at 15.30 the carrier spent just over two hours refuelling *Grenville.* At 23.10, when *Triumph* and her escort were 12 miles south-east of Start Point, the 6,997-ton Italian oil tanker *Alceo* collided with *Grenville.* The tanker's bow had ploughed into the destroyer's starboard quarter tearing a 30-foot hole in her side, damaging a gun turret and killing two officers, two senior ratings and three junior ratings. Although none of her crew were hurt, the tanker's bows were badly crushed and with damage to her cargo tanks there was a real risk of fire and an explosion. In order to minimize the risk a fire party was quickly mustered in *Triumph* and they were sent over to the tanker with foam equipment as it made its way slowly towards Plymouth. Meanwhile, *Triumph* escorted *Grenville* towards Plymouth Sound and at 09.00 the next morning tugs took the crippled destroyer in tow to secure her alongside Devonport Dockyard. Once the destroyer was safely inside the breakwater of Plymouth Sound, *Triumph* was secured to F buoy where she remained for three days. A subsequent Court Martial found that some responsibility for the collision lay with *Triumph's* commanding officer in that, as the senior officer, he failed to order an alteration of course of the formed units under his command in time to avoid the collision, and failed to inform *Grenville* that she should take independent avoiding action. On 5 October, this time in company with the destroyers *Wizard* and *Ulysses, Triumph* continued her flying training in the Channel and in the Irish Sea. On 26 October, off Torbay, Vampire jets used *Triumph's* deck for four days of landing practice, but on 30 October the carrier secured alongside North Corner Jetty to prepare for another trooping voyage to the Middle East.

On Friday 2 November, the men and equipment of the 3rd Infantry Division, which included the Royal Iniskilling Fusiliers, together with all their transport, were embarked and three days later *Triumph* sailed for Cyprus and Port Said. With what amounted to a guerrilla war being fought in the Suez Canal Zone, reinforcements were required to provide some relief for the troops already serving there, and Cyprus was being used as a springboard for the dispatch of men to the Egyptian garrison. *Triumph* arrived off Famagusta on 12 November, where some of the troops were disembarked, and three days later she secured in Port Said Harbour where the advance parties of the 39th Brigade and sections of the 1st Battalion The Buffs and the 1st Battalion Royal Iniskilling Fusiliers were disembarked. Meanwhile, further up the North African coast off Libya, *Ocean* was standing by in case she was required. During the forenoon of 16 November, with all the troops having left the ship, *Triumph* left Port Said to return to Portsmouth, where she arrived on 23 November. Three days later she returned to her role as a trials and training carrier, operating in the Channel and Irish Sea. During the first two weeks of December she operated aircraft of 736 and 738 Squadrons, but on 13 December she returned to Portsmouth for seasonal leave and for dockyard assisted maintenance, which included a period in dry dock. One of the tasks in the schedule was the painting of a 3° angled flight deck on *Triumph's* angled deck, but with her arrester wires remaining set for fore and aft landings, the aircraft, which would test the practicability of angled deck operations, would carry out only touch and go circuits. On 21 January 1952 *Triumph* was at sea again in the Irish Sea operating aircraft on her 'angled' deck, and these operations continued, with only short breaks, throughout February. At the end of February *Triumph* returned to Portsmouth Dockyard to undergo a nine-week refit.

On 28 April 1952, when *Triumph* returned to sea, she began a three-month period of intensive flying training in the Channel, Irish Sea and the Western Approaches. On 16 May, there was a crash on deck which resulted in the death of Lt (E) Bywater, and later that day, after *Triumph* had anchored in Torbay, his body was taken ashore for burial. Later in the month there was a weekend break at St Peter Port, Guernsey, and in early June there were further trials with Vampire jets. On Saturday 14 June, after distress calls from a US merchant ship, *American Miller, Triumph* was diverted from her flying operations to the area off Beachy Head, but she was beaten to the scene of the grounded vessel by the Newhaven lifeboat. Next day, whilst en route to Antwerp, an aircraft ditched into the sea ahead of the ship, but fortunately the carrier's sea boat rescued the pilot. For the ship's company the three-day break at Antwerp provided a break from flying operations, and this was followed by visits to Sheerness and Portsmouth. By 30 June, however, the intensive flying had started once again and this continued until 25 July when *Triumph* returned to Portsmouth. On 8 September, with the carrier back at sea, flying operations got under way again, and during the forenoon of the next day, in the Irish Sea, she was involved in the search for the pilot of a crashed RAF Meteor jet. In the event he was rescued by the merchantman *British Diligence,* but transferred to *Triumph* for medical attention. In mid-September the carrier took part in 'Exercise Mainbrace', which involved all the NATO countries, and included the fleet carriers *Eagle* and *Illustrious.* The exercise took *Triumph* north of the Arctic Circle, but severe storms hampered flying, and during the afternoon of 19 September she was released from the exercise to steam south for Rosyth. During October *Triumph* continued her flying training duties, operating in the Atlantic, with short breaks at Oban and Greenock, but by the third week of that month she was in the Channel carrying out trials with Rocket-Assisted-Take-Off-Gear (RATOG). Flying training continued into November when, in company with *Illustrious, Triumph* operated in the Channel, but on 27 November she returned to Portsmouth Dockyard for maintenance and seasonal leave. Since resuming her trials and training role *Triumph* had been extremely busy, having steamed some 43,285 miles and recording 6,349 deck landings. On 6 January 1953 there was a change of command when Captain H. P. Sears RN took over from Captain James and 14 days later *Triumph* left Portsmouth to continue her flying training with the aircraft of 737 Squadron from Eglinton. As before flying operations were intensive; on one day alone 100 deck landings were made by trainee pilots, but on 19 February there was some relaxation when the ship held a very successful Coronation Ball at Torquay. In the second half of February, 738 Squadron practised deck landings, but *Triumph's* career as an operational aircraft carrier was drawing to a close and on 27 February she returned to Portsmouth for conversion to a training ship.

An aerial view of *Triumph* at sea showing the remains of the 'angled' flight deck which was painted on in early 1952 for trials.
(Fleet Air Arm Museum, Cars T/30)

It had been decided that *Triumph* would replace the cruiser *Devonshire* as the naval cadets' sea-going training ship, and on 8 April she made the passage to Devonport where she was to undergo a refit during which modifications would be made to her accommodation in order to fit her for this new duty. With most of her hangar having been converted to classrooms *Triumph* would, in the future, only have space for up to three Sea Balliol training aircraft which would at least leave her with a limited capacity for operating aircraft. On Friday 8 May Captain Sears relinquished his command, and on Monday 7 September the officers, including Captain R. H. Wright DSC* RN, the ship's company and training staff transferred from *Devonshire* to *Triumph* and the ship was commissioned into the Home Fleet Training Squadron. On 22 September she put to sea for her machinery trials, and two days later she was ready to begin her training duties. Bill Campbell remembers that, 'The signature tune of the old *Devonshire* was carried over to *Triumph,* and whenever the occasion arose the Royal Marines Band would play, "To be a Farmer's Boy".' After a brief visit to Glengariff, in Ireland's Bantry Bay, *Triumph* set off for her first training cruise to the Mediterranean. On board she had 212 cadets, including 57 from Commonwealth countries, and Bill Campbell remembers, 'the young cadets coming down to the machinery spaces for tuition who always called us stokers "Sir", which I found a little embarrassing.' After leaving Gibraltar *Triumph* headed for Pollensa Bay, Majorca, but from there she was diverted to Argostoli on the Ionian Island of Cephalonia in Greece to deliver winter clothing collected from Valletta to the survivors of a serious earthquake which had devastated the area. From there she steamed to Navarin Bay and on to Athens, where she anchored in Phaleron Bay. During the return passage there were calls at Corfu, Malta, Aranci Bay, where a sailing regatta was held, and Gibraltar before, on 7 December, she arrived back at Devonport in plenty of time for Christmas.

Triumph's spring cruise began in late January 1954 and it was marked by a minimum of ceremonial with much recreation, including swimming, sunbathing and shore leave. After making her transatlantic crossing *Triumph's* first port of call in the Caribbean was Castries on the island of St Lucia and, as Bill Campbell remembers: 'The first sight of the majestic Pitons which loomed up out of the morning mist when we were still some miles away from the island was magical. The hub of entertainment for the ship's company was the Piccadilly Club, which one reached after walking a mile through the shanty town suburbs of Castries, but the result was well worth the effort. It boasted the biggest dance floor in the West Indies and music from the latest "Wurlitzer" jukebox which provided day and night dancing. The local girls were hostesses and there was even a floor show by Madame René Cabald, a Haitian dancer, as well as a magician.' From St Lucia *Triumph* called at Bridgetown, Barbados, where the visit coincided with the second Test Match between England and the West Indies. For those who were not interested in cricket there was the 'Old Brigade Calypso Tent', where there was good calypso music and a well-stocked bar. From Barbados *Triumph* steamed on to Port of Spain, Trinidad, and then to Beef Island, which was one of the British Virgin Islands. Bill Campbell remembers that, 'We were able to do a lot of swimming and sunbathing on a deserted, white sandy beach with just a small shack which sold soft drinks.' During the seven days at anchor off Beef Island one of the ship's officers was seriously injured in a swimming accident and after weighing anchor during the afternoon of 4 March, *Triumph* headed towards Puerto Rico where, as she approached the island, a US Navy helicopter flew out to pick up the injured officer and transfer him to hospital. *Triumph's* final port of call was Bermuda and during the afternoon of 11 March she secured alongside the naval base at Ireland Island, from where the ship's boats provided liberty men with a shuttle service between the base and the capital, Hamilton. *Triumph* left Bermuda on 18 March to set course for Gibraltar and then Devonport.

At 06.17 on Sunday 28 March, as *Triumph* was approaching Gibraltar, the troop transport *Empire Windrush**, with 1,276 passengers and a crew of 222 on board, was steaming westwards through the Mediterranean from the Far East, bound for Southampton. She was about 30 miles north-west of Cape Caxine when, suddenly, a massive fire broke out in the starboard boiler room and in the after funnel uptakes. It was quickly realized that the fire was beyond the means of the ship's firefighters and at 06.23, SOS messages were sent out. About 20 minutes later the first lifeboats full of passengers were launched, and fortunately the P&O Company's cargo vessel *Socotra* and three other merchantmen were in the vicinity, so it was not long before they were embarking the 1,496 passengers and crew from *Empire Windrush.* Most of them were disembarked at Algiers, and meanwhile, at Gibraltar, the C-in-C Mediterranean ordered the destroyers *Saintes* and *Whirlwind* to raise steam and proceed with all dispatch to the scene. In the event *Saintes* remained with the smoking and gutted hulk of the troopship and eventually took it in tow, whilst *Whirlwind* continued on to Algiers to begin the lift of passengers and crew. At 10.55 on 28 March *Triumph* anchored in Gibraltar Bay and two hours later she was ordered to Algiers in order to assist with the evacuation of the survivors. That day, as *Triumph* steamed towards Algiers, A and C hangars were prepared for the accommodation of the women and children from the crippled troopship, and at 10.25 on 29 March, as she approached Algiers Harbour, she passed *Saintes* which was preparing to take the wreck in tow. Two hours later *Triumph* secured stern first to a jetty at Algiers and after a pontoon had been secured on the starboard side, the embarkation began. At 16.00 that afternoon, with all the passengers aboard, the carrier left Algiers and set course for Gibraltar. Julian Best remembers that day: 'It was clear that the survivors would have to spend the night on board, so we had to fix up temporary wires across the hangar deck in order that they could sling hammocks. However, many of our passengers were women and children and it was great fun helping them to rig them up. It was even funnier for everyone when they tried to climb into their hammocks and I remember a lot of people just took them down and slept on the deck.' *Triumph* arrived alongside Gibraltar's south mole during the afternoon of 30 March, and an hour later the disembarkation of passengers had been completed. As for *Empire Windrush,* the tow continued at a speed of three knots, but at 00.30 on 30 March the troopship sank stern first into the waters of the Western Mediterranean. *Triumph* left Gibraltar during the forenoon of 1 April, and she arrived alongside 5 & 6 wharves of Devonport Dockyard four days later.

It was on 13 May that *Triumph* sailed again, and this time her training cruise began the next day with 'Exercise Loyalty' when, with the C-in-C Plymouth flying his flag on board, *Triumph* greeted Her Majesty The Queen who was returning from her Commonwealth tour in the royal yacht *Britannia. Triumph* also had on board a number of service chiefs and civic dignitaries for the occasion and at 11.00, with her ship's company and cadets manning the flight deck, *Triumph* steamed past the royal yacht, which was making her first voyage with the Queen embarked. Later that day *Triumph* returned to Devonport and three days later, with her faithful escort *Enard Bay,* she was at sea again, with three Sea Balliols and a helicopter flying from her flight deck. Next day she anchored off Glengariff in Ireland's Bantry Bay where, during one afternoon, the ship was opened to the public, with the boats providing a shuttle service between the ship and the shore. The ship's company were made very welcome by the local people, and the Guinness lived up to its reputation. From Ireland *Triumph* steamed north for Scotland's Loch Ewe and then to Rosyth, where all who lived north of the Tyne were granted a weekend's leave. On 8 June, after leaving Rosyth, *Triumph* set course for Copenhagen, arriving alongside the Langelinie Jetty in the Danish capital two days later. During the five-day visit a constant stream of visitors came to gaze at the ship, whilst ashore the ship's company

*HMT *Empire Windrush* was formerly the German passenger liner *Monte Rosa* which, since 1947, had been managed on behalf of the Minsitry of Transport by the New Zealand Shipping Company.

Flying operations in 1952. The remains of the painted 'angled' deck can still be seen.
(Fleet Air Arm Museum, Cars T/15)

enjoyed various entertainments which had been arranged, the most popular of which were the tours of the Carlsberg Brewery. As always in Copenhagen, the Tivoli Gardens provided almost every kind of entertainment, with restaurants, open-air cafes, dance halls, funfairs and theatres, and on one evening the Royal Marines Band added their talents to the Tivoli Gardens attractions. After Copenhagen *Triumph* spent five days at Fläm, which was followed by a visit to Bergen. After leaving Norway *Triumph* steamed to Invergordon, via Scapa Flow and Loch Erribol, but by 28 July she was back in Plymouth Sound. The last two days of the month were spent at Torquay where it was learned that, at the end of her autumn 1955 cruise, *Triumph* was to be paid off and placed in reserve. Meanwhile, in the short term, ahead lay her annual refit and by 3 August she was alongside 5 & 6 wharves of Devonport Dockyard.

Triumph remained at Devonport until 6 October 1954, when she set course for her autumn cruise, which took her into the Mediterranean. During the passage her Sea Balliols carried out flying practice, and during the afternoon of 11 October she carried out 'Operation Ethiopia'. This involved firing a 21-gun salute as she steamed past the cruiser *Gambia,* which was carrying Emperor Haile Selassie of Ethiopia. Three days later *Triumph* arrived in Villefranche and from there she steamed on to Aranci Bay and Malta. After leaving Grand Harbour on 4 November *Triumph* called at Palmas Bay, where there were sailing regattas, then Venice and Augusta. By 2 December she had returned to the Western Mediterranean and on 13 December, after seven days in Gibraltar, she arrived back at Devonport. On 31 December Captain V. C. Begg DSO DSC RN relieved Captain Wright in command of the training ship. On 24 January 1955, in company with the destroyer *Venus,* she left Devonport to make her second training cruise to the Caribbean. That evening, however, she was diverted from her course to the area of Wolf Rock in the Channel to search for the crew of a crashed RAF aircraft. In the event the only survivors were rescued by the merchantman *Scottish Eagle,* but *Triumph* and *Venus* continued to search for the pilot, sadly to no avail. On 29 January there was a brief stop at Praia Bay in the Azores, and on 7 February she anchored off Kingston, Jamaica. This was followed by visits to Port au Prince, Haiti, where the President of the Republic visited the ship, the island of Carriacou, Barbados and Antigua. Before leaving the Caribbean *Triumph* made an 11-day visit to Beef Island and on 24 March she arrived in the naval base at Bermuda. Finally, however, on the last day of March she set course for Devonport where, on 12 April, she arrived alongside No 8 wharf.

Triumph's summer cruise began on Monday 23 May 1955, when she and *Venus* left for Glengariff, before returning to Plymouth Sound where, on the last day of the month, she embarked the C-in-C Plymouth. That evening, after leaving the Sound she crossed the Channel, arriving in Brest the next day, where the C-in-C took part in an official wreath-laying ceremony and the Royal Marines provided a guard of honour. On 4 August, after returning the C-in-C to Plymouth Sound, *Triumph* sailed for the Baltic. At Copenhagen on 7 June the Danes gave the carrier a warm welcome and on one afternoon when she was opened to the public over 7,000 visited the ship. The

In 1953, as a cadet training ship, *Triumph* enters Grand Harbour.
(Michael Cassar)

next port of call was Aabenraa where, once again, the Danish people gave the ship an enthusiastic welcome. There was a successful ship's company dance and, with HMCS *Ontario* also in port, both ships' companies marched through the streets of the town. On 23 June, two days after leaving Denmark, *Triumph* arrived in Stavanger where the highlight of the stay was a brewery visit. The visit to Norway ended at the head of Sogne Fjord, over 100 miles from the open sea, at the town of Fläm and then, after almost a month in Scandinavia, *Triumph* returned to home waters. After carrying out full-power trials off Lossiemouth the carrier took part in helicopter flying training before putting in to Invergordon, where extensive use was made of the excellent sporting facilities. After leaving the Moray Firth on 18 July *Triumph* sailed to Bangor Bay, via Scapa Flow, and from there to Penzance for Regatta Week. During the festivities two of the ship's officers were given the task of choosing the town's regatta Queen, the Royal Marines beat Retreat along the Promenade, and *Triumph* herself gave a spectacular fireworks and searchlight display. The final call of the cruise was Torquay which, at the height of the holiday season, was a very popular run ashore for both the ship's company and the cadets. The visit ended with a party on board for 400 local children, many of whom were from orphanages in the area, and the BBC television service even came aboard to film the event. The cruise ended on Monday 8 August when *Triumph* returned to Devonport to begin a seven-week maintenance period.

When, on Monday 26 September, in company with *Venus, Triumph* left Plymouth Sound, it was to undertake her final cruise as a cadet training ship and three days later she arrived at Invergordon. On 6 October she arrived in Rosyth where the flag of the C-in-C Home Fleet, Admiral Sir Michael Denny, was hoisted. Next day *Triumph* sailed for an official visit to Leningrad (St Petersburg), and shortly after leaving the Firth of Forth she met with other units of the squadron, *Apollo, Chevron, Chieftain, Decoy* and *Diana,* and together they set course for the Baltic. On 9 October, as they steamed in thick fog in the Kattegat, four Soviet naval units, led by the cruiser *Sverdlov,* passed by bound for Portsmouth where they were to pay a goodwill visit. At dusk on 12 October the Soviet destroyer *Odyranny* escorted the British squadron to the entrance of the Morskay Canal, and from there they steamed slowly along the River Neva and into the heart of Leningrad, a passage which took over four hours. During this time crowds of curious, silent spectators on the canal and river banks gave little indication of the warmth of the reception which *Triumph* would receive when, on a dark night, she secured to head and stern buoys below the Schmidt Bridge. The river here is about the width of the Thames at London Bridge and the carrier was about 100 yards from the north bank. Here the reception was incredible. The crowds, most of whom had never seen a British warship before and had certainly never seen an aircraft carrier, had gathered in their thousands, cheering, shouting and singing. Much to their delight most of the ship's company manning the flight deck swapped alternate songs with them as they stood on the river bank. Every day during the whole of the stay the crowds would gather in the early morning and they would not disperse until late at night. *Triumph's* stay was well organized, with a heavy programme of entertainment each day. There were coach tours of the city, trips to the circus and ballet and to cinemas, where the sailors sat patiently through unintelligible Russian films. On 14 October all the ships of the squadron were opened to the public and large numbers of Russians took the opportunity to visit the ships where, on board *Triumph,* the three Sea Balliol training aircraft were closely inspected. During the evening of 15 October, strong winds which had been blowing suddenly turned into gales and as *Triumph's* stern buoy proved not strong enough to hold her, she began swinging towards the nearby landing stage. A quick-witted party of Russian and British seamen managed to drag a lighter between *Triumph* and the landing stage, which was an old hulk, as flood waters started to creep up into the streets of nearby Vasil'yevskiyo Island. Fortunately tugs arrived promptly on the scene and *Triumph* was soon out of danger and secured to new buoys. During the final afternoon of the visit there was a party for 400 local children in the ship's hangar and, as always, the event was very popular with both the children and the ship's company. During the afternoon of Monday 17 October, with the visit at an end, *Triumph* led the squadron down the River Neva and the Morskay Canal, past Kronstadt to the Leningrad lightship, where they anchored for the night. At the time it was reported that *Triumph* was the biggest warship to manoeuvre so far up the River Neva and, with strong gusts of wind frequently catching the ship, it was a remarkable feat of seamanship by Captain Begg.

On 19 October, during the return passage, *Triumph* again passed *Sverdlov* and her escorts and on the morning of 22 October the carrier anchored off Sheerness to disembark the C-in-C, before setting off on her final cruise into the Mediterranean. This took her to Pollensa, Villefranche, Malta, Aranci Bay and Barcelona. Finally on 8 December, after six days at Gibraltar, she sailed for Devonport. Three days later she carried out her final fixed-wing flying operations when her three Sea Balliols were flown off. During the forenoon of 13 December, after a night at anchor in Plymouth Sound, *Triumph* secured alongside Devonport's No 8 wharf. During the weeks which followed she was prepared for the Reserve Fleet, and on 23 January 1956 Captain Begg left the ship. Three months later, at 09.00 on 11 April, the ship was taken over by the dockyard and, with the remaining members of the ship's company having been discharged on leave or to HMS *Orion, Triumph* was paid off.

The blazing troop transport *Empire Windrush* off Algiers in late March 1953. *Triumph* took her passengers from Algiers to Gibraltar. *(Norman Pound)*

Chapter Sixteen

HMS *Triumph* May 1956 – February 1972

Unlike her sister ships *Glory, Ocean* and *Theseus,* when *Triumph* was placed in reserve in the spring of 1956, she was not placed on the disposal list and by the end of 1957 when it was announced that she was to be converted into a heavy repair ship to replace *Perseus,* it was clear that she was to be given a new lease of life. By early January 1958 she had been moved to Portsmouth Dockyard and work had started on the conversion, which it was thought would be completed by mid-1961. However, the decision in late 1959 to convert *Albion* to a commando ship took priority and work on *Triumph* was suspended. In mid-1962, with work on *Albion* well on the way to completion, conversion work on *Triumph* was restarted and by late 1964 she was almost ready for sea, having been designated an escort maintenance ship. In her new role, with deckhouses, workshops and a hangar having been built on her flight deck, she was almost unrecognizable as the light fleet aircraft carrier she had once been. Down below, in what had previously been the main hangar, and where hundreds of cadets had begun their sea-going careers, massive workshops and foundries had been constructed and in the mess decks, instead of hammock rails, the spaces were now fitted out with bunks. By this time she was the last of the Colossus-class ships still in naval service, and instead of catapulting aircraft she would provide maintenance facilities for the destroyers and frigates which formed the escort squadrons. She would enable the escort units to carry out their maintenance efficiently by providing a berth with overside services such as fresh water, steam and electrical

After her conversion to an escort maintenance ship, in October 1964 *Triumph* ran her contractor's sea trials. In this view the prewetting systems are tested. *(Fleet Air Arm Museum, Cars T/31)*

power, so allowing them to shut down, while workshops with facilities for almost any type of work were close alongside. Her new ship's company of 27 officers and 472 ratings would be supplemented by four maintenance units totalling 15 officers and 270 ratings skilled in a wide range of trades. In addition to the overside services *Triumph* would provide air-conditioned accommodation for the ships' companies of the largest destroyers, as well as medical and dental services, a chapel, a schoolroom, large galleys and a bakery, a clothing store and a canteen. Although her main role would be escort maintenance, she also had the space and facilities to undertake a variety of other tasks, including the carrying and maintenance of the small Wasp and the larger Wessex helicopters. In order to operate these machines a helicopter landing spot was retained at the forward end of the flight deck.

On 28 September 1964 *Triumph's* new commanding officer, Captain I. F. Somerville RN, joined the ship, and in the following month a reduced ship's company was drafted to her in order that she could undertake Phase One of her contractor's sea trials. These were due to begin on Friday 9 October 1964, but gale force winds prevented her from sailing that afternoon, and it was at 08.30 the next day that *Triumph* left Middle Slip Jetty for Spithead and the Channel for ten hours of full-power trials before returning to Spithead. Over the following four days *Triumph* ran her machinery trials in the Channel and, despite the additional weight of her new superstructure, she still managed 24 knots. The trials ended on 14 October with heeling trials at Spithead and next day she returned to Portsmouth Dockyard. Four days later, on Monday 19 October, *Triumph* began Phase Two of her contractor's trials and over three days she carried out fuel consumption and helicopter landing trials, before returning once again to Portsmouth Dockyard. At 11.00 on Thursday 7 January 1965 *Triumph* was finally commissioned into the fleet as an escort maintenance ship, with the guest of honour at the ceremony being Admiral Sir Wilfred Woods, who in 1940 had commanded the ninth *Triumph,* the T-class submarine which was lost in the Mediterranean. Next day *Triumph* began her post-conversion trials which continued for seven days, and included deck landings by Wessex helicopters of 829 Squadron. Having been allocated to the Far East Fleet stationed at Singapore Naval Base, which at that time was heavily involved in the Confrontation with Indonesia, *Triumph* left Spithead on 2 February. During the passage east she called briefly at Gibraltar and at Limassol in Cyprus before, on 12 February, she made her transit of the Suez Canal. Nine days after leaving Suez she anchored off Colombo and four days later she arrived at Singapore Naval Base where she took over from *Hartland Point.*

During her years on the Far East Station *Triumph* would spend most of her time swinging round C buoy in the Johore Strait, off the naval base at Sembawang on the north shore of the island, east of the Causeway which links Singapore Island with Johore Bahru. At least half of her officers and men were accompanied by their wives and children and they lived in married quarters either close to the naval base, or on the mainland at Johore Bahru. During *Triumph's* first four months on the station she took part in the annual FOTEX (Flag Officer's Tactical Exercises), and she spent seven days in Hong Kong, before she settled down in Singapore to assist four escort ships with their maintenance programmes. By the end of 1965, as well as making two more short trips to Hong Kong, no fewer than 37 different periods of maintenance had been carried out on 23 different fleet escorts, either alongside her huge bulk or in Singapore Dockyard. In addition extensive unprogrammed work was carried out on ships varying in size from aircraft carriers to minesweepers. Some of the more outstanding jobs included an entire boiler clean which was completed in less than 36 hours by a team of three ERAs and 17 M(E)s, working in watches, and the escort herself was back out on patrol within 48 hours. The removal of bearings from an engine room axial fan was completed within 11 hours; with work having started at 16.00, it was finished by 03.00 the next day. The maintenance teams were backed up by a hard-working ship's company which included the galley staff who provided 1,000 extra meals at any one time, using 556,400lb of potatoes, 48,000 sausages and 274,080 eggs in the space of nine months, as well as 109,640 tots of rum. The brief visits to Hong Kong provided some relief, and during one of these visits in late August the ship's divers earned considerable praise for their recovery work under difficult and dangerous conditions after a tragic air crash.

In April 1966 *Triumph* herself underwent a maintenance period in the King George VI dry dock, and in September that year there was a complete change of scenery when *Triumph* made a seven-day visit to Fremantle. Although she had returned to Singapore Naval base by mid-September, she did not remain there for long and on 20 September 1966 she sailed for Mombasa. With Rhodesia having issued a Unilateral Declaration of Independence in November 1965, the Royal Navy had the duty of enforcing the oil blockade outside the Portuguese East African port of Beira in Mozambique. Using Mombasa's Kilindini Harbour as their base, the Navy's escort ships were heavily involved in what had become known as the Beira Patrol, and maintaining the constant blockade over 4,000 miles from the nearest naval base necessitated special arrangements for the repair and maintenance of the ships and for the rest and relaxation of their ships' companies. For *Triumph* it was to become a major commitment, and during her first deployment to the East African base she remained at Kilindini Harbour for two months. During this time she assisted *Ashanti, Brighton, Caprice, Falmouth, Llandaff* and *Zulu* with their maintenance work. On Sunday 30

Tilting trials at Spithead in October 1964.
(Fleet Air Arm Museum, Cars T/32)

October, whilst she was at Mombasa, there was a change of command for *Triumph* when Captain P. G. La Niece RN, who had joined the ship two days before, took over from Captain Somerville. By 8 December 1966 *Triumph* was back in Singapore, and she remained in the naval base until March 1967 when she took part in the annual FOTEX manoeuvres in the South China Sea. During the last week of April *Triumph* left Singapore for her second deployment to East Africa, which kept her away for over ten weeks. During this second visit 40 men gave up their weekends to work at a missionary hospital at Kaloleni, about 40 miles inland from Mombasa. The work included whitewashing the church building, plastering the kitchen walls, restoring roof gutters and even repairing the operating table in the surgery. On 5 July, however, *Triumph* returned to Singapore where her arrival alongside in the dockyard was eagerly awaited by the families of the married men. At the end of September *Triumph* paid a two-week visit to Hong Kong, taking with her six Whirlwind helicopters which were to be based at Kai Tak. This was followed by a third stint at Mombasa, but she returned to Singapore on 22 December, just in time for Christmas.

On 7 February 1968, with *Devonshire* (flag FO2 FES Rear-Admiral E. B. Ashmore), *Dido, Euryalus, Zest* and RFA *Olna, Triumph* left Singapore to visit towns and cities in Australia. After a passage of ten days by way of the west coast of Australia, during which the maintenance ship joined in the squadron manoeuvres, on 17 February the ships arrived off Sydney. Crowds had gathered on top of the near-vertical cliff known as the North Head to welcome them, while others had a good view as they passed under the famous Harbour Bridge. The visiting ships did a circuit around the naval repair yard at Cockatoo Island, before returning under the bridge and securing alongside at the Australian naval base of Garden Island. Having spent ten days at sea the ships' companies took every opportunity for shore leave and recreation, and the legendary hospitality of the people of Sydney was as generous as ever. The weather was perfect and, besides the usual attractions of Bondi Beach and a trip over the bridge, many officers and men ventured further afield - to sheep stations or to visit relatives in other parts of Australia. However, there was also maintenance to be done, and whilst at Sydney Fleet Maintenance Units were employed on the frigates *Dido, Euryalus* and *Zest,* and the destroyer *Devonshire,* with one unit even travelling to Melbourne to carry out work on the destroyer *Daring.* Leaving Sydney on 5 March *Triumph* returned, via the Great Barrier Reef Channel and Torres Strait, direct to Singapore where she arrived on 15 March after steaming some 9,000 miles and circumnavigating the Australian subcontinent. On 13 May *Triumph* left Singapore for Hong Kong and eight days later, with the ship alongside the north wall of the colony's dockyard, Captain I. Easton DSC RN took over from Captain La Niece. Later that month the maintenance ship returned to Singapore where throughout the following weeks she took part in fleet exercises off Tioman in the South China Sea. On 2 August she held a Families Day, when wives and children of the ship's company were taken to sea and given a helicopter flying display. A few weeks later, on 20 September, having embarked 361 officers and men of the Royal Marines, as well as Army personnel and three SRN6 hovercraft, *Triumph* left Singapore to join an amphibious force which included *Albion, Intrepid, Caprice* and RFA *Tidespring,* for a major international naval exercise in the Solomon Sea and off Australia. The first troop landing practice took place in the Sulu Sea and on 25 September *Triumph* and her force met *Hermes, Defender, Diana* and other escorts, to set course for the Bismarck Sea where, on 30 September, 'Exercise Coral Sands' began. The main amphibious landing took place on 6 October in Shoalwater Bay, with *Albion's* helicopters landing *Triumph's* embarked force. Next day the remaining troops and stores were landed by hovercraft and when the exercise was completed *Triumph* paid visits to Vila, Noumea and Auckland. After nine days in New Zealand *Triumph* steamed west for Brisbane where, during the last week of October, she spent five days. Once again the passage from Australia to Singapore was made by way of the Great Barrier Reef Channel, and when she arrived in Singapore Naval Base on 8 November she was taken 'out of routine' for a three-month refit.

On Friday 17 January 1969, with her refit completed and with the ship's company having re-embarked from HMS *Terror, Triumph* returned to C buoy in the Johore Strait. Ten days later, after loading three SRN6 and one SRN5 hovercraft, *Triumph* left Singapore for her spring deployment which began with a visit to the Indonesian island of Bali, followed two days later by a call at the port of Ambon. With Confrontation over *Triumph* was the first British warship to visit Indonesia following the end of the hostilities. At Ambon the Commander of the Eastern Theatre of the Indonesian Navy, Rear-Admiral Susatyo Mardi, was welcomed on board by Captain Easton. On 6 February, when *Triumph* left the port, she was played out of the harbour by a band whose instruments were made from sea shells and bamboo which was an indication of the warmth of their reception and the fact that once again the friendship of the ordinary sailors had overcome politics. Once clear of the island *Triumph* set course for Hong Kong, where she arrived in time for Chinese New Year. On 5 March she returned to Singapore to undergo a major seven and a half-month refit, during which time her place as the escort maintenance ship for the Far East Fleet would be taken by *Berry Head.* With *Triumph* in refit the ship's company was reduced in number and Captain Easton relinquished his command. The work was carried out by the newly formed Sembawang Shipyard Co, and *Triumph* was their first major contract on a Royal Navy warship. To their credit it was completed six weeks ahead of schedule.

On 19 November 1969 *Triumph's* new commanding officer, Captain C. J. A. Johnson OBE DSC RN, was appointed to the ship and in early January 1970 she recommissioned to reassume her role as the fleet's maintenance ship. Once again over half of her ship's company had their wives and families on station, and it was not long before the old Colossus-class aircraft carrier became a familiar sight as the 'mother ship' for escort vessels on the Far East Station. Most of February was spent at Hong Kong and in April, with *Bulwark* and *Fearless,* she took part in 'Exercise Flying Fish' in the South China Sea. During the exercise, which took place over eight days in the Tioman area, *Triumph* operated 45 helicopters from her small flight deck, which was the busiest period of flying since her days as an operational aircraft carrier in 1953. She also transported 200 men of the 1st/2nd Gurkha Rifles from Singapore and put them ashore by landing craft and helicopter on the east coast of Malaysia. The exercise illustrated just how useful this heavy maintenance ship, with at least part of her flight deck still intact, could be for amphibious operations. The exercise was followed by a visit to Penang before, on 10 May, she returned to her buoy in Singapore's Johore Strait. On 11 June *Triumph* left Singapore bound for Hong Kong and three days later, when she was only hours from the port, she went to the assistance of a merchant ship, *Fair Transport,* which had broken down. In the event *Triumph's* engineers were able to disconnect three cooling water pipes and bring them back to the maintenance ship for welding. Although the repairs took the best part of 24 hours, once refitted *Fair Transport* was able to restart her main engine and resume her voyage. Fifteen hours later, at 15.30 on 15 June, *Triumph* arrived in Hong Kong, but by the end of the month she had returned to Singapore. When *Triumph* ventured out of Singapore again on 24 September, she had on board three Wessex helicopters of 847 Squadron, together with their maintenance crews, and once again she was bound for Hong Kong. This time, however, she spent only four days alongside the north arm and on 2 October she sailed for Japan. For the first time since leaving the port in September 1950, she was to visit Sasebo, where she spent four days before returning to Hong Kong on 12 October. Later the same day she was at sea again and carrying 300 men of 45 Commando, Royal Marines, the three Wessex helicopters of 847 Squadron and the Whirlwind helicopters of the RAF's No 28 Squadron. With the assault ship *Intrepid* she took part in 'Exercise Far Fling', the amphibious landing of troops in Hong Kong's New Territories. During the five days of the exercise *Triumph* carried out 112 helicopter deck landings, bringing her total for the commission to 187. Although the exercise was cut short by the approach of typhoon 'Joan', which at one stage looked as though it would pass directly over Hong Kong, in the event it remained 300 miles away, but even so it made its presence felt with Force 8 gales. This was enough to prevent any further amphibious landings, so *Triumph* rode out the high winds before returning briefly to Hong Kong, and then back to Singapore where she reverted to her primary role of fleet maintenance.

On Friday 13 November 1970, in the Bay of Bengal, devastating cyclones with wind speeds in excess of 120mph

The withdrawal of the Far East Fleet from the naval base at Singapore. *Albion* leads *Triumph* in a farewell steam-past, with the helicopters of 848 Squadron overhead. *(Author's collection)*

Flying her paying-off pennant, *Triumph* calls at Gibraltar on her way home in February 1972. There are two Wasp helicopters at the forward end of her flight deck. *(Michael Lennon)*

and torrential rain hit the coast of East Pakistan (Bangladesh), some 135 miles south-east of Dacca. The offshore islands of Hatia and Bhola in the Ganges delta were devastated when a 20-foot high tidal wave swept almost 2,000 people into the sea. Altogether, over 25,000 people died as a result of the storms and over two million were left without food or shelter, and continuing rough seas prevented small boats from getting supplies to the worst affected areas. It was clear that only helicopters would be able to deliver the urgently needed food, emergency clothing and other supplies. As a huge international relief effort got under way, during the afternoon of 18 November *Triumph* and the assault ship *Intrepid* were ordered to prepare to sail for the area. Two days later, having loaded tons of food, medicines and stores of all kinds, *Triumph* and *Intrepid* left Singapore to set course for the Ganges delta. It was at 01.00 on 24 November when they arrived at the mouth of the Ganges River, but so dangerous were the shallow waters, where huge deposits of mud had blocked what had once been shipping channels, that they had to anchor some 30 miles offshore. No sooner had they come to rest than the mercy mission began to swing into action, with sailors and marines in landing craft, inflatables and helicopters landing large quantities of stores and evacuating people from the worst hit areas. Within 24 hours *Triumph* and *Intrepid* had landed over 400 tons of food, medical supplies and clothing, as the helicopters on both ships flew day and night on the relief work. The operations came to an end at 22.00 on 1 December when, having landed 2,850 tons of supplies, built two schools,

On 9 December 1981, *Triumph* left Chatham under tow for her final voyage to the shipbreaker's yard at Castellon in Spain. *(Michael Lennon)*

repaired hospitals, jetties and various other buildings, *Triumph* and *Intrepid* sailed for Singapore. With their roles having been filled by civil aid agencies such as the British Oxfam team, the Navy's task was at an end, but the men of *Triumph* and *Intrepid* had generated an enormous amount of goodwill and they all felt they were doing a worthwhile job. *Triumph* arrived back in Singapore on 5 December and once again she reverted to her role as the fleet's maintenance ship.

In February and March 1971 *Triumph* spent four weeks in Hong Kong, and upon her return to Singapore she went into the King George VI dry dock for an overhaul. On 7 April she moved back alongside the sea wall, and two days later the 25th anniversary of her acceptance into the Royal Navy was marked by a *son et lumière,* featuring the eight *Triumphs* which had served the Navy. On 21 April there was a final change of command for the maintenance ship when Captain J. M. Forbes RN relieved Captain Johnson. Later that month he took *Triumph* to sea for two days of manoeuvres, and in June there was a ten-day visit to Hong Kong. In September there were three days of exercises in the South China Sea off Tioman, and when *Triumph* returned to Singapore Dockyard there followed a very busy three-week period while large quantities of stores and equipment were embarked as the Royal Navy prepared to withdraw from the Singapore Naval Base, just 34 years after it had been opened by the then Governor of Singapore, Sir Shenton Thomas. The Farewell Parade for the C-in-C Far East Station was held on 29 October, and all the Armed Forces were represented by colour guards. Next day, following the handover of the naval base to the newly formed ANZUK Force, *Triumph* left harbour with the rest of the fleet and on 31 October she formed part of a 20-ship steam past led by HMS *Glamorgan,* flying the flag of Rear-Admiral D. Williams, previously FO2 FES, but now Flag Officer, Second Flotilla. The fleet was reviewed by the C-in-C in RFA *Stromness* and the helicopters of 848 Squadron provided the main section of a helicopter fly-past. Most of the fleet then left Far Eastern waters but *Triumph* returned to Sembawang Shipyard (the former naval base), remaining alongside until 08.00 on Monday 8 November when, flying her paying-off pennant and with her ship's company manning the decks, she left Singapore for the last time, to take part in 'Exercise Curtain Call' off Penang. This ended on 13 November when *Triumph* set course for Mombasa, arriving eight days later. For over a month, whilst lying in Kilindini Harbour, the maintenance ship assisted a number of escorts, including *Argonaut, Achilles, Falmouth, Scylla, Minerva* and even the submarine *Finwhale,* with their maintenance programmes. In early January 1972, however, it was time to sail for home, via South Africa and South America, but not before she had embarked 100 boys from HMS *Ganges* and *Collingwood* who, within two months of joining the Royal Navy, were on board ship and east of Suez. During the passage home, as well as their schoolwork, they would also carry out seamanship duties, which included watchkeeping and bridge lookouts. During the voyage, in company with *Minerva, Triumph* called at Port Elizabeth, where she arrived on one of the hottest days of the year and where the

A final stern view of *Triumph* as she leaves Chatham for the breaker's yard. *(Michael Lennon)*

boys received an enthusiastic welcome. From South Africa *Triumph* and *Minerva* made the 11-day transatlantic crossing to the River Plate, arriving in Buenos Aires on 24 January. From there they steamed north to Rio de Janeiro, arriving on 3 February. Unfortunately, the visit was marred by the death of a rating who was caught in a burst of machine-gun fire as he sat in a taxi. Further shore leave was cancelled, but before the ships sailed Admiral Williams laid a wreath at the monument to Almirante Tamandare, Brazil's naval hero. After calling at Gibraltar, *Triumph* arrived home on a cold February day and after seven years in the Far East, she joined *Albion* and the redundant *Eagle* in Portsmouth Harbour. After a short stay in Portsmouth *Triumph* left for her old home port of Chatham, where she was the heaviest ship to enter the dockyard for many years. Soon afterwards she was paid off and after undergoing a refit she was placed in maintained reserve. She remained at Chatham until December 1981 when, having been sold to a Spanish shipbreaking company, she was towed away to be broken up. Over 45 years after she had first commissioned, *Triumph* was the last of the Colossus-class aircraft carriers to leave the service of the Royal Navy.

Commanding Officers:

Officer	Date
Captain H. W. Faulkner CBE DSO RN	9 October 1945
Captain E. M. C. Abel-Smith CVO RN	8 July 1947
Captain R. M. J. Hutton DSO** RN	5 April 1949
Captain A. D. Torlesse DSO RN	15 December 1949
Captain C. T. Jellicoe DSO DSC RN	2 April 1951
Captain U. H. R. James CBE RN	1 August 1951
Captain H. P. Sears RN	6 January 1953
Captain R. H. Wright DSC* RN	7 September 1953
Captain V. C. Begg DSO DSC RN	31 December 1954
Captain I. F. Somerville RN	28 September 1964
Captain P. G. La Niece RN	30 October 1966
Captain I. Easton DSC RN	20 May 1968
Captain C. J. A. Johnson OBE DSC RN	19 November 1969
Captain J. M. Forbes RN	21 April 1971

Battle Honours:

Armada 1588
Dover 1652
Scheveningen 1653
Four Days' Battle 1666
Solebay 1672
Texel 1673
Camperdown 1797
Malta Convoys 1941
Portland 1653
Gabbard 1653
Lowestoft 1665
Orfordness 1666
Schooneveld 1673
Cornwallis' Retreat 1795
Dardanelles 1915
Mediterranean 1941
Korea 1950

Chapter Seventeen

HMS *Warrior* October 1948 – February 1958

Although *Warrior* was not the last of the Colossus-class aircraft carriers to be completed, she was certainly the last one to enter service with the Royal Navy and when she was finally commissioned into the fleet two of the class had already been sold to foreign navies. *Warrior's* first keel plates were laid at Harland & Wolff's Belfast shipyard on 12 December 1942 and she was launched 17 months later on 20 May 1944. Soon after the launch *Warrior* was offered to the Royal Canadian Navy as a replacement for the badly damaged escort carrier *Nabob* which had been torpedoed during 'Operation Goodwood', (one of the air strikes on the German battleship *Tirpitz*), and to play a part in their contribution to the war in the Pacific. During the Second World War the Canadian Navy had provided the manpower for *Nabob,* which not only helped the Royal Navy out with the manning of the carrier, but also gave the Canadian Navy some valuable experience in naval aviation. This experience was something which they wished to continue after the war and they were offered *Magnificent* as well as *Warrior,* both of which were expected to complete in the latter half of 1945. However, when it became apparent that *Magnificent* would not be ready for service until spring 1948, *Warrior* was given on loan to Canada for two years. Although the ship's company of *Warrior* would be Canadian, the squadrons would be provided by the Fleet Air Arm for, despite the fact that the Canadian Government had refused to allow its forces to be involved in the recapture of Malaya and Singapore, the British Government considered all the Commonwealth navies to be part of a larger joint Royal Navy. *Warrior's* first commanding officer, who joined the ship at Belfast on 1 September 1945, was Captain F. L. Houghton CBE RCN,

Warrior on the stocks at Harland & Wolff's Belfast shipyard. She has been painted in the darker grey livery of the Royal Canadian Navy. *(Neg No 8983, Ulster Folk & Transport Museum)*

of Ottawa. Most of her Canadian ship's company joined the ship in December 1945, and she was actually commissioned into the Royal Navy at Belfast on 24 January 1946. The ceremony took place in the main hangar and it was attended by the Governor of Northern Ireland and the Canadian High Commissioner in London. After completing her trials and work-up *Warrior* left Portsmouth on 23 March 1946, arriving in her base at Halifax, Nova Scotia, at the end of the month to embark 803 (Seafire) Squadron and 825 (Firefly) Squadron, which formed the 19th Carrier Air Group. During her service with the Canadian Navy *Warrior* formed part of the Atlantic Fleet, along with three escort destroyers, and she took part in a number of 'showing the flag' and training cruises. These took her into the Mediterranean and European waters where she operated with the Home Fleet. In the New Year of 1948, however, she made a voyage to Belfast to deliver stores and key personnel to HMCS *Magnificent* which was nearing completion. In February 1948 *Warrior* sailed from Halifax to Bermuda, before making a transatlantic crossing to Portsmouth where she arrived on Monday 1 March. Here she was paid off and put to use as a depot and accommodation ship until her successor *Magnificent* was commissioned on 17 April 1948, whereupon *Warrior* was handed back to the Royal Navy. Before *Magnificent* sailed for Canada she shipped stores and equipment from *Warrior* in Portsmouth and it was in early May that the dockyard finally took *Warrior* over to refit her for her first, rather unusual, role in the Royal Navy.

By 5 May a small Royal Naval complement, including the Royal Marines Detachment, were on board manning *Warrior* and the dockyard was busy fitting what was to be known as a 'flexible deck'. With jet aircraft operating from the Navy's aircraft carriers, there was no longer a ground clearance required for propellers and it was proposed that jets (both Navy and RAF) without undercarriages could land onto a flexible, or yielding surface, and *Warrior* was chosen as the aircraft carrier on which this new and unusual idea would be tested. The 'flexible' deck, which was in effect a huge three and a half-inch thick rubber carpet, was superimposed on the existing flight deck, extending from the after end of the island to an athwartships line 150 feet from the round down. In addition a false steel deck was installed at the same level as the carpet, between the after end of the flexible deck and the round down. This area was 'funnel-shaped', and at its forward end it was the same width as the rubber carpet, but it tapered off aft until it ended in a short section at the round down. The false deck was marked with a 12-inch wide white line throughout its length, which also indicated the centre of the rubber mat, whilst the false round down was painted white. Towards the end of the subsequent trials the false steel decking aft was overlaid with a second flexible deck consisting of a single layer of seven-inch diameter pneumatic hoses covered with two layers of dinghy fabric. This was intended to provide a cushion in the event of a pilot touching down in this area after failing to level off, or because of the ship's movement. In retrospect, viewed from almost 55 years after the trials, it is difficult to take them seriously, but at the time it was thought that the weight-saving aspects would justify them.

On 1 September 1948, with most of the dockyard work having been completed, *Warrior's* new commanding officer, Captain P. S. Smith DSO RN, was appointed and soon afterwards, as she lay at Portsmouth's Middle Slip Jetty, the ship's company was brought up to strength. *Warrior* was commissioned in mid-October and at 08.00 on Tuesday 19 October she sailed to carry out her trials. These continued for most of the month and included 'crashed aircraft procedures' with *Cockade*, which was to act as planeguard during the forthcoming flexible deck trials. By 27 October she had returned to Portsmouth for a short break.

During the forenoon of Tuesday 9 November a trials party from RAE Farnborough embarked, among them Lewis Boddington, who was head of the Naval Aircraft Department and the man behind the idea of 'undercarriageless' deck landings, and that afternoon *Warrior* steamed into the Channel to begin the experiments. In the event, however, bad weather put paid to any landings that day and it was the forenoon of 12 November before the first aircraft left Farnborough and headed for *Warrior*. Flown by the Royal Navy's Chief Test Pilot, Lt-Cdr E. M. Brown DSC OBE AFC RN, the first specially adapted Vampire jet had the underside of its fuselage strengthened and fitted with skids and, since it was expected to penetrate well into the flexible deck, a device had been incorporated in the arrester hook to retract the flaps on landing and so keep them clear of the rubber mat. Although Lt-Cdr Brown had first made landings on a flexible runway at Farnborough in the summer of 1947, it was the first such attempt on an aircraft carrier and at 10.35, after two dummy runs, he approached the flight deck and, as he later reported: 'On the approach at about 100-102 knots (115-118 mph), I aimed at the white painted narrow funnel round down as the spot at which I would start levelling out to give myself 100 feet of run-up. Although my height above the round down was higher than I had anticipated, I found myself forced up to it by the moderate pitch at the stern, and the turbulence low over the round down.' Fortunately the landing went without a hitch, and once at a standstill the aircraft was lifted onto a trolley by a special crane, as the second stage of the trial consisted of striking down the aircraft as quickly as possible. Lt-Cdr Brown made three more landings that day and recalled: 'When attempting the fourth landing, the deck was pitching and heaving slightly and I just failed to pick up the arrester wire and, continuing on my flight path, struck the forward end of the flexible deck with

A specially adapted 'undercarriageless' Vampire jet takes the hook and is about to land on *Warrior's* flexible rubber deck which had been superimposed on the existing flight deck.
(Fleet Air Arm Museum)

sufficient force to record 0.4g and 2.0W on the accelerometers which were switched on, but the aircraft bounced off into the air at a fairly steep angle and remained airborne with little forward pressure on the stick. A successful landing was made at the next attempt.' Following the landings, take-offs were carried out by means of a detachable 'tricycle' undercarriage, which were the first such launchings from an aircraft carrier. The flexible deck trials continued throughout November and into the first week of December, but during one landing Lt-Cdr Brown reported that: 'The port wing of the aircraft struck the arrester wire which was rising on that side under roll. A successful landing was accomplished with minor damage to the leading edge of the port wing. The next two attempts at landing were unsuccessful, for although the arrester hook picked up the wire on both occasions, there appeared to be whip characteristics associated with tension of the supported span.' The first phase of the trials ended on 6 December when *Warrior* returned to Portsmouth Harbour for the trials party to disembark, following which the carrier steamed down Channel for Devonport where she spent Christmas and the New Year.

After returning to Portsmouth on 19 January 1949 *Warrior* once again embarked her flexible deck trials party, which also included an observer from the US Navy, and on 25 January she put to sea to resume the 'undercarriageless' landings on her flexible deck. By this time more pilots had been trained in this unusual landing technique, and Lt-Cdr Brown laid out three 'golden rules' for the landings: '1. Regard every attempt at landing as a potential miss, and be prepared to act accordingly. 2. Tend to err on the high side rather than try to ensure a contact by dipping low on to the arrester wire. 3. Keep on the fast side of optimum landing speed rather than on the low.' The trials continued for several weeks and by the time they were completed on Thursday 2 June over 200 landings had been made on *Warrior's* flexible flight deck They were meant to demonstrate that the technique could be used by all pilots and not just test pilots, but although the flexible deck trials were hailed as a great success, nothing came of them and the subsequent report was left to gather dust at RAE Farnborough. For his vital role in the trials Lt-Cdr Brown was awarded the Boyd Trophy for 1949. It was the end of another phase in the carrier's career, for on 15 June Captain Smith relinquished his command and *Warrior* herself was moved to No 6 buoy in Fareham Creek where she was reduced to a state of maintained reserve and her ship's company was much reduced. Later in June 1949 *Warrior* was towed to Pitch House Jetty where the dockyard removed the flexible deck, and in early September she was towed out to the buoys at Fareham Creek where her ship's company was exchanged with that of *Indefatigable,* which was being prepared for recommissioning in the Home Fleet Training Squadron. Shortly after this *Adamant* was secured alongside and thereafter the ship's company moved on board the depot ship, with only the duty emergency party sleeping aboard *Warrior.* During the time she was laid up in Fareham Creek *Adamant* left her and the battleship *Duke of York* took her place alongside *Warrior.* On 28 July 1950, however, following the outbreak of the Korean War,

May 1950 and *Warrior* is laid up at the dolphins in Fareham Creek, alongside the battleship *Duke of York.* *(Maritime Photo Library)*

Warrior leaving home waters on 15 January 1951 for a trooping voyage to Japan. She is carrying a deck cargo of aircraft and stores. *(Fleet Air Arm Museum, Cars W/14)*

Leaving Grand Harbour during her work-up period off Malta in March 1954. *(Michael Cassar)*

Warrior was towed from Fareham Creek to C lock and then into the floating dry dock where, with dockyard assistance, her small ship's company was employed in bringing the carrier forward for operational service. On 10 August 1950 *Warrior's* new commanding officer, Captain St John Cronyn DSO RN, was appointed and two weeks later, with the ship's company having been brought to steaming strength, Portsmouth Command became responsible for the administration of the ship as she was commissioned for service as a troop and cargo transport between the UK and the Far East.

On Sunday 20 August, after embarking naval drafts, including a new ship's company for the destroyer *Charity, Warrior* left Portsmouth to begin her first voyage to the Far East. First, however, she steamed north to Glasgow to load aircraft spares, equipment and stores. After leaving Glasgow on 24 August *Warrior* steamed east via Malta, Suez and Aden. In the Indian Ocean she passed her sister *Theseus* which was working up her squadrons on her way to Korea. At Singapore *Warrior* embarked Royal Marines, Army and RAF personnel, as well as replacement aircraft for the Navy at Iwakuni. On 23 September she arrived in Hong Kong and two days later she sailed for Sasebo. At 15.40 on 26 September, just 24 hours out from Hong Kong, *Warrior* went to the aid of a Greek cargo ship, *George H. Embricos,* and the carrier's surgeon was able to treat a member of the merchantman's crew. Two days later the carrier arrived at Sasebo where, during her eight-day stopover, she embarked homeward-bound drafts. She made her return passage via Hong Kong, Singapore, Trincomalee, where the RAF personnel who had joined on the outward passage left the ship, Aden, Suez, Malta and Gibraltar, arriving in Portsmouth on 21 November. A week later, having disembarked her passengers and cargo, Captain St John Cronyn relinquished his command and *Warrior* was towed to the floating dry dock where she remained until the end of the year.

On 2 January 1951, with *Warrior* alongside Portsmouth's North Corner Jetty, Captain A. F. Pugsley CB DSO RN took command and ten days later, having embarked drafts for the Far East, *Warrior* steamed north to Glasgow to embark aircraft for her second voyage to the Orient. Leaving Glasgow on 15 January 1951, she again sailed by way of Malta, Suez and Trincomalee, arriving in Singapore on 9 February. Here some of her aircraft were disembarked into lighters bound for RNAS Sembawang, and after leaving Singapore the carrier steamed on to Hong Kong and Sasebo where, on 20 February, her main drafts disembarked. That same afternoon she sailed for Iwakuni where, over a period of 48 hours, the remaining aircraft were unloaded into lighters and ferried ashore. After weighing anchor and leaving Iwakuni *Warrior* put into Kure for 24 hours, before starting her return passage by way of Sasebo and Hong Kong, arriving in Singapore Naval Base on Saturday 10 March. During her three days at Singapore a number of Army personnel were embarked for the return passage home, and one of these was Bill Markham, a bombardier with the Royal Artillery. He remembers the voyage thus: 'I had been serving with a Royal Battery based at Tampin in Malaya, having been detached from Hong Kong. Due to an oversight, in March 1951 it was suddenly discovered that 20 of us were close to the statutory three-year limit for overseas service and if we waited for the next troopship we would exceed this limit, so we were ordered to take passage in HMS *Warrior* which was homeward-bound. We embarked at the naval base shortly before she sailed and were allocated to a mess deck. Apart from the fact that we slept in hammocks aboard *Warrior,* living conditions and the food served were much better than on board the troopships. We were allocated to one of the specialist departments on the ship and so we received the added bonus of a daily tot of rum. I was lucky to be attached to the Shipwrights Department and I assisted a Petty Officer 'Chippy' who happened to be responsible for lowering the booms which accommodated the ship's boats when we were in harbour, so I was excused the obligatory spit and polish parade on the flight deck when we entered harbour. Another advantage over travelling on board troopships soon became clear when we entered harbour. Time ashore for the embarked forces in troopships was severely restricted and if the time in harbour amounted to ten hours, the troops on board would only be allowed ashore for two hours at the most. On board *Warrior,* with the leave being based on the port and starboard watch system, those off watch were down the gangway as soon as the ship had berthed and were not required to return to the ship until an hour or so before sailing time. Our first port of call was the naval base at Trincomalee, which was a change from Colombo where troopships normally called. The second port was Aden, and then Malta. Shortly after leaving the latter port the weather deteriorated and it became quite rough, with waves breaking over the gun sponsons and weather decks. By that time I thought I had become a real sailor and so I went to the forward end of the flight deck to enjoy the sensation of what felt like being in a giant lift while the bows rose and fell with the sea. However, my stomach soon told me that this had been a mistake, and the ship's company viewed my queasiness as a huge joke. By the time we reached Portsmouth we had made a number of friends amongst the ship's company and, being a non-smoker, I was asked to conceal a bit of contraband in my kit. We were assured that we would not be searched and, fortunately for me this proved to be the case, although most of the sailors and their kit bags were thoroughly searched.'

Warrior arrived in Portsmouth on 6 April, and she remained alongside Pitch House Jetty until the first week of June when, following a deterioration in the security in the Suez Canal Zone, she was required to carry Army

Warrior at Hong Kong during her 1954 commission in the Far East.
(Fleet Air Arm Museum, Cars W/3)

reinforcements to Cyprus. With one half of the 16th Independent Parachute Brigade having been embarked in the newly recommissioned *Triumph,* the other half of the brigade boarded *Warrior.* As well as troops *Warrior* loaded 140 tons of equipment and stores, 124 vehicles and two bulldozers on board. Finally, with the embarkation complete, on 5 June *Warrior* left Portsmouth and, in company with *Triumph,* she sailed for Cyprus where she arrived off Famagusta seven days later. With such a great deal of equipment to unload the carrier spent two days off Cyprus, but when she weighed anchor she made a direct passage to Portsmouth arriving alongside South Railway Jetty on 21 June. Five days later *Warrior* left Portsmouth to steam north for Glasgow, from where she was to make her next trooping voyage to the Far East. Once again she was carrying aircraft, equipment, stores and personnel and her passage to Sasebo took her by way of Malta, Suez, Aden, Trincomalee, Singapore and Hong Kong, arriving in Japan on 7 August. For the return to Portsmouth she carried home drafts of naval ratings who had completed their terms of foreign service on the Far East Station, plus a number of aircraft, and at Malta she embarked officers and men of the Grenadier Guards. When she arrived alongside Portsmouth's South Railway Jetty on 10 September relatives were allowed on board to welcome their loved ones and soon afterwards drafts of men left the ship for *Dolphin, Mercury,* the Royal Marines Barracks at Eastney, *Collingwood,* Lee-on-the-Solent, and the naval barracks at Portsmouth, Chatham and Devonport. On 27 September there was another change of command when Captain E. V. St John Morgan RN took over from Captain Pugsley and a month later, on 25 October, after embarking large drafts of naval personnel, of whom some 400 officers and men were destined for *Unicorn, Warrior* sailed for Glasgow to load her cargo. Sailing by way of the Mediterranean, Suez, Aden and Colombo, she arrived in Singapore Naval Base on 19 November. At Malta she had loaded 4,000 cases of local beer for the British Forces in the Suez Canal Zone, but most of her cargo and embarked passengers were disembarked during her nine days at Singapore. On her return passage, carrying men of the 8th Hussars from Korea and the Green Howards from Malaya, she called at Malta where she loaded aircraft and stores, including 130 Christmas trees which had come from Trieste, a number of cars and naval personnel. After a bumpy passage across the Bay of Biscay *Warrior* arrived in Plymouth Sound on 19 December where some of her passengers and cargo were disembarked before she left for Portsmouth the following day. When she arrived there the next day it was the end of *Warrior's* career as a troop transport.

In January 1952 *Warrior* was shifted from Pitch House Jetty to No 5 basin at Portsmouth Dockyard where destoring was carried out, and on 23 January she steamed down Channel to Devonport where, on the following day, she secured to a buoy at No 1 Capital Ship Trot. On 2 February Captain St John Morgan relinquished his command and at the end of that month, having been towed to No 5 basin, *Warrior* began a modernization refit in Devonport Dockyard. Among the tasks undertaken were the replacement of the tripod mast with an improved lattice structure, and the enclosing and enlargement of her bridge. The modifications were designed to allow *Warrior* to operate the latest aircraft, which would in turn permit her to take up the role of trade protection carrier. In January 1953, whilst lying in No 5 basin, a number of minor acts of sabotage, consisting mainly of damaged electrical cables, were perpetrated on board. Although the culprit was not discovered, the damage did not affect the course of the refit. On 18 August her new commanding officer, Captain P. J. Milner-Barry RN, was appointed to the ship, and a few weeks later, during the forenoon of Tuesday 8 September, a new ship's company marched down to the ship from the Royal Naval Barracks. At 12.00 *Warrior* was recommissioned and over the following ten days she carried out basin trials and inclining trials.

On Wednesday 14 October 1953 *Warrior* left Devonport to begin her post-refit trials, which continued through to the end of the month, with evenings at anchor in Plymouth Sound and weekends alongside Devonport Dockyard. On 11 November the C-in-C Plymouth, Admiral Sir Maurice Mansergh, inspected the ship and for the rest of the month the trials continued. On Wednesday 2 December *Warrior* began her flying trials off the Isle of Wight and at 08.30 an Avenger became the first aircraft to land on the flight deck since the Vampire trials in 1949. Christmas was spent at Devonport, but was marred by a number of acts of malicious damage in the main machinery spaces, which were discovered on Christmas Day. A number of gauge glasses had been deliberately smashed and with many of the ship's company about to start the second long leave period, all leave was stopped and the police were called in to investigate. This time a 21-year-old stoker mechanic was arrested and he was subsequently convicted and sentenced to two years' imprisonment. Fortunately the incident did not affect *Warrior's* operational capability.

The latter half of January 1954 was spent in No 10 dry dock for routine hull maintenance, and finally, on Monday 15 February, *Warrior* sailed to land on her squadrons off the Isle of Wight. After anchoring at Spithead the personnel of 825 (Firefly) Squadron and 811 (Sea Fury) Squadron were embarked and on leaving her anchorage during the forenoon of 17 February, she steamed down Channel to land on the aircraft. On 21 February she anchored in Gibraltar Bay for five hours and three days later she arrived off Malta to begin her work-up. During the whole of March, working out of Grand Harbour and Marsaxlokk Bay, the squadrons carried out intensive flying operations and on 3 March she went to the assistance of a small coaster which was in difficulties. Eight days later, at 10.05 on 11 March, a Firefly crashed into the sea in flames about a mile away from the ship, but fortunately both the pilot and observer were rescued by the ship's helicopter. The work-up continued into April, but during the afternoon of 1 April, whilst the carrier was operating off Tunisia, a Sea Fury and its pilot, Sub-Lt D. B. Evans, were lost. Three days later, at Malta, a memorial service was held.

On Saturday 17 April, having embarked the Royal Marines of 3 Commando Brigade, *Warrior* sailed from Grand Harbour to join the Far East Station. After leaving Malta the squadrons were landed on and during the afternoon of 20 April *Warrior* began her transit of the Suez Canal. That evening she anchored in the Great Bitter Lake where the Royal Marines were landed, and in the early hours of the next day she continued her passage south. On 25 April there was a stop of seven hours at Aden, before *Warrior* set course for Colombo. Twenty-four hours after leaving Aden, at 16.20 on Monday 26 April, the carrier passed the Shaw Savill liner SS *Gothic*, which was in service as a royal yacht and taking the Queen and Duke of Edinburgh on a Commonwealth tour. *Gothic* had left Colombo a few days earlier and she was bound for Aden and Malta where, for the final stage of the voyage home, the newly built royal yacht *Britannia* would take over from the liner. As *Warrior* passed *Gothic* a 21-gun salute was fired and the ship's company, who were manning the flight deck, cheered ship. Two hours later a signal was received thanking *Warrior* for her salute, with the command to 'Splice the Main Brace', which caused another cheer.

Warrior arrived in Colombo on 3 May, where the four days in harbour allowed for runs ashore to Kandy, Nuwara Eliya and Mount Lavinia. During the passage through the Bay of Bengal a heavy swell hampered flying operations, and on 12 May *Warrior* arrived in Singapore Naval Base and went straight into dry dock, whereupon the ship's company moved into shore accommodation at HMS *Terror*. Unfortunately, with civil unrest and riots in Singapore city, shore leave was restricted to Sembawang and Nee Soon, but by the end of the month, with the maintenance work having been completed, the carrier was back alongside the sea wall and the ship's company was back on board. On 1 June *Warrior* left Singapore to land on her squadrons and two days later she set course for Hong Kong where she arrived on 8 June. Although the Korean War had ended with an armistice in July 1953, the United Nations forces still had the task of monitoring the armistice line, which was fixed at the 38th Parallel. For the Royal Navy this meant maintaining a presence off the west coast of Korea and *Warrior* was ordered to join the UN monitoring force, where she would relieve HMAS *Sydney*. She left Hong Kong on 12 June, to make a five-day passage to Kure before proceeding to Sasebo. *Warrior's* first patrol began on 22 June and, together with the US Navy's carrier USS *Wright* and the destroyer HMCS *Crusader*, she patrolled the south-west coast of Korea. Although the aircraft flew reconnaissance missions over Korea there was not the urgency of wartime and on a number of occasions *Warrior* anchored off Inchon, where there was some limited shore leave at a nearby Army rest camp. The first patrol ended at Kure on 4 July, and after a break of eight days she sailed for her second patrol. During the afternoon of Wednesday 14 July, during flying operations, the ship's helicopter crashed into the sea abreast the port after Bofors sponson. The ship was stopped immediately and the sea boat quickly rescued the crew members. The last three days of the patrol were spent off Okinawa where the aircraft carried out flying exercises, then on 24 July *Warrior* arrived back at Kure for a short break.

After only four days *Warrior* left Kure for her third

patrol off south-west Korea, during which time she operated with the destroyer *Cockade*. She returned to Kure on 6 August but two days later, with the presence of a Commonwealth aircraft carrier off Korea no longer required, *Warrior* and *Cockade* were ordered to return to Singapore, where they arrived alongside on 16 August. For a week the carrier remained at Singapore, carrying out maintenance and replenishing stores and then, in the last week of August, she was ordered to put to sea and set course for the port of Haiphong in the northern zone of Vietnam.

After the end of the Second World War France had reoccupied her colonies in Indo-China (Vietnam, Laos and Cambodia) and by December 1945 she had over 20,000 troops in the country, mainly around Saigon (Ho Chi Minh City). However, that month also saw the start of Indo-China's war of independence, with the French Army facing a large and well-organized guerrilla army, the Viet Minh, led by Ho Chi Minh. The war had dragged on for over seven years until finally, the French, with 16,000 troops supported by artillery and light tanks, drew the Viet Minh into a set-piece battle at the small village of Dien Bien Phu. The French were confident that they would inflict a decisive defeat on the Viet Minh, but unknown to them Ho Chi Minh's forces had mustered over 50,000 men and even heavier artillery than the French. The battle started on 13 March 1954. After a long and bloody siege, during which the French forces suffered some 7,500 casualties, their garrison surrendered on 8 May 1954. The French defeat at Dien Bien Phu brought this unpopular colonial war to a close and, under the terms of the Geneva Peace Agreement, Vietnam was divided at the 17th Parallel by a Demilitarized Zone. French troops began evacuating the northern zone of Vietnam, which was to be ruled by Ho Chi Minh's Communist regime, and with their withdrawal due to be completed by October 1954, there was a rush of almost a million refugees, most of them Roman Catholics, to flee to the southern zone, which was to be governed by the United States-backed regime of Premier Ngo Dinh Diem. So immense was the refugee problem that the South Vietnamese Government appealed to the United Nations for assistance and as *Warrior* was still officially under the auspices of the UN, she was ordered to assist with the evacuation.

After leaving Singapore during the afternoon of 31 August, leaving her Air Group and the personnel at Sembawang, she set course for the North Vietnamese port of Haiphong. On board preparations to receive the refugees had been made by the dockyard, with the hangar being completely cleared and roped off with passageways around the sides. The after lift had been lowered to mid-level and accommodation ladders were fixed into place to allow the passengers access to the flight deck, where another large area had been cordoned off for their use. Beneath the after lift the dockyard staff had built male and female washbasins and showers, and two mess decks with easy access to the hangar were turned into an additional sickbay. The biggest problem turned out to be the toilet facilities, as the refugees would not wish to use the ship's western arrangements. Fortunately, the dockyard came to the ship's rescue and after landing the motor boats, rows of curious looking metal cubicles, complete with their own water supply, appeared in their place. In order to feed the passengers sacks of rice had been loaded and, finally, to help with the whole operation, three Army nurses, an interpreter and two Chinese women searchers from the police joined the ship. While in Singapore the additional toilets had obviously attracted attention for, shortly after leaving harbour *Warrior* received a signal from FO2 which read: 'You look very smart leaving harbour. Your new water-cooled anti-submarine weapons look most impressive.'

In September 1954 *Warrior* assisted with the evacuation of refugees from North Vietnam. Here they are boarding the carrier from French LCTs, just south of the port of Haiphong. *(Fleet Air Arm Museum, Cars W/17)*

The Vietnamese refugees, having staked out their deck space, packed into *Warrior's* main hangar and slept on their own rush mats. They were disembarked close to the Saigon River. *(Fleet Air Arm Museum, Cars W/18)*

The passage to Haiphong took three days and at 09.00 on Saturday 4 September *Warrior* anchored in the Passé Henriette, Ile de L'Union, several miles south of Haiphong itself, where she joined a fleet of French and American ships which were all involved in the evacuation. As no foreign ships were allowed to approach the main port of Haiphong, the refugees would be brought out to the ship by French LCTs while *Warrior* remained in sea routine. The Royal Marines Detachment had the task of providing searching parties and armed sentries on the gangway and in the hangar and, with the aid of two policewomen, all the refugees would be searched for arms and ammunition as they boarded the ship. At 13.30 two LCTs carrying 1,454 people, mostly women and children, approached the ship and the embarkation began. Most of the refugees were carrying what remained of their worldly possessions in the traditional style, slung at the end of a bamboo pole, and they were quite undeterred by the intermittent heavy rain which deluged them during the three-hour process. A few of the men and women were blind, a great many others were very elderly, there were several children without any relatives and many of the women had very young babies. The whole scope of the human tragedy that Vietnam's peace agreement had brought boarded *Warrior* that day, but the cheerfulness and the warmth of their reception from the carrier's ship's company helped to make them feel at home. On arrival on board all the refugees were dusted with DDT and searched for hand grenades and other weapons, and they were then guided to the hangar where they quickly established themselves on the hangar deck, marking out their own space with rush mats. They were delighted with their washing facilities under the after lift, and many of the children remained under the showers indefinitely. After some initial shyness, equal satisfaction was expressed with the temporary 'anti-submarine weapons' on deck outside the hangar. By 16.23 all the refugees from the two LCTs were safely on board and at 17.30 *Warrior* weighed anchor and set course south. During the passage two meals a day were served to the Vietnamese, consisting of rice and either fish or meat to accompany it. The only difficulty experienced was ensuring the correct consistency of the cooked rice, about which the refugees were fussy, but the galley staff soon got the hang of it and there were no complaints. The refugee sickbay did a roaring trade from anti-sea sickness tablets to stomach pumps, and a Vietnamese doctor, nurse and interpreter were on board to reinforce the ship's medical staff. Among the children were a number of cases of under nourishment and skin complaints and some of the women were pregnant, but the ship's staff took it all in their stride and coped admirably. Despite gale force winds and heavy seas during the voyage south, the flight deck took on the appearance of a school playground, except that the children were very, very ragged. Their initial shyness soon wore off and as their confidence grew, they were soon laughing and smiling at the sailors and repeating parrot-fashion English words which they were taught. The forward end of the flight deck refugee area was a favourite with the adults, many with tiny babies, who sat on deck watching the ship's company playing deck hockey. They particularly enjoyed the ship's volunteer band which, during the voyage south, spent long hours entertaining them with their music. At 08.00 on Tuesday 7 September *Warrior* anchored near Cape St Jacques (Vung Tau) off the Saigon River, which was as close as the ship could get to the city. The disembarkation into US Navy LCUs began at 10.00 and once again the whole of the ship's company, officers, sailors and marines, rose to the occasion. Burly marines carried the blind people down the accommodation ladder, whilst the sailors helped the women and children to carry their possessions and the whole difficult operation was carried out with the greatest good humour. By 13.00 the disembarkation was complete and just over five hours later *Warrior* was steaming north to embark more refugees. During the forenoon of 10 September the carrier anchored close to Haiphong for the second time, and at 18.00, with another 1,767 refugees embarked, *Warrior* set course for Saigon. This time, at 00.15 on 12 September a baby girl, Eu Thi Anh, was born in the refugee's hospital and, sadly,

After her modernization refit at Devonport and sporting a new partially angled flight deck, *Warrior* rejoined the fleet in August 1956.
(Fleet Air Arm Museum, Cars W/2)

three and a half hours later a young Vietnamese girl died. That morning speed was reduced and the funeral service was held for the child as her body was committed to the deep. Next day, at 08.15, *Warrior* anchored off Cape St Jacques for the second time and by mid-afternoon all the refugees were ashore. It was the end of *Warrior's* humanitarian mission for which the ship received a Citation from the President of South Vietnam. For the ship's company, however, the smiles on the faces of the refugees as they left the ship were reward enough, and even today there must be hundreds of Vietnamese people who remember their voyage to freedom in the aircraft carrier *Warrior.*

During the afternoon of 13 September *Warrior* left Vietnamese waters to return to Singapore, where she arrived two days later to begin cleaning up the ship and dismantling the special facilities which had been built for the refugees. A week later, on 23 September, *Warrior* sailed to land on her squadrons and to set course for Hong Kong. During the passage 'buzzes' about the ship's future programme were rife, but it was soon confirmed that the carrier would not be required to return to Korea. There was even better news when Captain Milner-Barry was able to announce that in October the ship would begin her passage home, via the Indian Ocean and South Africa. Whilst at Hong Kong, however, the carrier put to sea twice to carry out flying operations, on one occasion watched by the men of the 7th Hussars, but on 7 October she left the colony to sail home. Originally it had been thought that *Centaur* would relieve *Warrior* on the Far East Station, but following the decision to reduce the UN forces in Korea, the Royal Navy would no longer deploy an operational aircraft carrier in the Far East.

Warrior arrived in Singapore on 12 October, and four days later she left to start a 16-day passage across the Indian Ocean. During the afternoon of 23 October, Crossing the Line was celebrated in style, and three days later all the aircraft were launched to fly in formation over Port Louis, Mauritius. The Fireflies executed the fly-past in an 'anchor' formation with the Sea Furies in a 'W' formation, and by 16.00 they were safely back on board as the ship continued to steam west. At 08.30 on Monday 1 November *Warrior* arrived in Durban, where the legendary hospitality was extended to the ship's company and thousands of local people visited the ship during the four afternoons she was opened to the public. On one afternoon alone over 10,000 people flocked aboard. After leaving Durban on 8 November *Warrior* steamed south and after putting on a flying display over the town she put into Port Elizabeth for three days. The final port of call on the cruise to South African ports was Cape Town, and after securing alongside the Duncan Dock on 15 November, the ship's company spent four days enjoying the city's hospitality. From Cape Town *Warrior* set course into the Atlantic Ocean heading for the French West African port of Dakar in Senegal. On the last day of November there was another Crossing the Line ceremony and three days later she secured alongside No 1 Mole in Dakar's inner harbour. During the three-day visit *Warrior* was opened to the public and over 7,000 people came to look round. Finally, however, on 6 December she sailed for the final leg of her passage home and, six days later, the aircraft were flown ashore. Next day, 13 December, she anchored at Spithead where the squadron personnel were disembarked, and she then made an overnight passage to Devonport where, at 16.00 on 14 December, she secured alongside. Although *Warrior* was to undergo a modernization refit, she did not pay off until February 1955 and before this, in mid-January, more acts of malicious damage were committed when, during the afternoon of 16 January, some 15 gauge glasses in the boiler rooms and their fan flats were smashed. For a time all shore leave was stopped, but the culprit was not found. Soon afterwards the ship was paid off and taken over by the dockyard.

When *Warrior's* modernization refit started at Devonport it was planned that she would rejoin the fleet in 1956 as an operational aircraft carrier, before being replaced by *Hermes* in late 1959 or early 1960. In order to operate Sea Hawk jets and Gannet AEW aircraft she was fitted with a 5½° angled flight deck, new arrester gear and updated radar. Most of the work involved the addition of the angled flight deck, which meant moving sponsons on the port side and strengthening the surrounding areas of hull. She was the only aircraft carrier of the Colossus class to be fitted with an angled flight deck, but in the event the Royal Navy would not benefit from it. Altogether *Warrior* was out of commission for 18 months, but on 14 August 1956 her new commanding officer, Captain R. B. N. Hicks DSO RN, joined the ship. By the third week in August *Warrior's* complement was up to strength and at 12.00 on Tuesday 21 August the ship was commissioned for 'General Service'. Four days later she left Devonport for her trials and in September she operated from Spithead, carrying out flying trials with Avengers from RNAS Ford. At the end of September there was a weekend break at Portsmouth before *Warrior* continued her flying trials with helicopters, after which she returned to Devonport. During this period there was some thought that *Warrior* might be involved in the Suez Campaign, but in the event the naval air power was provided by *Eagle, Albion* and *Bulwark,* and she was not required. By mid-October the carrier was off the Isle of Wight once again and flying trials continued with a variety of aircraft using her new angled flight deck. At the end of October she took a weekend break at Portsmouth before setting course for Rosyth. From the Firth of Forth she made her way to Belfast by way of Scapa Flow, but severe gales prevented any flying during the voyage south through the Minches and her arrival at Belfast was delayed by some 24 hours. During the afternoon of Friday 9 November

Heavy weather during the first few days of *Warrior's* transatlantic voyage to the Pacific for the British hydrogen bomb tests, code-named 'Operation Grapple'. *(Fleet Air Arm Museum, Cars W/16)*

Warrior arrived alongside the Aircraft Wharf at Sydenham, close to Harland & Wolff's shipyard where, almost 11 years earlier she had first sailed for service with the Canadian Navy. From Belfast she returned to Devonport where she spent a short time in dry dock and the ship's company took their seasonal leave.

It had originally been intended that during 1957 *Warrior* would relieve *Bulwark* as the trials and training carrier but, in the wake of Suez, this plan was cancelled and in January 1957 *Warrior* was allocated to lead a special squadron of naval units to monitor Britain's hydrogen bomb tests which were to be carried out in the Pacific Ocean at Malden Island, some 400 miles south of Christmas Island. Before she joined the Pacific squadron, however, *Warrior* carried out a series of trials in the Channel off the Isle of Wight, which began on 3 January 1957. These consisted of prewetting trials and 'Emergency Stations' for radiation hazards, as well as co-ordination exercises with RAF Valiant bombers which flew low overhead as *Warrior* steamed down Channel. The hydrogen bombs were to be dropped by a Valiant bomber and the aircraft carrier would act as the Command Ship for the scientists from the Atomic Weapons Research Establishment. On Friday 11 January *Warrior* returned to Portsmouth Harbour, where she secured alongside Pitch House Jetty to make the final preparations for her voyage to the Pacific. During the three weeks in harbour there was an open day for relatives and friends of the ship's company, and two RAF Whirlwind helicopters, together with 103 Army and RAF personnel, joined the ship. *Warrior* left Portsmouth at 13.15 on Saturday 2 February 1957, a dull, damp and cold day, with steady drizzle falling. Off the Nab Tower she landed on a flight of two Avengers, which would be used for a variety of tasks during the atomic tests, before setting course down Channel. Once at sea the drizzle turned into heavy rain and as the ship steamed towards the Atlantic Ocean, wind speeds increased until they had become gales of considerable force. During the next five days there were times when the ship was almost blown to a standstill, with the needle of the wind-speed indicator being 'right off the clock'. The ship's boats suffered damage, some of the inflatable life rafts were washed overboard and down below mess traps were sent flying across the living spaces. Most of the Army and RAF personnel were victims of *mal de mer,* as were some of the younger ship's company members. On 11 February, with *Warrior* in the vicinity of the Azores, there were breaks in the clouds and the sun started to shine, allowing the mess decks to be squared off and the RAF helicopters to begin flying. Four days later the carrier arrived at Kingston, Jamaica, for a two-day break before reaching Cristobal at 05.30 on 19 February. Shortly afterwards she began her passage through the Panama Canal which, at Gatun and Pedro Miguel locks, was a tight squeeze, but by 23.00 that evening the carrier was heading for Christmas Island. During the passage, instead of damage control exercises there were radiation hazard exercises, and the helicopters and Avengers were able to 'spread their wings'. Finally, at 07.40 on Monday 4 March *Warrior* secured to a buoy off Christmas Island.

Warrior negotiates the Gatun Locks in the Panama Canal.
(Fleet Air Arm Museum, Cars W/19)

The shore base at which most of the servicemen were accommodated was a huge tented area, known to all who were there as 'Canvas City', but for *Warrior's* ship's company the limited shore leave was restricted mainly to a canteen in the base. Soon after the carrier's arrival a company of soldiers and airmen were embarked for a break from their tents, and at 12.00 on 7 March Captain Hicks was temporarily promoted to Commodore of the 16-ship 'Grapple' squadron, hoisting his broad pendant in *Warrior.* Two days later the carrier left Christmas Island for Honolulu where, on 13 March, she was met alongside Pier 40 by a troupe of Hula girls who performed a dance of welcome on the jetty. Willing hands assisted the girls up the gangway, where the dancing continued with the ship's company joining in, and with Commodore Hicks being selected for several dances. During the two days at Honolulu generous hospitality was received and returned in the best naval tradition. The short visit was a memorable one and it was to be the last real run ashore for some weeks, but it was soon time to return to Christmas Island, where *Warrior* arrived on 18 March. During the period of preparation for the nuclear tests, recreation on board consisted of deck hockey, volley ball, badminton, table tennis and uckers. There was a visit from the overall commander of 'Operation Grapple', Air-Vice Marshal W. E. Oulton. During April *Warrior* made several trips between Christmas and Malden Islands, carrying out meteorological duties and supplying fuel, food and water to Malden Island. On these occasions she operated mainly with the tank landing craft *Messina* and *Narvik,* the frigate *Alert* and the RFAs *Fort Rosalie* and *Wave Ruler.* On Tuesday 7 May *Warrior* left Christmas Island for Malden Island, where she arrived that evening. In the period before the nuclear explosions she operated off the island, and in addition to her weather reporting she carried out flying operations with her Avengers and helicopters. Each evening she would stop her engines at a safe distance from the island and drift with the wind and currents until the next forenoon, when she would get under way once again.

The first hydrogen bomb test took place during the forenoon of Wednesday 15 May, and *Warrior* got under way at 08.00 to operate her helicopters as they shuttled between the ship and shore carrying the scientists and their instruments. At 10.00 local time all hands who were not on watch were mustered on the flight deck and 20 minutes later, with the ship in a position Lat 03° - 39'S/Long 154° - 58'N, approximately 20 to 30 miles north-west of the island, all hands were ordered to 'stations for witnessing burst'. At 10.40 a Valiant bomber, commanded by Sqdn-Ldr D. Roberts RAF with a crew of four, approached Malden Island. John Carr, an Air Electrical Mechanic, remembers the events: 'Lower deck was cleared and, apart from those on watch, the whole ship's company mustered on the flight deck. We were wearing our No 8 action working rig, anti-flash gear, dark goggles and a special radiation detection badge. We had to sit on the flight deck, face away from the direction of the explosion and cover our goggles with our hands. As we sat there, over the ship's tannoy we could hear everything that was going on, including the voice of the Valiant pilot as he flew in high

Three members of the ship's company, having removed their protective goggles and their anti-flash hoods, watch the awe-inspiring sight of a hydrogen bomb burst above Malden Island. *(John Carr)*

over Malden Island. We heard him announce that the bomb had gone, and then there was a countdown before the burst. When the bomb exploded, with a noise like a deep, heavy, rumbling thunder, we could feel the heat of it through our shirts and although we had been warned to expect a blast wave, it did not materialize. After ten to 15 seconds we were told we could stand up and face the direction of the explosion, but we had to keep our goggles on. A few seconds later we were told to remove the goggles, and the sight was awe-inspiring. There, in the sky over the island, was a huge boiling fireball and rolling around within it were enormous red flames. It was like a boiling red and yellow sun hanging there in the sky, with the flames boiling within it. Then, slowly, from the top and centre of the fireball, came white smoke which, as incongruous as it may sound, reminded me of white sauce covering a Christmas pudding and slowly running down its sides. After this the distinctive mushroom cloud started to form and our Whirlwind helicopters flew ashore to pick up samples from the island and bring them back on board. Before they had returned our two Avengers were waiting to be launched, and as soon as the samples had been transferred the two aircraft were catapulted off to Christmas Island. I believe the samples were flown by Canberra bombers back to the UK and had arrived at their destination before the end of the day. Although I was an Air Electrical Mechanic, when the helicopters had completed their flying between the ship and Malden Island, I had to help wash them down. By the time of the third test on 19 June, we had all become very nonchalant about the whole experience and as we had not felt any blast from the first two explosions, we did not expect any from the third. This time, however, it took us all by surprise and we felt the ship being buffeted by the shock wave.'

Soon after each explosion RAF Canberra bombers flew through the mushroom cloud to collect samples and *Warrior's* helicopters flew towards the target area on the island taking radiation readings and collecting instruments and earth samples for testing. That first evening at 20.00, *Warrior* stopped her engines and drifted less than a mile from Malden Island and on 17 May she set course to return to Christmas Island. By 30 May, however, she was back off Malden Island, and at 10.41 the next day the second hydrogen bomb was exploded over the Pacific Island. The final nuclear test of the series took place at 10.40 on Wednesday 19 June and *Warrior's* log records events as follows:

09.37	Assume Damage Control State 1A.
10.40	Thermo-nuclear explosion obscured by Malden Island.
12.15	Course 210°, speed 15 knots to close Malden Island.
13.10	Flying Avengers.
13.46	Commodore left ship for Malden Island.
14.46	Courses to close Malden Island.
15.45	Stop both engines. Lower port after ladder. Ten minutes' notice for steam.

That evening *Warrior* again drifted off the contaminated island, but during the forenoon of 21 June, with her role in the nuclear tests over, she returned to Christmas Island.

On 4 July *Warrior* made a voyage to Pearl Harbor and back to Christmas Island, but upon her return she stayed just long enough to land stores and to embark 50 additional passengers in the form of Army and RAF personnel who had volunteered to make the voyage home in *Warrior*, rather than await the arrival of a troopship. As *Warrior* was sailing by way of the Pacific and Atlantic Oceans, the opportunity was taken to extend her passage and incorporate 'showing the flag' visits to some remote Pacific islands and to four major South American ports.

Warrior at anchor off Raratonga during her passage home from her 'Operation Grapple' duties. *(John Carr)*

At anchor off Pitcairn Island on 31 July 1957. She lay off the island for just 11 hours and is almost certainly the only Royal Navy aircraft carrier to make a post-war visit to the island. *(John Carr)*

On 23 July the carrier arrived at her first port of call when she anchored off Raratonga which, in 1957, was both undeveloped and unspoiled. Many from the ship consumed rather too much of a locally produced alcoholic drink made from orange juice, and on the second day of the visit islanders boarded *Warrior* to sell souvenirs while a troupe of grass-skirted girls entertained the ship's company with singing and dancing. After leaving Raratonga on 25 July, *Warrior* set course for Pitcairn Island where the islanders ferried liberty men ashore to the Bounty Bay landing stage. Many of the local people came on board to sell souvenirs, and they did a roaring trade in wood carvings and fruit. During the Pacific voyage news came through of the post-Suez cuts in defence expenditure, which meant that many ships, including *Warrior,* would be reduced to reserve with manpower drastically reduced. As far as *Warrior* was concerned the two Avengers of the ship's flight fell victim to early 'defence cuts' when, with due ceremony, they were catapulted into the Pacific Ocean.

Warrior's next port of call was Callao in Peru, where the President of the country visited the carrier. From there *Warrior* moved on to Valparaiso where she arrived on 17 August for a four-day visit. It was here that two Chilean Navy Bell 47 helicopters took part in some joint flying practice with the RAF Whirlwinds, and the local people flocked on board to look round. From Valparaiso *Warrior* made the 1,500 mile passage to the Falkland Islands, ploughing through heavy seas and gale force winds on the way before anchoring in Stanley's outer harbour during the forenoon of 27 August. Despite the heavy rain many went ashore to the tin-roofed pubs to sample the draught Guinness. After three days *Warrior* left the remote British colony and sailed for Argentina and the naval base of Puerto Belgrano. During the passage she rendezvoused with the frigates *Lynx* and *Mounts Bay* and a Royal Marines Band joined the ship by jackstay. With *Lynx* flying the flag of Flag Officer South America and South Atlantic, the visit to Argentina was to be more high-profile than the previous ports and during the forenoon of 2 September the squadron arrived alongside the North West Wall of Puerto Belgrano. Rumours were circulating on board that the Argentine Navy had more than a passing interest in *Warrior,* and for one member of the ship's company this seemed to be confirmed when, '..hordes of Argentine sailors, complete with kit bags, came aboard for the passage to Buenos Aires, as well as the C-in-C of the Argentine Navy'. After leaving Puerto Belgrano on 4 September the carrier and her escorts sailed for the River Plate, arriving in the Argentine capital two days later. On 9 September the President of Argentina inspected Divisions on board, and three days after that *Warrior* arrived in Montevideo. When the ship was opened to visitors the flight deck became a heaving mass of people, and when rumours circulated among the crowds that the gangway was about to be shut the police had to be called to restore order on the dockside as people fought to get aboard. The final, and most popular South American port, was Rio de Janeiro and on 19 September *Warrior* and her escorts, which had been supplemented by the frigate *Burghead Bay,* entered harbour to secure alongside the city's commercial wharf. Four days later *Warrior* was heading for home, and after 48 hours at anchor in Gibraltar Bay she set course for Portsmouth. *Warrior* arrived alongside Portsmouth's North Corner Jetty at 07.15 on Friday 11 October, and after her passengers had disembarked, the ship's company started their special 'Grapple' leave. By 8 November *Warrior* had been moved into C basin and on 28 November, after she had been taken over by the dockyard, Commodore Hicks left the ship. During the next two months *Warrior* was destored and at sunset on 10 February 1958 the White Ensign was lowered for the last time. Three weeks later, on 5 March, the last naval personnel left the carrier, which became part of the Reserve Fleet.

Just four months after being placed in reserve, *Warrior's* future became clear when it was announced that the head of Argentina's Naval Purchasing Mission in London had signed an agreement to purchase the carrier. Some members of the Argentine Establishment had not been enthusiastic about the proposed deal and one of those who resigned over the issue was the country's Ambassador in London, who thought that his country's money would be better spent on agricultural equipment. In the event, however, the Argentine Navy had its way and on 4 July 1958 the sale was completed. On 24 July, as the carrier was refitted in Portsmouth Dockyard, she was renamed *Independencia,* and in September 26 officers and 300 ratings of the Argentine Navy were brought to Portsmouth by the transport *Bahia Buen Suescesco,* in order to familiarize themselves with their new aircraft carrier. On 8 December 1958 *Independencia* sailed from Portsmouth for trials, and as she left harbour a helicopter from HMS *Vernon* carried the new Argentine Ambassador to London, who was a senior naval officer, together with other VIPs, out to the ship. Two days later she sailed for Buenos Aires and during her 12 years' service with the Argentine Navy she operated Corsairs and AT-6 Harvards. In 1970, 12 years before the Falklands War, and following the acquisition of *Veinticinco de Mayo*,* she was withdrawn from service and in March 1971 she was broken up.

Commanding Officers:

Captain F. L. Houghton CBE RCN	1 September 1945
Captain P. S. Smith DSO RN	1 September 1948
Captain St J. Cronyn DSO RN	10 August 1950
Captain A. F. Pugsley CB DSO RN	2 January 1951
Captain E. V. St J. Morgan RN	27 September 1951
Captain P. J. Milner-Barry RN	18 August 1953
Captain R. B. N. Hicks DSO RN	14 August 1956

Battle Honours:

The Saintes 1782
Copenhagen 1801
Jutland 1916

* See Chapter Four – HMS *Venerable*

Colossus-Class Aircraft Carriers: Principal Particulars:

Length Overall:	All ships 695ft	
Beam:	All ships 112ft - 6in	
Draught:	All ships 23ft - 5in	
Standard Displacement:	All ships 13,190 tons	
Armament:	*Colossus* -	6 quadruple 2pdr pom-poms 10 single 20mm Oerlikons
	Vengeance -	6 quadruple 2pdr pom-poms 19 single 40mm Bofors
	Venerable -	6 quadruple 2pdr pom-poms 11 twin 20mm Oerlikons 10 single 20mm Oerlikons
	Glory -	4 quadruple 2pdr pom-poms 16 single 40mm Bofors
	Ocean -	6 twin 40mm Bofors 16 single 40mm Bofors
	Theseus -	6 quadruple 2pdr pom-poms 16 single 40mm Bofors
	Triumph -	6 quadruple 2pdr pom-poms 19 single 40mm Bofors
	Warrior -	4 twin 40mm Bofors 18 single 40mm Bofors
Aircraft:	All ships up to 42	
Main Propulsion Machinery:	All ships, twin shaft, two sets Parsons geared steam turbines. Four Admiralty three-drum boilers. 40,000 SHP. 25 knots	
Complement:	All ships 1,300.	

Acknowledgements:
My thanks to the following for their help and, in many cases, for the loan of valuable photographs: -
Tom Abbey, Fleet Air Arm Museum, Yeovilton: Charles Adams, Lancaster: Kenneth Anderson, Ulster Folk & Transport Museum, Holywood, Belfast: D. L. G. Barratt, Rochester, Kent: Roger Beecham & staff, Cheltenham Reference Library: Julian Best, Llanelli, Carmarthenshire: Geoffrey Broxup, Alnwick, Northumberland: Graham Burns, Fleet, Hampshire: Bill Campbell, Belfast: John Carr, Acocks Green, Birmingham: George Cashmore, Rugby, Warwickshire: Michael Cassar, Valletta, Malta: George Chadwick, Stockport, Cheshire: Peter Chamberlain, Shiremoor, Tyne & Wear: Glyn Collins, Methyr Tydfil, Mid Glamorgan: Brian Conroy, Farnborough, Hampshire: Peter Cook, Morpeth, Northumberland: W. H. Cooper, Bridlington, Yorkshire: Michael Dunne, Hastings, Sussex: Ray Ellis, West Drayton, Middlesex: Geoffrey Ellison, Bradford, Yorkshire: George Gardner, University of Glasgow: Alan Gordon, Stockton-on-Tees: Bill Grice, Normanton, Yorkshire: Peter Harbinson, Harland & Wolff, Belfast: Ray Hill, Ramsgate, Kent: Peter Josiah, Morden, Surrey: J. C. Keeble, Gosport, Hampshire: Kenneth Lambert, Peterborough: Derek Lander, Newmarket, Suffolk: Michael Lennon, Waterlooville, Hampshire: Brian Lloyd, Burnham, Buckinghamshire: Brigadier R. J. McGarel-Groves OBE RM, Lymington, Hampshire: Bill Markham, Kings Lynn, Norfolk: Ted Moore, Stourport-on-Severn, Worcestershire: John Morris, Dalgety Bay, Fife: James Murphy, Kentish Town, London: Rod Newell, Swansea: Tony Perrett, Gosport, Hampshire: Norman Pound, Poulton-le-Fylde, Lancashire: Jerry Shore, Assistant Curator, Fleet Air Arm Museum, Yeovilton: Ian Spashett, FotoFlite, Ashford, Kent: R. L. Turnham, Sunbury-on-Thames: G. Woolley, Huntingdon, Cambridgeshire: Adrian Vicary, Maritime Photo Library, Cromer, Norfolk: Finally, to my wife Freda and my daughter Louise for all their help and support.

Readers wishing to purchase photographs from the Fleet Air Arm Museum collection should write to: Records & Research, Fleet Air Arm Museum, Box No D6, RNAS Yeovilton, Somerset BA22 8HT, England, quoting the reference number(s) shown.